Abstracts from the
Land Records of Dorchester County, Maryland

Volume J

1790-1795

Libers HD #3, HD #4,
HD #6, and HD #8

James A. McAllister Jr.

Colonial Roots
Millsboro, DE
2015

ISBN 978-1-68034-033-4
Published May 2015

© Copyright 1967 James A. McAllister Jr.
All rights reserved
Printed in the United States of America

NOTES

The figures at upper left of each abstract represent the Liber and Folio, in the original records, on which the abstracted material begins.

For the most part, each abstract includes a deed and all supporting documents (Power of Attorney, Bond, etc.) recorded with the deed.

References in the Index are to liber and folio in the original records, as shown at upper left of each abstract.

This volume (Volume J) is a merger of Mr. McAllister's Volumes 30, 31, 32 and 33.

3 HD 1. September 3, 1790. Robert Gilmor of the town of Baltimore, Merchant, on behalf of himself and William Bingham of Philadelphia, Pennsylvania, his partner in merchandise, to John Smoot of Dorchester County, Gent.: lands of Eben Hill, containing 451 acres, taken by said Gilmor and Bingham by Court action in settlement of a judgment against the said Eben Hill; the said John Smoot having paid to Gilmor and Bingham the principal, interest and costs due by virtue of their judgment against Hill. Witnesses: John Smith, John Usher. Acknowledged before George Salmon and Thos. Elliot, Justices for Baltimore County. Wm. Gibson, Clk.

3 HD 4. June 10, 1790. Samuel Muir of Dorchester County to Nathan Griffin of the same county, planter: part of "Muirs Inspection" in Town Point Neck, adj. John Mackeel's part of said tract and containing 72 acres. Witnesses: Henry Lake, Moses LeCompte. Acknowledged before Henry Lake and Moses LeCompte, Justices.

3 HD 6. November 29, 1790. Henry Ennalls of Dorchester County, Gent., and Sarah his wife to Charles Goldsborough of the same county, Gent.: part of "Teverton" on Fishing Creek, formerly devised to John Goldsborough by his father Robert Goldsborough, deceased; a 1/9 part of the said tract having passed to the said Sarah at the death of her brother, the said John Goldsborough. Witnesses: Edward Noel, Soln. Birckhead. Acknowledged before Edward Noel and Soln. Birckhead, Justices.

3 HD 8. December 2, 1790. Daniel Godwin of Dorchester County, planter, to Charles Daffin of the same county, Merchant: part of "Goodridges Choice" between Trot's Creek and the mouth of Hunting Creek, containing 51 acres more or less. Also part of "Walkers Lott" or "Walkers Chance" at the mouth of Hunting Creek, adj. "Chesums Gore" and containing 100 acres more or less. Also "Chesums Gore" at the mouth of Hunting Creek, containing 13 acres more or less. Also land in New Market conveyed by James Sulivane to said Charles Daffin and by said Daffin to said Daniel Godwin. (Mortgage). Witnesses: Jno. Smoot, D. Sulivane. Acknowledged before Jno. Smoot and Danl. Sulivane, Justices.

3 HD 10.. December 13, 1790.. Henry Ennalls and Sarah his wife of Dorchester County to John Rogers of the same county: parts of tracts called "Muirs Good Luck," "Appleby" and "Harwoods Choice" all lying on Fishing Creek, adj. "Brannocks Chance" and Thomas Brannock's part of "Harwoods Choice" and containing 343 acres more or less. Witnesses: Thos. Jones, Soln. Birckhead.

Acknowledged before Thos. Jones and Soln. Birckhead, Justices.

3 HD 14. November 3, 1790. Nathaniel Elliot of Dorchester County, planter, from Zechariah Keene of the same county: part of "Wallaces Meadow" at the bead of Meekinses Creek, containing 10 acres. Witnesses: Benj. Keene, Henry Lake. Acknowledged by Zechariah Keene and Kitturah his wife before Benj. Keene and Henry Lake, Justices.

3 HD 15. January 28, 1782. John Wallace of Dorchester County to Aaron Wallace of the same county: Bond to convey "Good Luck to Wallace." Witnesses: Jobn Burne, Ezekiel Johnson.

3 HD 16. December 14, 1790. Joseph Trippe of Dorchester County to James Hodson of the same county: "Trippes Marsh" on Chicamacomico River, containing 50 acres more or less. Also "Trippes Discovery" on Chicamacomico River, containing 229 acres more or less. Also "Trippes Inclosure" on Chicamacomico River, containing 191 acres. Also the interest of said Joseph Trippe in lands devised by Wm. Trippe to John Trippe and since devised by said John Trippe to said Josepb Trippe. Witnesses: Tho. Jones, Jno. Tootell. Acknowledged before Tho. Jones and Jno. Tootell, Justices.

3 HD 18. December 14, 1790. John Dawson of Dorchester County, planter, to Charles LeCompte, son of Philemon, of the same county: part of a tract originally called "Howards Lott" but since resurveyed and now called "Dawsons Lott," containing 50 acres more or less. Witnesses: Tho. Jones, Jno. Tootell. Acknowledged by John Dawson and Elizabeth his wife before Tho. Jones and Jno. Tootell, Justices.

3 HD 20. November 23, 1790. Joseph Andrews of Dorchester County and Elizabeth his wife to Joseph Robbins of the same county: part of "Callis" adj. Wm. Shorter's land and containing 1 3/4 acres more or less. Witnesses: Henry Lake, Benj. Keene. Acknowledged before Henry Lake and Benj. Keene, Justices.

3 HD 21. November 23, 1790. Matthew Keene of Dorchester County to Joseph Andrews of the same county: part of "Keenes Discovery" containing 181 acres more or less. Witnesses: Benj. Keene, Henry Lake. Acknowledged by Matthew Keene and Sally his wife before Benj. Keene and Henry Lake, Justices.

3 HD 23. October 26, 1790. William Whittington, Junr. of Dorchester County to

Isaac Whittington and William Whittington, Senr. of Somerset County: "Francis's Cottage" on the east side of Transquakin River, containing 51 acres more or less; part of "Stewarts Second Beginning" on the east side of Transquakin River, containing 155 acres; and "Cambridge," containing 6 1/4 acres. (Mortgage). Witnesses: Dan Sulivane, Jno. Tootell. Acknowledged before Dan Sulivane and Jno. Tootell, Justices.

3 HD 25. August 18, 1790. Tabitha Brodess, widow, of Dorchester County to her son Jonathan Brodess: Negro slaves, livestock and furniture. Witness: Jno. Eccleston.

3 HD 25. December 1, 1790. Charles Daffin of Dorchester County, Merchant, to Daniel Godwin of the same county, planter: lot in the village of New Market, part of a tract called "New Market" purchased by said Charles Daffin from James Sulivane. Witnesses: Jno. Smoot, D. Sulivane. Acknowledged before Jno. Smoot and D. Sulivane, Justices.

3 HD 27. October 14, 1790. Adam Muir of Dorchester County to William Barrow of the same county: 1/2 acre, part of "Nevitts Double Purchase," lying at the back of the dwelling house of said William Barrow, on the south side of "the new street called Gay Street," adj. land of Mrs. Ann Muse. Witnesses: Moses LeCompte, Soln. Birckhead. Acknowledged before Moses LeCompte and Soln. Birckhead, Justices.

3 HD 29. December 23, 1790. Thomas Harper of Dorchester County, planter, to Thomas Thompson of the same county, planter: one sorrel mare and 16 barrels of corn. Witness: D. Sulivane. Acknowledged before D. Sulivane, Justice.

3 HD 30. January 1, 1791. Thomas Taylor of Dorchester County, planter, to John North of the same county, planter: lease of the plantation where Richard Covey now lives. Witnesses: Levin Marshal, Samuel Wheelear.

3 HD 31. September 11, 1790. Charles Wheatley of Dorchester County to Charles Russell of the same county: part of "Levertons Chance" between the Northwest and Northeast Forks of Nanticoke River, containing 56 acres more or less. Witnesses: Jno. Smoot, Dan Sulivane. Acknowledged before Jno. Smoot and Dan Sulivane, Justices.

3 HD 33. December 3, 1790. William Ennalls Hooper of Dorchester County to Mary Hooper of the same county: part of "Upper Black Walnut Landing," near

Crotchers Ferry on the Northwest Fork, late the property of Ann Hooper deceased, ("a further reference had to the last will and testament of Henry Hooper Esquire bearing date September seventeen hundred and ninety containing whatever quantity of acres it may"). Witnesses: Jno. Smoot, Dan Sulivane. Acknowledged by Wm. Ennalls Hooper and Sarah his wife before Jno. Smoot and Dan Sulivane, Justices.

3 HD 35. January 17, 1791. William Ratcliff of Dorchester County to Negro Jacob: Manumission. Witnesses: George Ward, Mary Ward. Acknowledged before Edward Noel, Justice.

3 HD 35. January 17, 1791. William Vans Murray, Esq. and Charlotte his wife to Solomon Birckhead (all of the town of Cambridge): "Ennalls Outrange," containing 11 acres. Witnesses: Tho. Jones, Moses LeCompte. Acknowledged before Tho. Jones and Moses LeCompte, Justices.

3 HD 38. January 29, 1791. Mary Woodard of Dorchester County to Dinah Macer: Manumission. Witnesses: Moses LeCompte, T. Pattison. Acknowledged before Moses LeCompte.

3 HD 38. January 29, 1791. William Vickars 2nd to the State of Maryland: Bond as Inspector at Whites Warehouse, with Saml. Hooper and Arthur Whiteley Junr. as Sureties. Witnesses: Richard Keene, John Stewart. Proved by witnesses before Tho. Jones, Justice.

3 HD 39. January 25, 1791. William Keene of Dorchester County to Joseph Andrews: livestock, and other personal property. Witness: Edwd. Staplefort. Acknowledged before Henry Lake.

3 HD 40. January 18, 1791. Thomas Colston of Dorchester County, carpenter, and Betsy his wife to John Williams of the same county, Merchant: part of "Colstons Industry" adj. "Outlet" and containing 14 ½ acres; part of "Green Bank" adj. "Head Range," on the road from Blackwater Bridge to Fishing Creek, adj."Cornwell" and containing 13 ½ acres; and "Tryangle" adj. "Outlett" and containing 1 3/4 acres. Witnesses: Tho. Jones, Moses LeCompte. Acknowledged before Tho. Jones and Moses LeCompte, Justices.

3 HD 42. January 23, 1791. Receipt from Richard Stanford, Celia Stanford and Elizabeth Stanford for money paid them by Medford Andrews "in consideration of our full claim against a legacy left him by William Medford late of

Dorchester County deceased amounting to one hundred pounds six shillings current money of Maryland in virtue of a Judgement obtained by us against William Medford Executor of said William Medford deceast." Witnesses: Danl. McDonnell, Abner Toppan.

3 HD 43. February 4, 1791. Henry Ennalls of Dorchester County to George Ward and Mary Ward his wife of the same place: land at the head of Gutty Wilsons Creek, on the road from Ennalls Ferry to Cambridge, adj. lands of Richard Sprigg and Joseph Ennalls and containing 300 acres. Witnesses: Tho. Jones, Soln. Birckhead. Acknowledged by Henry Ennalls and Sarah his wife before Tho. Jones and Soln. Birckhead.

3 HD 45. February 8, 1791. John Pitt to the State of Maryland: Bond as Inspector at Ennalls Ferry Warehouse, with Thos. Hill Airey and William Pitt as sureties. Witnesses: Jos. Ennalls, Nathaniel Hooper. Proved by witnesses before soln. Birckhead, Justice.

3 HD 46. February 5, 1791. John Hooper of Dorchester County to Thomas Stevens: Negro slave Jems Roberts. Witness: Cala Stevens.

3 HD 47. April 1, 1791. John Ball to the State of Maryland: Bond as Inspector of Tobacco, with Thomas Hicks and John Maguire as sureties. Witnesses: Daniel Akers, Jno. Murray. Proved by witnesses before Soln. Birckhead, Justice.

3 HD 48. February 7, 1791. Levin Smith of Dorchester County to Archibald Patison of the town of Cambridge: part of "Norths Range" near Blackwater River, devised by George North to his daughter Rebecca Smith, containing 50 acres more or less. Witnesses: Edward Noel, Soln. Birckhead. Acknowledged before Edward Noel and Solomon Birckhead, Justices.

3 HD 50. January 31, 1791. William Tucker of Dorchester County, planter, to John Blair of the town of Cambridge, Merchant: Lot No. Four of the Prison lands in Cambridge, sold by the Justices of Dorchester County under Act of Assembly to Ann Smith and. la ter conveyed by said Ann Smith to said William Tucker. Witnesses: Soln. Birckhead, Edward Noel. Acknowledged before Edward Noel and Soln. Birckhead, Justices.

3 HD 53. October 8, 1790. Michael Hall Bonwell, Jacobus White and Elizabeth his wife, all of Dorchester County, to Anthony Manning of the same county: part of "Bonwills Expitible Lott"; part of "Bonwills Lott"; and part of "Turkey

Neck." The said three tracts adj. "Johns Delight," "Tripps Inclosure" and land of Nancy Jones, widow of Morgan Jones, and cont. 156 3/4 acres. Witnesses: James Shaw, Rob Dennis. Acknowledged by Michael Hall Bonwill and Mary his wife, Jacobus White and Elizabeth his wife before James Shaw and Rob Dennis, Justices.

3HD 56. October 8, 1790. Michael Hall Bonwill and Mary his wife, Jacobus White and Elizabeth his wife of Dorchester County to Anthony Manning of the same county: part of "Bonwills Expitible Lott" near Mrs. Ann Jones's barn, adj. "Johns Delight" and containing 33 acres more or less. Witnesses: James Shaw, Rob Dennis, Jno. Tootell. Acknowledged before James Shaw, Rob Dennis and Jno. Tootell, Justices.

3 HD 59. February 1, 1791. Henry Hodson of Dorchester County to Anthony Manning of the same county: "Pound Second Addition Corrected," containing 30 ½ acres. Witnesses: James Shaw, Jno. Tootell. Acknowledged by Henry Hodson and Elizabeth his wife before James Shaw and Jno. Tootell, Justices.

3 HD 62. February 1, 1791. Joseph Trippe of Dorchester County to Anthony Manning of the same county: "Tripps Inclosure" adj. "Bonwills Expetible Lott" containing 31 acres. Witnesses: James Shaw, Jno. Tootell. Acknowledged before James Shaw and Jno. Tootell, Justices.

3 HD 65. February 4, 1791. William Hayward Stewart of Dorchester County to Thomas Stewart (son of James) of the same county: part of "Phillips's Discovery" on the main street leading into Cambridge, with a dwelling house, containing ½ acre and 15 sq. perches (lot No.1 on the plat and certificate returned by the Sheriff May 21, 1790 of lands of Wm. Hayward Stewart and Sarah Stewart). Witnesses: Tho. Jones, Soln. Birckhead. Acknowledged before Tho. Jones and Soln. Birckhead, Justices.

3 HD 67. February 26, 1791. Joseph Thompson of Dorchester County, planter, and Priscilla his wife to Thomas Williams of the same county, planter: part of "Partnership," containing 15 acres more or less. Witnesses: Jno. Smoot, Rob Dennis. Acknowledged before Jno. Smoot and Rob Dennis, Justices.

3 HD 69. February 26, 1791. Joseph Thompson of Dorchester County, planter, and Priscilla his wife to William Thompson of the same county, planter: "Venture," containing 50 acres more or less, on the north side of a tract called "Thompsons Meadows." Also part of "Thompsons Meadows," containing 42

acres more or less. Witnesses: Rob Dennis, Jno. Smoot. Acknowledged before Jno. Smoot and Rob Dennis, Justices.

3 HD 72. December 3, 1790. William Ennalls Hooper of Dorchester County to Sarah Ennalls, wife of Bartholomew, of the same county: "Cow Garden," late the property of Ann Hooper deceased (see Will of Henry Hooper Esq. dated September 1790). Witnesses: Jno. Smoot, Dan Sulivane. Acknowledged by Wm. Ennalls Hooper and Sarah Hooper his wife before Jno. Smoot and Dan Sulivane, Justices.

3 HD 74. December 1, 1790. Henry Ennalls, Jno. Stevens and Nathan Wright of Dorchester County to Edward Adams of the same county: part of "The End of Strife," in Northwest Fork, containing 86 ½ acres more or less. Witnesses: Jno. Smoot, Dan Sulivane. Acknowledged by Henry Ennalls and Sarah his wife, John Stevens and Frances his wife and Nathan Wright before Jno. Smoot and Dan Sulivane, Justices.

3 HD 76. November 23, 1790. Joseph Andrews and Elizabeth his wife of Dorchester County to Wm. Shorter of the same county: lands called "Callis," "Middle Range" and "Fourth Callis" on the west side of Blackwater River, on Sandy Island Creek, containing 148 acres in all. Also ½ of "Third Callis" on the east side, of Blackwater River, containing 46 ½ acres. Witnesses: Henry Lake, Benj. Keene. Acknowledged before Henry Lake and Benj. Keene, Justices.

3 HD 78. March 12, 1791. Thomas Stainton of Dorchester County to Thomas Logan of the same county: part of "Staintons Industry," adj. 3 acres of said tract conveyed to Sarah Abbot about 4 years ago; 21 acres more or less, hereby conveyed. Witnesses: Jno. Smoot, Rob Dennis. Acknowledged by Thomas Stainton and Nancy his wife before Jno. Smoot and Rob Dennis, Justices.

3 HD 81. January 29, 1791. Thomas More of Sussex County, Delaware, Administrator of Charles Laing, and John Laing to Patrick Braughan of Dorchester County: part of a tract on the west side of Cratchers Ferry, called "Discovery," containing 100 acres more or less. Witnesses: Jno. Smoot, D. Sulivane. Acknowledged by Thomas More and Sarah his wife, John Laing and Rosanna his wife, before Jno. Smoot and D. Sulivane, Justices.

3 HD 83. March 18, 1791. Jeremiah Pattison of Dorchester County to John Brohawn of the same county: part of "Pattisons Priviledge" on Slaughter Creek, adj. "Davids Chance" and land of David Sare and containing 5 acres more or

less. Witnesses: Thomas Jones, Moses LeCompte. Acknowledged by Jeremiah Pattison and Nancy his wife before Thos. Jones and Moses LeCompte, Justices.

3 HD 85. March 18, 1791. Jeremiah Pattison and Nancy his wife of Dorchester County to Thomas North of the same county: part of "Pleasant Grove," adj. land of John Edmondson and containing 9 3/4 acres more or less. Witnesses: Tho. Jones, Moses LeCompte. Acknowledged before Thos. Jones and Moses LeCompte, Justices.

3 HD 86. March 12, 1791. Bartholomew Fletcher and Margery his wife, of Dorchester County, to Daniel Nicolls of the same county: part of "Stantons purchase," adj. Isaac Cauter's part of the said tract and containing 147 1/4 acres more or less. Witnesses: Jno. Smoot, Rob Dennis. Acknowledged before Jno. Smoot and Rob Dennis, Magistrates.

3 HD 89. February 26, 1791. Thomas Pritchet, Executor of Daniel Payne of Dorchester County, deceased, to Daniel Nicolls of the same county: part of "Neighbourly Kindness," containing 100 acres more or less. Also "Henrys Delight" adj. a tract called "Long Ridge," formerly the property of David Harper, containing 8 1/4 acres more or less. Witnesses: Jno. Smoot, Rob Dennis. Acknowledged before Jno. Smoot and Rob Dennis, Magistrates.

3 HD 91. January 29, 1791. Benjamin Bright of Dorchester County to William Wheatley Junr. of the same county: "Waters Last Choice" on the east side of the Northwest Fork of Nanticoke River, containing 117 ½ acres more or less. Witnesses: Jno. Smoot, Danl. Sulivane. Acknowledged by Benjamin Bright and Elizabeth his wife before Jno. Smoot and Dan Sulivane, Justices.

3 HD 94. March 12, 1791. George Gale of Dorchester County to Edward Wheatley of the same county: part of "Hogg Yard" on the east side of the Northwest Fork of Nanticoke River, containing 74 ½ acres more or less. Witnesses: Jno. Smoot, Rob Dennis. Acknowledged before Jno. Smoot and Rob Dennis, Justices.

3 HD 96. March 12, 1791. George Gale of Dorchester County, Gent., to Ezekiel Wheatley of the same county, planter: land on the north side of Nanticoke River called "Hog Yard," adj. land of William Wheatley, also adj. "Denwoods Resurvey" and land of William Fletcher, and containing 194 acres more or less. Witnesses: Jno. Smoot, Rob Dennis. Acknowledged before Jno. Smoot and Rob Dennis, Justices.

3 HD 98. March 12, 1791. George Gale of Dorchester County, Gent., to William Fletcher of the same county, planter: part of "Hog Yard" on the north side of Nanticoke River, adj. Mrs. Bradley's land and containing 114 ½ acres more or less. Witnesses: Jno. Smoot, Rob Dennis. Acknowledged before Jno. Smoot and Rob Dennis, Justices.

3 HD 101. March 12, 1791. George Gale of Dorchester County to Parris Chipman of the same county: part of "Hog Yard" on the east side of the Northwest Fork of Nanticoke River, adj. a lot laid out for John Smoot, containing 74 3/4 acres more or less. Witnesses: Jno. Smoot, Rob Dennis. Acknowledged before Jno. Smoot and Rob Dennis, Justices.

3 HD 103. March 12, 1791. Doctor George Gale of Dorchester County to John Elliott of the same county: part of "Hog Yard" on the east side of the Northwest Fork of Nanticoke, adj. John Smoot's land and Bradley's land and containing 200 acres more or less. Witnesses: Jno. Smoot, Rob Dennis. Acknowledged before Jno. Smoot and Rob Dennis, Justices.

3 HD 105. March 12, 1791. George Gale of Dorchester County, Gent., to Purnal Bradley and Kelbey Bradley of Dorchester County, planters: part of "Hog Yard" on the north side of Nanticoke River, containing 100 ½ acres more or less. Witnesses: Jno. Smoot, Rob Dennis. Acknowledged before Jno. Smoot and Rob Dennis, Justices.

3 HD 107. February 7, 1791. Roger Foxwell of Dorchester County to Shadrach Foxwell of the same county: "Foxwells Venture," containing 45 acres more or less; and "Rogers Chance," containing 47 acres more or less. Witnesses: Henry Lake, Benj. Keene. Acknowledged before Henry Lake and Benj. Keene, Justices.

3 HD 109. December 1, 1790. Henry Ennalls, John Stevens and Nathan Wright of Dorchester County to Matthew Smith of the same county: part of a tract in the Northwest Fork called "The End of Strife," containing 139 1/4 acres. Witnesses: Jno. Smoot, Dan Sulivane. Acknowledged by Henry Ennalls and Sarah his wife, John Stevens and Frances his wife and Nathan Wright before Jno. Smoot and Dan I Sulivane, Justices.

3 HD 111. February 7, 1791. Thomas Wingate of Dorchester County, planter, to Naboath Hart of the same county: part of "Bettys Desier" on Feirm Creek, adj. "Hog Quarter," adj. lands of Joseph Andrews and Isaac Andrews and containing

9 acres more or less. Also part of "Feirm" on Feirm Creek, containing 40 acres more or less. Also "Insleys Prevention," containing 51 acres more or less. Witnesses: Henry Lake, Benj. Keene. Acknowledged before Henry Lake and Benj. Keene, Justices.

3 HD 113. March 12, 1791. Joshua Wright and Sarah his wife of Sussex County, Delaware to William More of Dorchester County: part of "Kings Chance" on the east side of the Northwest Fork of Nanticoke River, containing 51 acres more or less. Witnesses: Jno. Smoot, Rob Dennis. Acknowledged before Jno. Smoot and Rob Dennis, Justices.

3 HD 115. March 23, 1791. William Badley of Dorchester County, planter, to John Stevens of the same county, shoemaker: part of 'Bradleys Intention," containing 7 1/4 acres more or less. Witnesses: Moses LeCompte, Soln. Birckhead. Acknowledged before Moses LeCompte and Soln. Birckhead, Justices.

3 HD 117. December 31, 1790. Peter Harrington of Dorchester County to Richard Bright of the same county: "Brights Addition to the Grove" containing 357 acres; "Foresight' containing 12 acres; and "Taylors Range" containing 50 acres more or less. Witnesses: Thos. Jones, Benj. Keene. Acknowledged before Tho. Jones and Benj. Keene, Justices.

3 HD 119. December 31, 1790. Richard Bright of Dorchester County to Peter Harrington of the same county: "Brights Addition to the Grove," containing 100 acres. Witnesses: Tho. Jones, Benj. Keene. Acknowledged before Tho. Jones and Benj. Keene, Justices.

3 HD 121. December 31, 1790. David Rogers of Dorchester County and Susannah his wife to Peter Harrington of the same county: part of "Meekins Hope" in Meekins Neck, containing 24 acres more or less. Witnesses: Tho. Jones, Benj. Keene. Acknowledged before Tho. Jones and Benj. Keene, Justices.

3 HD 122. December 31, 1790. Richard Bright of Dorchester County to Edward Streets of the same county: 4 acres of "Foresight" and 129 acres of "Brights Addition to the Grove," located on a branch of Blackwater called Charles Branch. Witnesses: Tho. Jones, Benj. Keene. Acknowledged before Tho. Jones and Benj. Keene, Justices.

3 HD 124. March 23, 1791. Thomas Colsten Senr. and Thomas Colsten Junr. of Dorchester County, planters, to Richard Tubman of the same county, planter: part of "Colstens Despute" in Blackwater swamps, containing 75 acres more or less. Witnesses: Moses LeCompte, Soln. Birckhead. Acknowledged before Moses LeCompte and Soln. Birckhead, Justices.

3 HD 127. March 23, 1791. John Rogers of Dorchester County to Thomas Colsten of the same county: part of "Harwoods Choice" and part of "Appelbe," on Sylvys Cove and Fishing Creek, containing 155 1/4 acres. Witnesses: Moses LeCompte, Soln. Birckhead. Acknowledged before Moses LeCompte and Soln. Birckhead, Justices.

3 HD 130. March 23, 1791. Richard Keene of Dorchester County, Merchant, to Thomas Colsten of the same county, carpenter: part of "Keens Outlett," containing 11 3/4 acres. Witnesses: Moses Lecompte, Soln. Birckhead. Acknowledged before Moses Lecompte and Soln. Birckhead, Justices.

3 HD 133. March 15, 1791. Francis Elliott of Caroline County, blacksmith, to Thomas Stevens, cabinet maker, son of Peter Stevens of Talbot County: house and lot in New Market, being part of a tract called "New Market," containing 1 acre more or less. Witnesses: J. Richardson, P. Edmondson. Acknowledged by Francis Elliott and Elizabeth his wife before Joseph Richardson and Peter Edmondson, Justices for Caroline County. Thos. Richardson, Clk.

3 HD 136. March 25, 1791. Thomas Colsten, son of Thomas, and Thomas Colsten, Carpenter, of Dorchester County, to Levin Wall of the same county, planter: part of "Addition to Small Profit," containing 8 ½ acres; and part of "Colstens Dispute" containing 24 acres. Witnesses: Moses Lecompte, Soln. Birckhead. Acknowledged before Moses Lecompte and Soln. Birckhead, Justices.

3 HD 137. March 26, 1791. James Busick of Dorchester County, planter, and Anne his wife to Thomas Jones Junr. of the same county: part of "Maces Purchase" on the west side of Hudsons Branch; and part of "Outlett" bought by Jonathan Wood from Josias Mace. Witnesses: Moses Lecompte, Soln. Birckhead. Acknowledged before Moses Lecompte and Soln. Birckhead, Justices.

3 HD 139. March 30, 1791. Rachel Goldsborough and William Goldsborough, both of Dorchester County, to Charles Goldsborough of the same county: their

interest in "Teverton" on Fishing Creek, inherited from their brother John Goldsborough deceased, the said tract having been devised to said John Goldsborough by his father Robert Goldsborough deceased. The said Charles Goldsborough is also mentioned as a brother of said Rachel and William. Witnesses: Moses LeCompte, Soln. Birckhead. Acknowledged before Moses Lecompte and Soln. Birckhead, Justices.

3 HD 142. March 12, 1791. Bartholomew Easum of Dorchester County to Joseph Wheatley of the same county: "Easons Venture" near the Northeast Fork of Nanticoke, containing 51 acres more or less. Witnesses: Jno. Smoot, Rob Dennis. Acknowledged before Jno. Smoot and Rob Dennis, Justices.

3 HD 145. March 29, 1791. Robert Harrison of Dorchester County, Gent., to James Rule Stevens of the same county, Gent.: lease of a house and lot in Cambridge now in the tenure and occupation of Charles McMahan, adj. a lot bought by Nicholas Hammond Esq. from Capt. Robert Ewing. Witnesses: John Done, Moses Lecompte. Acknowledged before John Done and Moses Lecompte, Justices.

3 HD 148. March 21, 1791. William Hayward of Dnrchester County to William Tucker of the same county: "Francis Cottage," "Addition to Francis Cottage" and "Haywards Regulation" (1/4 undivided interest in each), in accordance with the Wills of John Hayward and Francis Hayward deceased. Witnesses: Soln. Birckhead, Henry Lake. Acknowledged before Soln. Birckhead and Henry Lake, Justices.

3 HD 150. April 8, 1791. Nicholas Hammond of the town of Cambridge to James Rule Stevens of the same place, Gent.: lease of land in Cambridge now in the occupation of said James Rule Stevens, adj. lands of Anne Muse .and Robert Harrison. Witnesses: Henry Dickinson, Jno. M. Stevens. Acknowledged before Robt. Harrison and Soln. Birckhead, Justices.

3 HD 155. February 7, 1791. John Stewart McNemara of Dorchester County to James Booze of the same county: "Paris" on the south side of Blackwater River. Witnesses: Henry Lake, Benj. Keene. Acknowledged by John Stewart McNamara and Lovey his wife before Henry Lake and Benj. Keene, Justices.

3 HD 157. February 3, 1791. Henry Sterling of Dorchester County to William Bramble of the same county: personal property. Witness: Priscilla Bramble. Acknowledged before Henry Lake, Justice.

3 HD 158. February 7, 1791. Letter of John Muir concerning Celia and Elizabeth Stanford, daughters of Capt. Rd. Stanford. Witnesses: Patrick Braughan, Robert Muir.

3 HD 158. March I, 1791. Letter from William Hayward to Archibald Patison, Edwd. Stephens and Levin Stephens. Witnesses: James Shaw, Peter Gordon.

3 HD 159. February 26, 1791. Certificate of Levin Marshall, Danl. Nicols, William Paddison and Joseph Thompson concerning a bounded stump of Isaac Bell's dwelling plantation, identified by Patrick Braughan.

3 HD 159. February 9, 1791. Garner Bruffit of Dorchester County to Negro slave Lish, aged 25 years, and her son Harry, aged about 2 years, formerly the property of John Greenwood, deceased: Manumission. Witnesses: Robert Goldsborough, Jno. Murray. Acknowledged before Soln. Birckhead, Justice.

3 HD 160. March 1791. Proceedings concerning lease of part of the prison lands in Cambridge to Thomas Lockerman.

3 HD 164. January 12, 1788. Henry Travers of Sussex County, Delaware and Elizabeth Travers, widow, of Dorchester County, to Richard Pattison Junr. of Dorchester County: Bond to convey "Taylors Folly" on Taylors' Island, which formerly belonged to Henry Travers, son of Col., adj. lands of Capt. Jacob Pattison and Levin Travers' heirs. Witnesses: Robson Barns, Henry Traverse Proved by oath of Robson Barnes, one of the witnesses, before Moses LeCompte, Justice.

3 HD 165. March 2, 1791. Henry Dare of Dorchester County, tailor, to Robert Dennis and Thomas Hingson, Merchants: personal property. Witnesses: Arthur Pritchard, Nehemiah Nichols.

3 HD 166. March 2, 1791. Andrew Insley of Dorchester County to John Insley of the same county: furniture and other personal property. Witnesses: Benj. Todd, Joseph Ryder.

3 HD 167. January 14, 1791. James Hodson, Administrator with will annexed of John Trippe deceased; Henry Trippe; Joseph Trippe both for himself and as guardian for William Trippe; Ann Trippe; Mary Trippe; Thomas Ennalls for himself and as guardian of Joseph Ennalls; William Ennalls; John Eccleston as guardian of John Ennalls; Ann Ennalls; and Elizabeth Ennalls, being all of the

representatives and devisees of said John Trippe deceased, to Negro slaves Alce, Stephen and Keziah and her child: Manumission, in accordance with the Will of the said deceased. Witnesses: James Shaw, John Hodson Senr. Acknowledged before James Shaw, Justice.

3 HD 168. October 11, 1790. - March 22, 1791. Commission to Nathan Wright, Richard Pattison, Jonathan Patridge, Thomas Jones Junior and Samuel Hooper of Dorchester County, Gent., to perpetuate bounds of Richard Keene's land, part of "End of Controversy," and Return. Deposition of Elizabeth Chezum, aged about 60 years, mentions her brother Edward Dorsey about 42 years ago. Deposition of Edmond Brannock, aged about 51 years, concerns a post fixed about 8-10 years ago for Ezekl. Keene, as the first bounder of said land. Depositions of William Vickarse of Sarah, aged about 63 years, and Levin Mills, aged about 50 years, who, about 19 years ago, were chain carriers when the said land was divided between Robt. Goldsborough deceased, Levin Dorsey and Ezekl. Keene, guardian to Richard Keene. Certification mentions Howes Goldsborough Esq. of Talbot County, Guardian to Howes Goldsborough of Robert. Also locates bounded post near the dwelling houses of John Dorsey and Richard Keene, and states that a line was surveyed by Richard Pattison, with Levin Fooks and Jacob Mills as chain carriers.

3 HD 172. March 30, 1791. Thomas Ross of Dorchester County, planter, to Nehemiah Beckwith of the same county, planter: livestock and other personal property. Witnesses: Levin Woolford, Moses Lecompte. Acknowledged before Moses Lecompte.

3 HD 173. April 6, 1787. William Ennalls Hicks and Thomas Hicks, both of Dorchester County, Gent., to John Scott: Bond to convey part of "Darley" on the east side of Blackwater River, adj. a tract called "Buck-field" and containing 175 acres (mentions Sarah, wife of Thomas Hicks). Witnesses: Henry Hooper Qs., Richard Pattison Junr. Proved by witnesses before Moses LeCompte, Justice.

3 HD 175. April 6, 1787. William Ennalls Hicks and Thomas Hicks to John Scott: Bond to convey 115 3/4 acres of "Darley" on the east side of Blackwater River (mentions Sarah, wife of Thomas Hicks). Witnesses: Henry Hodson Qs., Richard Pattison Junr. Proved by witnesses before Moses Lecompte, Justice.

3 HD 177. February 18, 1791. Negro Levi (formerly the slave of Wm. Pitt of Dorchester County and by said Pitt manumitted and set tree) of Dorchester

County, laborer, to Henry Hooper Qs.: Negro woman slave called Nell, and her four children Levi, Sal, Moll and Jem (Mortgage). Witness: Jno. Tootell. Acknowledged before Jno. Tootell, Justice.

3 HD 178. May 6, 1785. Ezekiel Reed of Dorchester County to John Clark of the same county: Bond to convey part of "Golden Grove," adj. "Cripples Lott" and containing 28 acres more or less. Witnesses: Paris Chipman, Thos. Briley.

3 HD 180. April 25, 1791. John LeCompte to Negro slaves Cato and others: Manumission. Witnesses: Moses Lecompte, James R. Stevens. Acknowledged before Moses Lecompte, Justice.

3 HD 180. May 9, 1791. Mary Lay ton of Dorchester County, widow of Charles Lay ton, to Negro slaves Moll and others: Manumission. Witness: Soln. Birckhead. Acknowledged before Soln. Birckhead, Justice.

3 HD 181. April 15, 1791. James Trego of Dorchester County, planter, to Henry Keene of the same county: part of "Robinsons Lott" on Taylors Island, containing 134 acres more or less. Witnesses: Tho. Jones, Moses Lecompte. Acknowledged before Tho. Jones and Moses Lecompte,

3 HD 183. November 23, 1790. Zachariah Keene of Dorchester County, planter, and Kitty (Catherine) his wife to Matthew Keene of the same county: part of two tracts called "Addition to Keenes Delight" and "Addition to Whitelys Choice" containing 8 1/4 acres more or less; and 43 3/4 acres more or less adj. lands of John Griffith and Nathaniel Elliot. Witnesses: Benj. Keene, Henry Lake. Acknowledged before Benj. Keene and Henry Lake, Justices.

3 HD 185. May 6, 1791. Matthew Keene of Dorchester County, planter, to Joshua Meekins of the same county: part of two tracts on the west side of Stapleforts Creek, called "Keenes Rest" and "Johnsons Contrivance," 20 acres more or less hereby conveyed, adj. "Moseleys Addition." Witnesses: Benj. Keene, Henry Lake. Acknowledged before Benj. Keene and Henry Lake, Justices.

3 HD 187. May 20, 1791. Isaac Reed of Sussex County, Delaware, to Thomas Insley of Dorchester County: "Reeds Regulation," containing 6 ½ acres more or less. Witnesses: Tho. Jones, Soln. Birckhead. Acknowledged by Isaac Reed and Eby his wife before Thos. Jones and Son. Birckhead, Justices.

3 HD 189. May 20, 1791. Isaac Reed of Sussex County, Delaware, to Thos. Insley of Dorchester County: part of "Yorkt," part of "Harpers Third Purchase" and part of "Isaac Venture," all included in another tract called "Reeds Regulation" on Gladsons Branch, adj. land of Daniel Layton and containing 142 ½ acres more or less (also adj. lands called "Hog Range" and "Dixons Discovery"). Also part of "Dixons Discovery," containing 9 1/4 acres more or less. Witnesses: Tho. Jones, Soln. Birckhead. Acknowledged by Isaac Reed and Eby Reed his wife before Tho. Jones and Soln. Birckhead, Justices.

3 HD 192. May 20, 1791. Isaac Reed of Sussex County, Delaware, to Daniel Layton of Dorchester County: part of "Reads Regulation," containing 20 acres more or less. Witnesses: Soln. Birckhead, Thos. Jones. Acknowledged by Isaac Reed and Eby Reed his wife before Soln. Birckhead and Tho. Jones, Justices.

3 HD 195. April 26, 1791. Certificate of Nathan Bradley, Jno. Stevens, Theo. Marshall and Thomas Stevens concerning a bounder of "Andertons Desire," mentions Henry Dickinson, Capt. James Sulivane and Daniel Godwin as interested parties.

3 HD 195. February 7, 1791. Anthony Manning of Dorchester County to Joseph Trippe of the same county: "Pounds Second Addition," containing 3 1/4 acres. Witnesses: James Shaw, Jno. Tootell. Acknowledged before James Shaw and Jno. Tootell, Justices.

3 HD 198. May 18, 1791. Richard Keene of Dorchester County to John Keene of the same county: "Keens Neglect" between the head of Hungar River and Slaughter Creek. Witnesses: Benj. Keene, Moses Lecompte. Acknowledged before Henj. Keene and Moses Lecompte, Justices.

3 HD 199. February 7, 1791. Thomas Ross and Rebeccah Ross his wife of Dorchester County, planters, to Abraham Mister of the same county, planter: part of two tracts called "Safford" and "Stanaways Forrest" between Hunger River and Farham Creek, containing 158 acres more or less. Description mentions a locust post standing by Todd's path. Witnesses: Henry Lake, Benj. Keene. Acknowledged before Henry Lake and Benj. Keene, Justices.

3 HD 202. June 13, 1791. John Eccleston to the State of Maryland: Bond as Collector of the Fund Tax of Dorchester County, with Charles Goldsborough and Thos. Green as Sureties. Witnesses: Robt. Harrison, Henry Hooper Qs., Jos. Ennalls.

3 HD 202. April 25, 1791. John Willen of Pitt County, North Carolina, planter, to Levin McNamara and Shadrick Wingate of Dorchester County, planters: part of "Fair Dealing" adj. "Wadles Desire," near the head of Goose Creek, adj. "Wingates Inclosure" and "Steple Bumstead" and containing 31 acres more or less. Also "Addition to Fair Dealing," containing 34 ½ acres more or less. Also "Timber Swamp" on the west side of Goose Creek which issues out of Fishing Bay, containing 24 acres more or less. Also "Addition to Timber Swamp," containing 18 acres more or less. Also part of "Black Swamp," containing 24 acres more or less. Witnesses: Henry Lake, Benj. Keene. Acknowledged before Henry Lake and Benj. Keene, Justices.

3.HD 206. April 30, 1791. Agreement between Levin McNamara and Shadrick Wingate concerning division of lands bought from John Willen, adj. "Maiden Lot" and "Waddles Desire." Witnesses: Benjamin Todd, John McNamara.

3 HD 206. March 21, 1791 - May 13, 1791. Commission to Moses LeCompte, Jonathan Patridge, Nathan Wright, Benjamin Woodard and Richard Keene (Fishing Creek) of Dorchester County, Gent., to perpetuate bounds of land of Stevens Woolford Junior called "Hackron," and Return. Deposition of Roger Woolford, aged about 63 years, mentions John Jones about 40 years ago.

3 HD 209. June 20, 1791. John Eccleston to the State of Maryland: Bond with John Eccleston Junr. and William Ennalls as sureties. Witnesses: Jas. Hodson, Jno. Stevens. Proved by witnesses before Soln. Birckhead, Justice.

3 HD 210. July 2, 1791. Richard Goldsborough of Dorchester County, Physician, to William Vickers of the same county: part of a tract called "Bellefield" on the road from the meeting house to the head of Fishing Creek, adj. "Goldsboroughs Outlett" and containing 150 acres more or lesse Witnesses: Robt. Harrison, Soln. Birckhead. Acknowledged before Robt. Harrison and Soln. Birckhead, Justices.

3 HD 213. April 29, 1791. Certificate of Theophilus Marshall concerns Mr. James Hodson and "a small branch that empties itself into the branch between the dwelling plantation where said Hodson now lives and Jonathan Wards plantation, as mentioned in the last Will and Testament of Thomas Ennalls bearing date the 19th of Novr. 1789 to be the division between his brother John and Thomas Ennalls Hodson, in the dwelling plantation."

3 HD 213. March 3, 1791. Howes Goldsborough of Talbot County, Gent., and

Rebecca his wife, who was one of the daughters of Robert Goldsborough late of Cambridge, Atty at law, deceased, to Richard Goldsborough, one of the sons of said Robert Goldsborough: the interest of the said Howes and Rebecca in lands devised by said Robert to his son Robert Goldsborough (brother of Rebecca) who has since died intestate and without issue, called "Woodyard" (bought by the said testator from Mrs. Mary Hicks); part of "Busby" conveyed by Richard Glover and wife to Charles Goldsborough, son of the testator, and by said Charles to the said testator; part of "Ennalls Luck" bought by testator from Henry Ennalls Junr.; part of "Woolfords Interest" bought by testator from Levin Woolford; part of "Cotmans Swamp" not included in the Indian lands; and a resurvey of the aforesaid several tracts called "Clifton," all lying near the head of Jenkins Creek. Also 50 acres of woodland, part of testator's tract called "Goldsboroughs Outlett." Witnesses: R. Goldsborough, Wm. Goldsborough. Acknowledged before R. Goldsborough, one of the Judges of the General Court of Maryland.

3 HD 216. March 31, 1791. John Eccleston Junr. of Dorchester County, Gent., to John Scott of the same county, Gent.: land on the west side of Transquakin River called "Travers's Lott," alias "Ennalls Town." Witnesses: Robt. Harrison, Soln. Birckhead. Acknowledged before Robt. Harrison and Soln. Birckhead, Justices.

3 HD 218. July 25, 1791. Archibald Patison of Dorchester County, Esq., to Bartholomew Ennalls and Robert Ewing, Admr. of Patrick Ewing deceased: Negro slaves and livestock, to indemnify said Ennalls and Ewing as sureties on Patison's bond. Livestock is located at Patison's farm on Little Choptank, at Glasgow farm, at Patison's house in Cambridge, at his farm on Transquakin River and on his farm on said river where Denton Carroll is overseer. Witness: Peter Gordon. Acknowledged before Soln. Birckhead, Justice.

3 HD 221. February 4, 1791. Henry Ennalls of Dorchester County, Gent., to Joseph Dowson of Cambridge, Mcht.: part of lots 14 and 15 in Cambridge, adj. the Court House land and lands of Peter Rea and the heirs of Doctor Henry Murray deceased. Witnesses: Tho. Jones, Soln. Birckhead. Acknowledged by Henry Ennalls and Sarah his wife before Tho. Jones and Soln. Birckhead, Justices.

3 HD 224. July 29, 1791. Richard Waters of Dorchester County to Levin Winder and Thomas Woolford: 800 acres, part of two tracts called "Hogg Yard" and ! "Rohobath," which the said Richard holds as "tenant by the Curtesy"; also

200 acres due said Richard from the State of Maryland for his services during the late War with Great Britain, lying in Allegany County to the westward of Fort Cumberland; and Negro slaves, livestock, and other personal property.(Mortgage). Witness: J. Toy. Chase. Acknowledged before J. Toy. Chase, one of the Judges of the General Court.

3 HD 226. February 10, 1791. John Macnemara Pritchett of Dorchester County, planter, and Elizabeth his wife, to George Dean of the same county: "Tarkill Ridge" containing 17 acres more or less; and part of "Black Swamp" containing 38 acres, between Charles Creek and Blackwater River. Witnesses: Henry Lake, Benj. Keene. Acknowledged before Henry Lake and Benj. Keene, Justices.

3 HD 229. March 9, 1791. Division of "Venture" and "Discovery" between Absolum Willey and his nephew, Littleton Willey, mentions adjoining tracts called "Worlds End" and "Hoopers Range."

3 HD 230. July 29, 1791, John Cryer, Jr. of Dorchester County to Negro slaves: Manumission. Witnesses: Moses Lecompte, Richard Keene. Acknowledged before Moses Lecompte, Justice.

3 HD 231. March 8, 1791. Elizabeth Wheatley of Dorchester County, widow of Augustus, to Major Ezekiel Vickars of the same county, planter: 140 acres called "Whores Harbour" or "Chance," where Augustus Wheatley now lives. (Mortgage). Witnesses: Solne Birckhead, Edward Noel. Acknowledged before Soln. Birckhead and Edward Noel, Justices.

3 HD 234. August 9, 1791. Amos Griffith of Dorchester County, planter, to Patrick Carroll of the same county, Mcht.: land west of Fort Cumberland due to said Amos under Act of Assembly as a soldier in the late American Army as certified under the hand of John Callahan, Register. Witnesses: Moses Lecompte, Soln. Birckhead. Acknowledged before Moses Lecompte and Soln. Birckhead, Justices.

3 HD 236. August 9, 1791. Richard Goldsborough of Dorchester County to Peter Rea of the same county: part of "Bellfield" adj. "Johns Desire" and land of John Blair, on the road from Cambridge to Fishing Creek, adj. land of William Barrow and containing 51 acres more or less.
Witnesses: Tho. Jones, Moses Lecompte. Acknowledged before Tho. Jones and Moses Lecompte, Justices.

3 HD 239. August 9, 1791. Joseph Dowson of Dorchester County to John Eccleston of the same county: "Trices Chance" which said Joseph Dowson bought of George Trice. Also "North Division," containing 47 3/4 acres, also bought from George Trice. Witnesses: Moses Lecompte, Solno Birckhead. Acknowledged before Moses Lecompte and Soln. Birckhead, Justices.

3 HD 242. August 8, 1791. William Willoughby of Dorchester County to Abraham Lee of the same county: Negro slaves. Witnesses: Moses Lecompte, Charles Hodson. Acknowledged before Moses Lecompte, Justice.

3 HD 243. August 2, 1791. John Brohawn of Dorchester County to Negro slave Moses: Manumission. Witnesses: Moses Lecompte, Richard Pattison. Acknowledged before Moses Lecompte, Justice.

3 HD 244. August 15, 1791. Robert Ewing, Administrator of Patrick Ewing deceased, of Dorchester County, to John Finley of Dorchester County: lot No.1 of the Prison lands in Cambridge. Witnesses: Robt. Harrison, Soln. Birckhead. Acknowledged before Robt. Harrison and Soln. Birckhead, Justices.

3 HD 246. August 20, 1791. McKeel Connerly and Rebecca his wife of Dorchester County to William Rumble of the same county: "Tryall," containing 13 3/4 acres more or less. Witnesses: E. Richardson, Jno. Crapper. Acknowledged before E. Richardson and Jno. Crapper, Justices.

3 HD 249. August 20, 1791. Henry Travers of Wm. and Teresa his wife of Northumberland County, Virginia, to Thomas Brome Travers of Dorchester County: part of "Robsons Lott" on Taylors Island (mentions divisions between Thomas Travers and Levin Woolford and between Thomas Travers and Matthew Travers), containing 61 3/4 acres (sold to, Thomas Travers by John Edmondson). Witnesses: Tho. Jones, Moses Lecompte. Acknowledged before Tho. Jones and Moses Lecompte, Justices.

3 ED 251. .May 6, 1791. Benjamin Keene and Nancy his wife of Dorchester County to their son Benjamin Keene 3d. of the same county: part of "Exchange" on the west side of Transquakin River in accordance with the Last Will and Testament of William Stephens, in Fork Neck. Also "Poplar Neck." Witnesses: Henry Lake, Moses Lecompte. Acknowledged before Henry Lake and Moses Lecompte.

3 HD 253. August 24, 1791. Mary Payne of Dorchester County to Samuel

Wright of the same county: Bond to convey her interest in part of "Hampton" now belonging to Daniel Nicolls, and part of "Addition" now belonging to said Nicolls. Witnesses: Theophilus Marshall, John McCotter, Jacob Wright.

3 HD 254. August 15, 1791. Moses Delahay of Dorchester County, planter, to John McGuire of the same county: Bond to convey part of "Sarah Land" and "Sarah Land Addition" and to defend all right claimed by William Tucker and wife and Mary James. Qitnesses: James Shawl William McCollister.

3 HD 254. August 27, 1791. Bartholomew Ennalls, James Hudson and Trustram Thomas, Commissioners, to John McGuire: lands of Cloudsbury Jones, sold per attachment issued out of Dorchester County Court for Patrick Ewing and other creditors of said Cloudsbury Jones, called "Sarah Land" and "Sarah Land Addition," containing 130 acres more or less. Witnesses: Robt. Harrison, Soln. Birckhead. Acknowledged before Robt. Harrison and Soln. Birckhead, Justices.

3 HD 257. August 29, 1791. Nathan Harrington, Henry Mowbray and James Mowbray to Edward Anderson and Joseph Anderson: Negro woman named Daphne. Witness: Jno. Stevens. Acknowledged before Jno.Stevens, Justice.

3 HD 257. September 1, 1791. Kenneth McKenney of Dorchester County to Daniel Nicolls of the same county: personal property. Witnesses: Jno. Stevens. Jona. Pinkney.

3 HD 259. July 1, 1791. Thomas Green of Dorchester County to Walter Rawley of the same county: part of "Appin Forrest" adj. "Sector" and containing 236 acres more or less. Witnesses: Soln. Birckhead, Jno. Stevens. Acknowledged by Thos. Green and Mary his wife before Soln. Birckhead and Jno. Stevens, Justices.

3 HD 264. August 23, 1791. Joshua Johnson of Dorchester County and Mary his wife to Thomas Creighton of the same county: "New Town" and "Addition to New Town," containing 87 acres more or less. Also 5 acres bought by said Joshua Johnson from Thomas Travers. Witnesses: Tho. Jones, Moses Lecompte. Acknowledged before Tho. Jones and Moses Lecompte, Justices.

3 ED 267. June 12, 1791. William Ratliff of Dorchester County, Taylor, to William Hayward of the same county, Mcht.: part of "Ratliffs Addition" on the south side of Great Choptank River and the east side of Chapel Creek, adj. the old tract called "Contention," and containing 12 acres. Witnesses: Tho. Jones,

Soln. Birckhead. Acknowledged before Tho. Jones and Soln. Birckhead, Justices.

3 HD 271 September 2, 1791 Richard Pattison of Dorchester County to Negro slave Esther:: Manumission. Witnesses: Moses Lecompte, Nancy Lecompte.

3 HD 272 August 2, 1791. Thomas Thompson of Dorchester County, planter, to Dorsey (Vival) Wyvill, Doctor, of Dorchester County: part of "Whitehaven" containing one acre of land. Witnesses: Tho. Jones, Moses Lecompte. Acknowledged by Thomas Thompson and Priscilla his wife before Thomas Jones and Moses Lecompte, Justices.

3 ED 275. September 10, 1791. William Thomas of Dorchester County, Mariner, and Alce (Alice) his wife to William Vickars 2nd. of the same county, planter: parts of three tracts called "Chance" "Addition" and "Middle Land," on a creek called Preston or Vickars's Creek, on the road to Town Point, and containing 158 1/4 acres more or less in all. Witnesses: Tho. Jones, Moses Lecompte. Acknowledged before Tho. Jones and Moses Lecompte, Justices.

3 HD 279. August 9, 1791. Richard Goldsborough of Dorchester County, physician, to William Barrow of the same county, surveyor: part of a tract called "Bellfield," adj. "Johns Desire," "Stewarts Lot," Wm. V.. Murray's fence, "Murray's Settlement," land of Peter Rea and the road from Cambridge to Fishing Creek, and containing 110 acres more or less. Witnesses: Tho. Jones, Moses Lecompte. Acknowledged before Tho. Jones and Moses Lecompte, Justices.

3 HD 282. June 13, 1791. Henry Ennalls of Dorchester County to Negro Oliver, lately the property of Richard Goldsborough: Manumission. Witnesses: Thos. Hill Airey, George Ward. Acknowledged before Soln. Birckhead, Justice.

3 HD 282. October 4, 1791. Thomas Loockerman as Trustee of Thomas Hooper Junr., an insolvent debtor, to Jacob Wright: part of "Bradford," containing 95 acres more or less. Witnesses: Moses Lecompte, Soln. Birckhead. Acknowledged before Moses Lecompte and Soln. Birckhead, Justices.

3 HD 284. September 14, 1791. Nathan Harrington of Dorchester County, planter, to Benjamin Collison of the same county, planter: land formerly the property of James Hooper called "Goodridges Choice." (Mortgage). Witnesses: E.. Richardson, Jnoo Stevens. Acknowledged before E. Richardson and Jno.

Stevens, Justices.

3 HD 286. October 29, 1791. Charles Hodson to the State of Maryland: Bond as High Sheriff of Dorchester County with John Eccleston and Samuel Hooper as sureties. .Witnesses: Robt. Harrison, Moses Lecompte.

3 HD 287. August 11, 1791. Stanley Byus of Dorchester County planter, to William Lecompte of the same county: "Good Intent" between Great Choptank River and the head of Little Choptank River, containing 15 acres more or less. Witnesses: Soln. Birckhead, Jno. Stevens. Acknowledged before Soln. Birckhead and Jno. Stevens, Justices.

3 HD 289. September 14, 1791. Charles Daffin of Caroline County to William Ennalls Hooper of Dorchester County: Bond concerning a tract of 334 acres in Dorchester County purchased by said Charles Daffin from Patrick Braughan. Mable Daffin is mentioned as wife of the said Charles Daffin. Witness: Solomon Corner Junr.

3 HD 290. August 25, 1791. Charles Daffin of Caroline County to William Ennalls Hooper of Dorchester County: 334 acres bought by said Daffin from Patrick Braughan. Witnesses: Henry Downes, John Hardcastle. Acknowledged before Henry Downes and John Hardcastle, Justices for Caroline County. Thomas Richardson, Clk.

3 HD 293. October 5, 1791. Bartholomew Fletcher of Dorchester County to Daniel Nicols of the same county: Negro man named Isaac. Witness: Thomas Kirkman.

3 ED 294. September 9, 1791. Sarah Ratcliff of Dorchester County to Negro slaves: Manumission. Witnesses: Wm. Ratcliff, Sally Mitchell.

3 HD 295. October 1, 1791. McKeel Connelly of Dorchester County and Rebeccah his wife to William Paddison of the same county: part of "Tryall" between the Northwest and Northeast Forks of Nanticoke River, containing 23 acres more or less. Witnesses: Jno. Crapper, E. Richardson. Acknowledged before Jno. Crapper and E. Richardson, Justices.

3 HD 297. October 7, 1791. James Moore and Mary his wife of Dorchester County to Robert Griffith of the same county: part of "Marshalls Chance" near "Cathergene," containing 100 acres. Witnesses: Jno. Stevens, E. Richardson.

Acknowledged before Jno. Stevens and E. Richardson, Justices.

3 HD 299. October 7, 1791. John Stevens and Frances his wife of Dorchester County to Robert Griffith of the same county: parts of "Carthagenia" purchased by said John Stevens from John and Henry Dickinson and from Theophilus Marshall and wife, containing 44 1/4 acres in one part and 200 acres in the other. The part purchased from Theophilus Marshall was left to said Theophilus by his father Thomas John Marshall by Will. Witnesses: E. Richardson, John Crapper. Acknowledged before E. Richardson and Jno. Cropper. Justices.

3 HD 302. October 24, 1791. John Robinson, blacksmith, of Sussex County, Delaware, to James Smith of Dorchester County: "Robinsons Discovery" on a branch of Blackwater River. containing 177 acres more or less (excepting the part held by the heirs of James Edmondson). Also "Robinsons Craft" (excepting the part held by the heirs of James Edmondson). Also "Chance" containing 12 acres more or less. Also "Busicks Tryal" containing 14 acres more or less. Also "Obscurity," containing 50 acres more or less. . Witnesses: Robt. Harrison, Moses Lecompte. Acknowledged before Robt. Harrison and Moses Lecompte, Justices. .

3 HD 304. October 25, 1791. James Byus of Dorchester County to Richard Tubman of the same county, planter: part of "Blackwater Range," containing 83 3/4 acres more or less. Witnesses: Thos. Jones, Henry Lake. Acknowledged before Tho. Jones and Henry Lake, Justices.

3 HD 306. October 22, 1791. William Ratcliff of Dorchester County to Thomas Ratcliff of the same county: 11 acres of "Littleworth" and 7 ½ acres of "Ratcliffs Addition" on the east side of Castle Haven Creek, containing 18 ½ acres in all. Witnesses: Robt. Harrison. Soln. Birckhead. Acknowledged before Robt. Harrison and Soln. Birckhead, Justices.

3 HD 308. May 5, 1791. Ayres Busick and Henry Dean of Dorchester County to Samuel Keene of the same county: Negro woman named Maryah. Witnesses: Benj. Keene, Richard Keene.

3 HD 309. March 21, 1791 - July 27, 1791. Commission to John Stevens, Theophilus Marshall, Jacob Wright and Isaac Lowe of Dorchester County, Gent., to perpetuate bounds of Peter Webb's land called "Kings Misfortune," and Return. Deposition of Richard Alford, aged about 69 years, mentions Edward Trippe, Doctor William Murray, Anthony Murray, William Green and

James Green, about 40 years ago. Also mentions Joseph Webb who lived on the said land some years later. Deposition of John McCotter, aged about 44 years, mentions Peter Webb of Talbot County about 17 years ago. Deposition of John Trice, aged about 39 years. Marked stone set down in the presence of Thomas Thompson, Nathan Wright (of Samuel), Henry Anderson (of Thos.) and James Brinchfield.

3 HD 312. October 25, 1791. Philip King Sherwood and William LeCompte of Dorchester County, Merchants, to Doctor Daniel Sulivane of the same county: part of a tract called "New Market," nearly opposite a house in New Market belonging to Mr. Charles Daffin. One acre more or less, hereby conveyed. Witnesses: E. Richardson, Jno. Stevens. Acknowledged by Philip King Sherwood, Wm. LeCompte and Ann Sherwood, wife of. said Philip King Sherwood, before E. Richardson and Jno. Stevens, Justices.

3 HD 315. October 12, 1791. Jonathan Jacobs and Elizabeth his wife to Jacob Jacobs of the same county: part of "Addition to Reeds Chance" on the Northwest Fork of Nanticoke River. Witnesses: E. Richardson, Jno. Crapper. Acknowledged before E. Richardson and Jno. Crapper, Justices.

3 HD 318. October 25, 1791. Jacob Jacobs of Dorchester County to Jonathan Jacobs and Elizabeth his wife of the same county: part of "Addition to Reeds Chance" on the Northwest Fork of Nanticoke River. Witnesses: E. Richardson, Jno. Stevens. Acknowledged by Jacob Jacobs and Rachel his wife before E. Richardson and Jno. Stevens, Justices.

3 HD 322. October 5, 1791. Henry Killman of Dorchester County to Thomas North of the same county: "Piney Grove," adj. "Gum Swamp" and containing 50 acres. Witnesses: Tho. Jones, Moses Lecompte. Acknowledged by Henry Killman and Delilah his wife before Tho. Jones and Moses Lecompte, Justices.

3 HD 324. October 26, 1790. Thorms Hill Airey of Dorchester County, Farmer, to John Pitt of the same place: part of "Aireys Regulation" adj. lands of Newton Trego and William Pitt and containing 161 acres. Witnesses: Tho. Jones, Jno. Stevens. Acknowledged before Tho. Jones and Jno. Stevens, Justices.

3 HD 326. September 19, 1791. Robert Griffith of Dorchester County to John Barns of the same county: bond concerning arbitration by Moses Lecompte and Benjamin Todd. Witnesses: Jacob Todd, Levin Keene. This arbitration concerns lands called "Hogg Ridge" and "Hogg Quarter."

3 HD 327. October 26, 1791. Award by Moses Lecompte and Benjamin Todd concerning dispute between Robert Gritfith and John Barns of Thos.

3 HD 328. November 3, 1791. Deposition of William LeCompte of John, aged about 59 years, concerning the Will of old John LeCompte deceased, mentions James and John, the sons of old John LeCompte.

3 HD 329. November 4, 1791. William Vans Murray, Attorney at Law, of Dorchester County to Thomas James Pattison of the same county, planter: parts of "Hailes's Choice," "Stokes's Priviledge, "Stokes Adventure" and "Addition to Skinners Choice" and part of a late resurvey called "Hay-Land" made by R. Goldsborough, conveyed to Wm. Dail and by him to said Murray exchanged for 50 acres of equal value. Witnesses: Robt. Harrison, Soln. Birckhead. Acknowledged by Wm. Vans Murray and Charlotte his wife before Robt. Harrison and Soln. Birckhead, Justices.

3 HD 333. November 7, 1791. John Eccleston Junr. of Dorchester County to John Eccleston Senr. of the same county: part of "Batchelders Hope" where said John Eccleston Senr. now lives, containing 113 acres more or less. Witnesses: Robt. Harrison, Soln. Birckhead. Acknowledged before Robt. Harrison and Soln. Birckhead, Justices.

3 HD 335. November 7, 1791. Rachel, Charles and Richard Goldsborough of Dorchester County to William Goldsborough of the same county: houses and lots in Cambridge devised by Robert Goldsborough deceased by Will dated 1 December 17, 1788 to his son Robert Goldsborough, who has died intestate whereby the title to said lots has descended to his brothers and sisters as tenants in common. Witnesses: Robt. Harrison, Soln. Birckhead. Acknowledged before Robt. Harrison and Soln. Birckhead, Justices.

3 HD 338. July 2, 1791. Henry Ennalls of Dorchester County and Sarah his wife to Richard Goldsborough of the same county: their interest in lands devised by Robert Goldsborough (father of said Sarah Ennalls and Richard Goldsborough) by Last Will and Testament dated December 17, 1788, to his son Robert, who has since died intestate and without issue. The said lands were bought by the testator from Mary Hicks deceased and are known as "Woodyard," part of "Busby" conveyed by Richard Glover and wife to Charles Goldsborough, son of the testator, and by him to the testator; "Ennalls's Luck" bought by testator from Henry Ennalls; "Woolfords Interest" adj. thereto, bought by testator from Levin Woolford; part of "Cotmans Swamp"; and a late resurvey of said several tracts

called "Clifton," all lying near the head of Jenkins Creek. Also 50 acres of "Goldsboroughs Outlett," adj. ."Woolfords Interest." Witnesses: Robt. Harrison, Soln. Birckhead. Acknowledged before Robt. Harrison and Soln. Birckhead, Justices.

3.HD 341. July 25, 1791. William, Charles and Rachel Goldsborough of Dorchester County to Richard Goldsborough of the same county: their interest in 478 acres called "Clifton," near the head of Jenkins Creek, and 50 acres of "Goldsboroughs Outlet," devised by Robert Goldsborough deceased to his son Robert who has since died intestate and without issue. Witnesses: Moses LeCompte, Soln. Birckhead. Acknowledged before Moses LeCompte and Soln. Birckhead, Justices.

3 HD 345. August 15, 1791. Richard Goldsborough of Dorchester County, Physician, to John Blair of said county, Mcht.: part of a tract called "Bellfield," adj. "Johns Desire" and part of "Bellfield" laid out for Peter Rea; also adj. land of Wm. Vickars, on the road from Cambridge to Fishing Creek, and containing 50 acres more or less. Witnesses: Soln. Birckhead, Jno. Stevens. Acknowledged before Soln. Birckhead and Jno. Stevens, Justices.

3 HD 347. October 8, 1791. Rubin Mitchel of Dorchester County to Negro slaves: Manumission. Witnesses: James B. Jones, Sarah Ratcliff. Acknowledged before Soln. Birckhead, Justice.

3 HD 348. November 13, 1791. Abraham Lee of Dorchester County, planter, to his son Thomas Lee: part of "Nimcock" on Armstrongs Bay, containing 100 acres more or less. If said Thomas Lee dies without heirs, the said land is to go to Edward Lee, son of said Abraham Lee. Witnesses: Robt. Harrison, Soln. Birckhead. Acknowledged before Robt. Harrison and Soln. Birckhead, Justices.

3 HD 351. June 2, 1791. Nathaniel Elliott of Dorchester County, planter, to Aron Wallace of the same county: Bond concerning part of "Pinkneys Chance," adj. "Wallaces Chance" (mentions bounded tree proved by Thomas Wallace). Witnesses: Matthew Keene, Wm. Vase.

3 HD 352. February 5, 1750. Staplefort Wallace to Joseph, Thomas and Matthew Wallace: Bond concerning lands of their mother Beththuly Wallace. Witnesses: Lewis Griffith, Henry Fisher.

3 HD 352. November 15, 1791. Certificate of Aaron Wallace concerning his

mark.

3 HD 353. November 21, 1791. John Cook Stewart to Elizabeth G. Ennalls: 18 black cattle and a negro slave called Jim, about 8 years of age. (Mortgage). Witness: Soln. Birckhead. Acknowledged before Soln. Birckhead, Justice.

3 HD 354. November 29, 1791. Rachel Goldsborough to Negro slave named Jack: Manumission. Witnesses: Hy. Ennalls, Sarah Ennalls. .Acknowledged before Robt. Harrison, Justice.

3 HD 355. November 21, 1791. Frederick Gootee and Priscilla Gootee, both of Dorchester County, to Edmondson Bramble of the same county: "Hazzard" containing 211 acres; and "Addition to Second Chance" on the road down Gootees Neck, adj. "Second Chance" and containing 29 acres more or less. Witnesses: Jno. Stevens, E. Richardson. Acknowledged before Jno. Stevens and E. Richardson, Justices.

3 HD 350. November 16, 1791. Alexander L. Smoot of Dorchester County, Merchant, to William L. Bond of the same county: Power of Attorney. Witness: Jno. Stevens. Acknowledged before Jno. Stevens, .Justice.

3 HD 354. November 29, 1791. Indenture between Dr. James Sykes and Elizabeth his wife of Dover, Delaware of the first part; Charles Goldsborough of Dorchester County of the second part; William Goldsborough of the same county of the third part; Dr. Richard Goldsborough of the same county of the fourth part; Rachel Goldsborough of the same county of the fifth part; Henry Ennalls and Sarah his wife of the same county of the sixth part and Howes Goldsborough and Rebecca his wife of Talbot County of the seventh part (the said Elizabeth, Charles, William, Richard, Rachel, Sarah and Rebecca being seven of the children of Sarah Goldsborough, daughter of Richard Yerbury late of London, Mcht.) concerning real estate and personal property in Great Britain devised to them by the Last Will and Testament of said Richard Yerbury. Witnesses: Joseph Cummins, Jno. Goldsborough.

3 HD 361. December 24, 1791. Patrick Carroll of Caroline County, Mcht., to Samuel Smith and James A. Buchanan of Baltimore County: merchandise, etc. Witness: Robt. Harrison.

3 HD 363. June 6, 1791. William Harrison LeCompte, Fanny Griffin and Rebecca LeCompte of Dorchester County to Lemuel Beckwith of the same

county: part of "Addition to LeComptes Chance" adj. "Contention" and containing 39 3/4 acres more or less. Witnesses: Thos. Jones, Soln. Birckhead. Acknowledged before Thos. Jones and Soln. Birckhead, Justices.

3 HD 366. November 2, 1791. John Tootell of Dorchester County, Gent., to Thomas Coleson of the same county, carpenter, trustee for the creditors of Thomas Kallendar: Release of Mortgage on part of a tract called "Tootells Venture," containing 500 acres. Witness: Moses LeCompte. Acknowledged before Moses LeCompte and Soln. Birckhead, Justices.

3 HD 369. December 12, 1791. Edmond Mace, son of Edmond, of Dorchester County, to Thomas Colsten, Carpenter, of the same county: part of "Maces Back Range," containing 9 3/4 acres. Witnesses: Soln. Birckhead, Thos. Jones. Acknowledged before Thos. Jones and Soln. Birckhead, Justices.

3 HD 371. December 12, 1791. Thomas Colsten, Carpenter, of Dorchester County, to William Mace of the same county, planter: part of "Addition to Green Bank," adj. "Maces Back Range" and containing 9 3/4 acres. Witnesses: Thos. Jones, Soln. Birckhead. Acknowledged before Thos. Jones and Soln. Birckhead, Justices.

3 HD 374. December 12, 1791. William Mace of Dorchester County, planter, to Edmond Mace of the same county, planter: part of "Cornwell," beginning at the end of a division "between old Edmond Mace and Thomas Mace his brother" and containing 9 3/4 acres. Witnesses: Thos. Jones, Soln. Birckhead. Acknowledged before Thos. Jones and Soln. Birckhead, Justices.

3HD 377. December I, 1791. Deposition of Richard Alford, aged about 70 years, concerning division line between Gen. Henry Hooper and Henry Withgot, shown to deponent by John Dannelly, Mark Littleton and Henry Withgot. This deposition was taken in the presence of Joshua Willis, Wm. Withgott, Nathan Harrington, Benjamin Collison, Levin Marshall, Joseph Withgott and Hooper Elliott, by Jno. Stevens.

3 HD 377. October 28, 1791. William Meddis of Dorchester County, planter, to Ezekiel Fitchew of the same county, planter: land on Church Creek, on a division line between said William Meddis and Roger Jones, and containing 2 acres more or less. Witnesses: Jno. Stevens, Thos. Jones. Acknowledged before Jno. Stevens and Thos. Jones, Justices.

3HD 380. April 15, 1791. Levin Woolford of Dorchester County, planter, to James Tregoe of the same county: part of "Robinsons Lott" on Taylors Island, beginning at a division post between William Traverse and Thomas Traverse and containing 105 acres more or less. Witnesses: Thos. Jones, Moses LeCompte. Acknowledged by Levin Woolford and Molley his wife before Thos. Jones and Moses LeCompte, Justices.

3 HD 383. October 5, 1791. Samuel Muir of Dorchester County, Mariner, to Nathan Griffin of the same county: part of "Muirs Inspection" near "South Preston," on Smiths Creek, containing 23 3/4 acres more or less. Witnesses: Henry Lake, Moses LeCompte. Acknowledged before Henry Lake and Moses Lecompte, Justices.

3 HD 386. December 19, 1791. James LeCompte and Elizabeth his wife, Samuel Mullican and Sarah his wife of Dorchester County to Ann Ennalls of Blackwater, widow: parts of "Murrays Friendship' and "Ennalls Outrange" on branches of Blackwater River, containing 108 acres more or less. Witnesses: Thos. Jones, David Smith. Acknowledged before Thos. Jones and David Smith, Justices.

3 HD 389. October 28, 1791. William Skinner and Elizabeth his wife of Dorchester County to Ezekiel Vickars of the same county: "Fookes's Regulation" containing 363 acres more or less, in which said Elizabeth is seised of an estate tail, hereby conveyed in fee simple in accordance with Act of Assembly of 1782-83. Witness: Thos. Jones, Jno. Stevens. Acknowledged before Thos. Jones and Jno. Stevens, Justices.

3 HD 391. October 28, 1791. Ezekiel Vickars of Dorchester County to William Skinner and Elizabeth his wife of the same county: "Fookes Regulation" containing 363 acres more or less, to said Wm. and Elizabeth for the term of their natural lives, and at the death of the survivor of them then to Joseph Fookes Stewart, Levin Stewart, James Skinner and Zachariah Skinner. Witnesses: Thos. Jones, Jno. Stevens. Acknowledged before Thos. Jones and Jno. Stevens.

3 HD 394. December 23, 1791. Richard Goldsborough of Dorchester County to Horatio Ridout of Annapolis and Rachel his wife (formerly Rachel Goldsborough): land in Cambridge devised to said Richard Goldsborough by his late father Robert Goldsborough. Witness: Hy. Ennalls. Acknowledged before R. Goldsborough, one of the Judges of the General Court.

3 HD 395. August 10, 1791. Charles Goldsborough, Executor of Robert Goldsborough deceased, to William Dail of the same county: 50 acres of "Hayland," adj. "Hails Choice," in accordance with the Will of said deceased. Witnesses: Moses Lecompte, Soln. Birckhead. Acknowledged before Moses Lecompte and Soln. Birckhead.

3 HD 397. December 29, 1791. Joseph Harper of Kent County, Delaware to Iseac Bell of Dorchester of County: "Harpers Meadows" adj. "Discovery" and containing 158 3/4 acres more or less by patent dated April 5, 1775; hereby conveyed in accordance with bonds of said Harper to Thomas Connelly, assigned by Connelly to Henry Willis of Caroline County and by Willis to said Isaac Bell. Witnesses: Jno. Crapper, David Smith. Acknowledged by Joseph Harper and Hetty his wife before Jno. Crapper and David Smith, Justices.

3 HD 400. January 16, 1792. William Vickars 2d. to the State of Maryland: Bond as Inspector at Whites Warehouse, with Levin Woolford and Nehemiah Whiteley as sureties. Witnesses: Sam Hooper, Soln. Frazier. Proved by witnesses before Thos. Jones and Jno. Stevens, Justices.

3 HD 402. December 24, 1791. Charles Brown and Rebeccah his wife of Dorchester County to William Wheelton of the same county: part of "Scholarship" on Connerlys Branch, adj. "Wrights Discovery," on the road from Hunting Creek Church to James Payne's Mill, adj. Arthur Bell's land end containing 21 acres more or less. Witnesses: Jno. Crapper, Jno. Stevens. Acknowledged before Jno. Crapper and Jno. Stevens, Justices.

3 HD 404. December 1, 1791. Ebenezer Newton of Dorchester County to Richard Sweeting of the same county: part of "Newtons Interest" adj. a tract formerly called "Addition," also adj. the new Indian line, also adj. "Newtons Regulation" and "Partnership," and containing 41 acres more or less. Witnesses: E. Richardson, Jno. Stevens. Acknowledged before E. Richardson and Jno. Stevens, Justices.

3 HD 406. January 30, 1792. William Harrison LeCompte of Dorchester County to Elizabeth Cook, wife of Hodson Cook of the same county and sister of said Wm. Harrison LeCompte: "Indian Ridge" between the head of Chapple Creek and Wrights Creek, containing 127 acres more or less. Witnesses: Thos. Jones, Jno. Stevens. Acknowledged before Thos. Jones and Jno. Stevens, Justices.

3 HD 408. January 30, 1792. William LeCompte (son of Anthony) of

Dorchester County, planter, to Hudson Cook of the same county, planter: part of "BuckRange" adj. Thomas Wheeler's part of said tract, adj. "Whores Harbour," adj. "Sewers Land" and containing 164 acres more or less. Witnesses: Thos. Jones, Jno. Stevens. Acknowledged before Thos. Jones and Jno. Stevens, Justices.

3 HD 410. May 19, 1791. Survey and division of "Indian Ridge," "Addition to White Fryers" and "Addition to Killmons Folly" (adj. "Whores Harbour" and "Wrights Lott") between Fanny Griffin, William LeCompte, Becky LeCompte and one Lisbor from the Western Shore, who married one of the heirs.

3 HD 411. February 25, 1792. John Pitt to the State of Maryland: Bond as Inspector of Tobacco at Ennalls Warehouse, with Thos. Hill Airey and William Pitt as Sureties. Witnesses: Wm. Hayward, Levin Keys. Proved by witnesses before Jno. Stevens, Justice.

3 HD 412. October 5, 1791. Samuel Muir of Dorchester County, Mariner, to Nathan Griffin of the same county: "Grove" adj. Snake Point" and containing 150 acres more or less. Witnesses: Henry Lake, Moses LeCompte. Acknowledged before Henry Lake and Moses LeCompte.

3 HD 414. February 6, 1792. William Goldsborough of Dorchester County to Charles LeCompte of the same county: Bettys Inlargement" on the main branch of Transquakin River, near "Exchange," "Rodely" and "Maids Choice" and containing 136 acres more or less. Witnesses: Thos. Jones, Jno. Stevens. Acknowledged before Thos. Jones and Jno. Stevens, Justices.

3 HD 416. March 3, 1792. William C. Angell and Nancy his wife of Dorchester County to John McGuire of the same county: lot No.22 in Vienna, on Thomas Street, containing 3/4 acre. Witnesses: Jno. Eccleston, David Smith. Acknowledged before Jno. Eccleston and David Smith, Justices.

3 HD 419. March 17, 1792. John Ball to the State of Maryland: Bond as Inspector of Tobacco, with Thomas Hodson and Thomas Hodson Senr. as sureties. Witnesses: Geo. Brown, James Shaw Junr. Proved by witnesses before David Smith.

3 HD 420. January 19, 1792. Daniel McCollister of Dorchester County, planter, to John Hutchinson of the same county, planter: personal property. Witness: Jno. Stevens. Acknowledged before Jno. Stevens, Justice.

3 HD 422. December 10, 1791. Edward Wheatley of Dorchester County to Negro slaves: Manumission. Witnesses: White Brown, Humphriss Brown. Acknowledged before E. Richardson, Justice.

3 HD 423. November 21, 1791. Priscilla Gootee, widow of Andrew, of Dorchester County to Joseph Andrews of the same county: the remainder part of "Calliss" on the west side of Blackwater River. Witnesses: Jno. Stevens, E. Richardson. Acknowledged before Jno. Stevens and E. Richardson, Justices.

3 HD 424. February 16, 1792. William Keene of Dorchester County to Joseph Andrews: personal property and two acres of "Addition to Brambles Hope." Witness: Wm, Willey.

3 HD 425. October 16, 1780. William Jones of Cabin Creek in Dorchester County, planter, to Benjamin Collison of the same county, planter: part of "Goodridges Choice" containing 209 acres, on Cabin Creek. Witnesses: Jos. Richardson, Thos. Jones. Acknowledged by William Jones and Delitha his wife before Jos. Richardson and Thos. Jones, Justices.

3 HD 428. October 22, 1791. William Jones of Rockingham County, North Carolina, planter, to Benjamin Collison of Dorchester County, planter: 209 acres of "Goodridges Choice" on Cabin Creek. Henry Waggaman and Nicholas Hammond Esquires are named as attorneys for Jones to acknowledge this deed in Court. Witnesses: Timothy Corkran, Edward Collinson, Jonathan Bird. Proved by witnesses and acknowledged by attorneys in Dorchester County Court March 22, 1792. H. Dickinson, Clk.

3 HD 431. November 9, 1791. Henry Lord of Kent County, Delaware to Daniel Nicols of Dorchester .County: part of "Travers' s Purchase" or "Regulation" adj . "Staitons Purchase" adj. John Braughan's land and containing 10 acres more or less. Witnesses: E. Richardson, Jno. Stevens . Acknowledged before E. Richardson and Jno. Stevens, Justices.

3 HD 434. June 29, 1790. Frederick Willey, Amelia Smith and Sarah Willey to George Willey: Bond to convey land of Rachel Willey, their mother, deceased, called "Timber Swamp." Witnesses: Levi Foxwell, Wm. Carroll.

3 HD 434. December 26, 1791. Thomas Hicks of Dorchester County, planter, to John Scott of the same county: part of "Buckfield" adj. a part of "Darley" formerly conveyed by said Hicks to said Scott, and containing 126 acres more

or less. Witnesses: Robt. Harrison, Thos. Jones. Acknowledged before Robt. Harrison and Thos. Jones, Justices.

3 HD 437. January 7, 1792. Henry Ennalls, son of Henry, of Dorchester County, Gent., and Sarah his wife to John Scott of Dorchester County: part of "Ennalls's Outrange," containing 3 ½ acres more or less, on the road to New Market, in the forks of the road near Cambridge. Witnesses: Jno. Crapper, Jno. Stevens. Acknowledged before Jno. Crapper and Jno. Stevens, Justices.

3 HD 439. March 3, 1792. Samuel Muir of Dorchester County to William McBryde and Co. of the same county: Negro slaves. Witnesses: David Smith, Saml. Stanford. Acknowledged before David Smith, Justice.

3 HD 440. March 5, 1792. James Rule Stevens of Dorchester County to Andrew McDonald of the same county: Negro girl named Clea, about 16 years of age. Witness: Thos. Stewart. Acknowledged before Levin Woolford, Justice.

3 HD 442. March 5, 1792. Richard Goldsborough of Dorchester County, Physician, to John Scott of the same county: part of "Bellfield" within the lines of "Ennalls's Outrange," which was sold by Henry Ennalls and wife to said John Scott. Witnesses: Jno. Stevens, Levin Woolford. Acknowledged before Jno. Stevens and Levin Woolford, Justices.

3 HD 444. March 5, 1792. William H. LeCompte {son of Anthony LeCompte, deceased), Hodson Cook and Elizabeth his wife of Dorchester County to Thomas Hubbert of the same county, planter: parts of "Indian Ridge," "Kilmons Folly" and "Addition to Kilmons Folly" (description refers to the first bounder of "Kilmons Folly or White Fryers"), adj. lands of John Ratcliff and containing 127 acres more or less. Witnesses: Jno. Stevens, Levin Woolford. Acknowledged before Jno. Stevens and Levin Woolford, Justices.

3 HD 447. December 24, 1791. Cyrus Mitchell and Sarah his wife of Dorchester County to Eccleston Brown of the same county: part of "Addition to Moores Meadows," containing 21 acres more or less. Also "Sandy Hill" {part in Caroline County) adj. "Windsort" and containing 100 acres more or less. Witnesses: Jno. Stevens, David Smith. Acknowledged before Jno. Stevens and David Smith, Justices.

3 HD 450. February 25, 1792. John Jones {son of Morgan) of Dorchester County to Thomas Kilman of the same county: part of "Lockermans

Regulation" adj. land of Henry Kilman and containing 9 acres more or less. Witnesses: Thos. Jones, Moses LeCompte. Acknowledged by John Jones and Lunaria (Lurania) his wife before Thos. Jones and Moses LeCompte, Justices.

3 HD 452. February 25, 1792. John Jones {son of Morgan) of Dorchester County, planter, to Henry Kilman of the same county: part of "Lockermans Regulation" adj. Thomas Kilman's land and containing 16 3/4 acres more or less. Also part of the same tract adj. Robert Willson's land and containing 24 acres more or less. Witnesses: Thos. Jones, Moses LeCompte. Acknowledged by John Jones and Lurania his wife before Thos. Jones and Moses LeCompte, Justices.

3 HD 455. December 24, 1791. James Sykes of Dover, Delaware and Elizabeth his wife (formerly Elizabeth Goldsborough) to Richard Goldsborough of Dorchester County: her 1/8 interest in land called "Wood Yard" or "Clifton" devised by her father Robert Goldsborough to her brother Robert Goldsborough, who has since died unmarried and intestate. Witness: Horatio Ridout. Acknowledged before R. Goldsborough, one of the Judges of the General Court.

3 HD 457. December 24, 1791. Charles Brown and Rebeccah his wife of Dorchester County to John Charles of the same county: part of "Scholarship Improved" on the road from Hunting Creek Church to Payne's Mill, adj. Wm. Connerly's land and containing 8 1/4 acres more or less. Witnesses: Jno. Stevens, Jno. Crapper. Acknowledged before Jno. Stevens and Jno. Crapper, Justices.

3 HD 460. December 6, 1791. Henry Mobray of Dorchester County to Nathan Harrington of the same county: part of "Goodridges Choice" on the north side of Cabin Creek, adj. Bromwell's land and land of Wm. Jones, and containing 310 acres more or less. Witnesses: E. Richardson, Jno. Stevens. Acknowledged before E. Richardson and Jno. Stevens, Justices.

3 HD 463. February 1, 1792. Levin Stack of Dorchester County to his son Levin Stack of the same county: part of "Priviledge" adj. "Taylors Neglect" and containing 63 acres more or less. Witnesses: E. Richardson, Jno. Stevens. Acknowledged before E. Richardson and Jno. Stevens, Justices.

3 HD 464. October 28, 1791. Award by Moses Lecompte and Robt. Griffith in a dispute between Vachel Keene and Matthias Travers, concerning a mistake in the Will of Zebulon Keene Senr., deceased, in which a tract of 59 acres is called

"Keenes Security" instead of "Keenes Inclosure," its proper name. Bond from Vachel Keene to Matthias Travers.

3 HD 466. February 17, 1792. Elizabeth Travers of Dorchester County to Negro slave named Nedd, aged 35 years: Manumission. Witnesses: Peggy Creaton, Richd. Pattison. Acknowledged before Richd. Pattison, Justice.

3 HD 467. March 20, 1792. William Pitt of Dorchester County to Negro Jem, aged 10 years: Manumission. Witnesses: Richd. Pattison, Peregrine Beaston. Acknowledged before Richd. Pattison, Justice.

3 HD 467. March 21, 1792. James Tall of Dorchester County to Thomas Tregoe of the same county: 4 acres called "Talls First Venture." Witnesses: Thos. Jones, Henry Lake. Acknowledged before Thos. Jones and Henry Lake, Justices.

3 HD 469. November 14, 1791. Isaac Wheatley and Charles Wheatley of Dorchester County to John Vickers of the same county: part of "Levertons Chance," part of "Willsons Chance" and part of "Isaac Venture," containing 230 ½ acres more or less. Witnesses: Jno. Crapper, Jno. Stevens. Acknowledged by Isaac Wheatley and Mary his wife and by Charles Wheatley before Jno. Crapper and Jno. Stevens, Justices.

3 HD 472. March 21, 1792. Joseph Thomas of Dorchester County to John Cook of the same county, planter: part of a tract formerly called "Indian Quarter," now "Thomas's Chance" adj. "Brooks Outhold," on the north side (of Hudsons Creek, on Little House Cove, containing 39 3/4 acres more or less. Witnesses: Henry Lake, Thos. Jones. Acknowledged before Henry Lake and Thos. Jones, Justices.

3 HD 474. March 20, 1792. Award by Charles Eccleston and Joseph Hubbard, Arbitrators, in a controversy between Reuben Thomas and John Cook, concerning 62 acres, part of a tract called "Indian Quarter."

3 HD 475. February 4, 1792. McKeel Connerly and Rebecca his wife of Dorchester County to Jesse Williams of the same county: land in Northwest Fork, called "Tryall," containing 36 acres more or less. Witnesses: Jno. Crapper, Jno. Stevens. Acknowledged before Jno. Crapper and Jno. Stevens, Justices.

3 HD 477. December 17, 1791. Anthony Ross and Mary his wife of Caroline County to Jesse Williams of Dorchester County: lands in Northwest Fork being

79 ½ acres of "Addition to Hog Quarter," parts of "Tryall," and "Phillips' Lot" containing 29 ½ acres more or less. Witnesses: E. Richardson, Jno. Crapper. Acknowledged before E. Richardson and Jno. Crapper, Magistrates.

3 HD 480. March 20, 1792. John Laing and Hosanna his wife and Anne Records of Dorchester County to William McBryde and James Richie of the same county: lots in Vienna, adj. lands of Alexander Douglass and James Shaw, "which the said John Laing and Anne Records hath any Right or Title either by the Last Will and Testament of his father Alexander Laing or as Heir to his said Father or a Heir to his said Mother Eleanor Lang." The said land was lately occupied by William Bond and Co. as a storehouse, but is now vacant. Witnesses: David Smith, Jno. Crapper. Acknowledged before David Smith and Jno. Crapper, Justices.

3 HD 483. March 21, 1792. Joseph Hubbard of Dorchester County to William Thomas of the same county: part of a tract near the head of Hodsons Creek, formerly called "Indian Quarter," now called "Thomas Chance." Witnesses: Thos. Jones, Henry Lake. Acknowledged before Thos. Jones and Henry Lake, Justices.

3 HD 485. November 14, 1791. George Messick and Eliza his wife of Dorchester County to John Robertson Senr. of Somerset County: part of "Levertons Chance," part of "Adams Venture" and part of "the Small Tract," containing 97 3/4 acres in all. Witnesses: Jno. Stevens, Jno. Crapper. Acknowledged before Jno. Stevens and Jno. Crapper, Justices.

3 HD 487. November 4, 1791. Charles Wallace and John Muir of Annapolis, Merchants, to Isaac Wheatley of Dorchester County: "Cumberland," part of "Ross's Lott," part of "Harpers Folly," part of "Harpers Seat," part of "Adams Dear Purchase" and part of "Increase," containing 249 acres more or less in all, conveyed June 28, 1788 to said Wallace and Muir by David Weems and William Scrivener, and formerly conveyed by John Ross to Morgan Jones of Ann Arundel County and by said Morgan Jones to said David Weems. Witness: J. Toy. Chase. Acknowledged before J. Toy. Chase, one of the Judges of the General Court.

3 HD 489. March 21, 1792. Benjamin Keene of Dorchester County, Gent., to his son Levin Keene of the same county: "Keenes Regulation" on the road from the head of Hungar River to Worlds End Bridge, containing 47 ½ acres more or less. Also 5 other tracts or parts of tracts near the main road from where Capt.

John Bennett formerly lived to the bridge across Worlds End Creek, to wit, "Stapleforts Desert" containing 5'0 acres more or less "Keenes Timber Yard" containing 36 acres more or less; "Pinckneys Chance" in two parts, containing 95 acres more or less and "the Jib" containing 3 3/4 acres more or less. The use of the said lands is to be retained by the said Benjamin Keene and Nancy his life during their natural lives. Witnesses: Thos. Jones, Levin Woolford. Acknowledged before Thos. Jones and Levin Woolford.

3 HD 491. March 3, 1792. Richard Badley of Dorchester County, Farmer, and Jane his wife, to Thomas Hodson of the same county, Farmer: part of "Friends Discovery," patented to Christopher Short Badley and conveyed to his son Richard Badley for 117 ½ acres more or less; 63 acres of this tract having already been conveyed by said Richard to the said Thomas Hodson, 54 ½ acres is hereby conveyed. Witnesses: Jno. Eccleston., David Smith. Acknowledged before Jno. Eccleston and David Smith, Justices.

3 HD 493. March 15, 1792. George Ward to John Molock, formerly the slave of Levin Traverse and purchased this day by said George Ward: Manumission. Witnesses: Hy. Ennalls, Bartho. Ennalls. Acknowledged before Levin Woolford, Justice.

3HD 494. March 13, 1792 . William Tull and Mary Tull his wife of Sussex County, Delaware, to Charles Russell of Dorchester County: Bond for conveyance of their part of "Addition to Reeds Chance" between the branches of Nanticoke River, adj. John Ross's part of the said tract and containing 18 ½ acres. Witnesses: Charles Wheatley, Joseph Wheatley.

3 HD 495. June 7, 1790 - July 23, 1791. Commission to Thomas Jones, Levin Woolford, William Stevens and Jonathan Patridge of Dorchester County, Gent., to perpetuate bounds of Abraham Lee's part of "Nimcock," and Return. Deposition of Andrew Marshall, aged about 61 years, mentions Mr. Joseph Byus about 18-20 years ago. Deposition of John Frazier, of full age, mentions Joseph Byus and William Lee about 18-20 years ago. Deposition of Jonathan Patridge, aged 59 years, re land surveyed 20 years ago on the road to Cooks Point. ..

3 HD 499. March 3, 1792. Samuel Muir of Dorchester County to Alexander Douglass of the same county: Negro slave called George. Witnesses: Jno. Eccleston, James Shaw. Acknowledged before Jno. Eccleston, Justice.

39

3 HD 500. March 21, 1792. Thomas Tregoe of Dorchester County to James Tall of the same county: 4 acres, part of three tracts called "Ending," "Talls Regulation" and 'Tregoes Venture." Witnesses: Thos. Jones, Henry.Lake. Acknowledged before Thos. Jones and Henry Lake, Justices.

3 HD 502. March 21, 1792. Thomas Wright and John Soward of Dorchester County, planters, to Levin Hubbert of the same county, planter: part of a tract formerly conveyed to said Thomas Wright by Thomas Taylor and wife and afterwards sold by Thomas Lockerman, High Sheriff, under Fieri Facias issued at suit of Henry Tregoe, for part of two tracts called "Rosses Range" and "Addition to Rosses Chance" on the east side of Hodsons Creek, adj. lands of Hugh McCall and John Arnal and containing 20 acres more or less. Witnesses: Henry Lake, Richd. Pattison. Acknowledged by Thomas Wright, John Soward and Nancy Wright, wife of said Thomas, before Henry Lake and Richd. Pattison, Justices.

3 HD 505. March 23, 1792. William Thomas of Dorchester County to Joseph Hubbard of the same county: part of a tract near the head of Hodsons Creek, formerly called "Indian Quarter," now called "Thomas's Chance." Witnesses: Henry Lake, Thos. Jones. Acknowledged before Thos. Jones and Henry Lake, Justices.

3 HD 507. March 21, 1792. Reubin Thomas of Dorchester County to John Cook of the same county, Carpenter: part of "Thomas's Chance" on the Northeast side of Hodsons Creek, containing 62 ½ acres more or less. Witnesses: Henry Lake, Thos. Jones. Acknowledged before Henry Lake and Thos. Jones, Justices.

3 HD 510. March 20, 1792. Henry Macoter of Dorchester County to William Martain of the same county: "White Oak Range" on a branch of Blackwater River in Peters Neck, adj. "Sandwitch" and containing 50 acres more or less. Witnesses: Richd. Pattison, Levin Woolford. Acknowledged before Richd. Pattison and Levin Woolford, Justices.

3 HD 512. March 20, 1792. Samuel Hooper of Dorchester County, planter, to William Martin of the same county: part of "Hoopers Beginning," containing ½ acre more or less. Witnesses: Levin Woolford, Richd. Pattison. Acknowledged before Levin Woolford and Richd. Pattison, Justices.

3 HD 514. March 19, 1792. Levin Woolford of Dorchester County to John Jones of the same State, Mariner: "Fishing Creek Point Regulated," containing

128 acres more or less. Also the Moiety of "Fishing Creek Point" which Robert Goldsborough purchased of John Hill, containing 75 acres more or less. Witnesses: Thos. Jones, Moses LeCompte. Acknowledged by Levin Woolford and Anne his wife before Thos. Jones and Moses LeCompte, Justices.

3 HD 517. March 28, 1792. Charles Crookshanks, Gent., and Archibald Moncrieff, Gent., of . Baltimore Town, to Gustavus Scott Esq. of Dorchester County: part of "Loockermans Regulation," also known as "Glasgow," mortgaged by Archibald Pattison during his lifetime to Archibald Moncrieff and now sold by authority of the said Patison's Last Will and Testament. This tract adj. land of William Murray Robertson and lies on the road from Cambridge to the late Richard Glover's Farm. .Witnesses: John Done, Robt. Harrison. Acknowledged before John Done, Judge, and Robert Harrison, Associate Justice of Dorchester County Court.

3 HD 520. March 29, 1792. Charles Crookshanks and Archibald Moncrieff to Gustavus Scott Esq. of Dorchester County: land on the main street of Cambridge, mortgaged by Archibald Patison during his lifetime to Archibald Moncrieff and now sold by authority of said Patison's Last Will and Testament, located near lands of Charles Goldsborough and Robert Ewing. Witnesses: John Done, Moses LeCompte . Acknowledged before John Done, Judge, and Moses LeCompte, Associate Justice of Dorchester County Court.

3 HD 523. March 28, 1792. Charles Crookshanks and Archibald Moncrieff to William Murray Robertson of Dorchester County: part of "Lockermans Regulation" mortgaged by Archibald Patison during his lifetime to Archibald Moncrieff and now sold by authority of said Patison's Last Will and Testament. Witnesses: John Done, Robt. Harrison. Acknowledged before John Done, Judge, and Robt. Harrison, Associate Justice.

3 HD 526. November 21, 1791. Priscilla Goutee of Dorchester County to Henry Edgar of the same county: part of "Callis" containing 200 acres, and "Goutees Choice" containing 25 acres, Witnesses: E. Richardson, Jno. Stevens. Acknowledged before E. Richardson and Jno. Stevens, Justices.

3 HD 529. April 9, 1792. Peter Rea, Dealer, to Gustavus Scott, Barrister, both of the town of Cambridge: part of "Loockerma.ns Regulation," containing 1 ½ acres more or less. Witnesses: Levin Woolford, Stanley Byus. Acknowledged before Levein Woolford, Stanley Byus, Justices.

3 HD 532. April 9, 1792. Gustavus Scott to William Murray Robinson: lots 6 and 7 of "Glasgow"; and lot No. 1, opposite lot No.6, for his own use and as trustee for the public, for a highway. Witnesses: Levin Woolford, Stanley Byus. Acknowledged by Gustavus Scott and Margaret Scott his wife before Stanley Byus and Levin Woolford.

3 HD 535. April 9, 1792. Margaret Trippe and William Murray Robinson (Robertson) to Gustavus Scott as trustee for the public: land in Cambridge, for use as a street, adj. land now occupied by John Kenny and land of John Murray. Witnesses: Levin Woolford, Stanley Byus. Acknowledged before Levin Woolford and Stanley Byus, Justices.

3 HD 537. April 4, 1792. Henry Hicks of Thomas of Dorchester County to David Smith of the same county: part of "Partnership" on the east side of the main road from Vienna to Crotchers Ferry, containing 6 1/4 acres more or less. Witnesses: Jno. Eccleston. Jno. Stevens. Acknowledged before Jno. Eccleston and Jno. Stevens, Justices.

3 HD 540. April 16, 1792. Joseph Ennalls Junr. of Dorchester County to Anthony Manning of the same county: part of "Strife." Witnesses: Jno. Stevens, Levin Woolford. Acknowledged before Jno. Stevens and Levin Woolford, Justices.

3 HD 544. March 1, 1792. John Breeden and Mary Breeden of Marlborough County, South Carolina, to Abraham Lewis of Dorchester County: Power of Attorney concerning "Coles Venture" or "Coles Regulation" on Coles Creek (the said Mary Breding was formerly the wife of George Cole). Witness: Aaron Lewis. Acknowledged before J. Winfield, Clk. of Court, Marlborough County, S. C.

3 HD 545. March 12, 1792. Isaac Nichols and Dolly his wife of Guilford County, North Carolina, to Abraham Lewis of Dorchester County: Power of Attorney (Dolley is the daughter of George Cole) concerning "Coles Venture" or "Coles Regulation." Witness: Aaron Lewis. Acknowledged before William Gray, Justice for Guilford County, N. C. John Hamilton, Clk.

3 HD 541. April 16, 1792. Abraham Lewis of Thomas of Dorchester County to Thomas McNamara of the same county: "Coles Regulation," "Coles Venture" and "B rambles Hope." Witnesses: Levin Woolford, Stanley Byus. Acknowledged before Levin Woolford and Stanley Byus, Justices.

3 HD 549. April 16, 1792. Richard Goldsborough of Dorchester County to Peter Rea of the same county: part of "Belfield" adj. John Blair's part of said tract, on the road to Fishing Creek, adj. the Meeting House Survey and William Vickers' part of "Belfield," and containing 29 acres more or less. Witnesses: Jno. Stevens, Levin Woolford. Acknowledged before Jno. Stevens and Levin Woolford, Justices.

3 HD 552. April 2, 1792. Charles Goldsborough of Dorchester County to Thomas Stewart of the same county: land in Cambridge, adj. Mrs. Muse's garden, on the main street, and adj. the brick house now in the possession of Miss Mary Ennalls. Witnesses: Jno. Stevens, Levin Woolford. Acknowledged before Jno. Stevens and Levin Woolford, Justices.

3 HD 555. March 21, 1791 - August 8, 1791. Commission to Moses LeCompte, Richard Pattison, Nathaniel Manning, Charles Eccleston and Thomas Lynthecum of Dorchester County to perpetuate bounds of John Phillips' land, part of "Nimcock," and Return. "Nimcock" and the second course of "Cedar Point" were surveyed by William Barrow Esq. by direction of the said Commissioners. The second bounder of "Cedar Point" was identified by Elijah Marshall. John Phillips and Hugh Spedding are mentioned as parties concerned. The Commissioners also settled the division of "Nimcock" between John Phillips and Abraham Lee, in accordance with a division made by Wm. Lee deceased between his sons Abraham and John Lee, on the road to Cooks Point.

3 HD 559. June 11, 1792. Charles Hodson to the State of Maryland: Bond with Jno. Eccleston and Samuel Hooper as Sureties. Witnesses: H. Dickinson, Jno. M. Stevens. Proved by witnesses before Thos. Jones.

3 HD 560. March 15, 1792. George Ward, Henry Ennalls and Bartholomew Ennalls, trustees of the Poor of Dorchester County, to James Murphey of Dorchester County: Indenture of John Pursom, aged 10 years, and John Patison, aged 8 years, to serve as apprentices until age 21 to learn the occupation of farming. Witness: Thos. McKeel

3 HD 561. March 15, 1792. George Ward. Henry Ennalls and Bartholomew Ennalls, Trustees of the Poor of Dorchester County, to William B. Murphey of Dorchester County: Indenture of Nancy Fitzgerald to serve as apprentice until age 16 years (she being now 9 years of age). Witness: Thos. McKeel.

3 HD 562. March 21, 1792. Henry Ennalls, John Hooper and Bartholomew

Ennalls, Trustees for the Poor of Dorchester County, to Andrew Kirwan: Indenture of John Seers to serve as apprentice until age 21 years (he being now 19 years of age), to learn the trade of shoemaker. Witness: Thos. McKeel.

3 HD 564. March 21, 1792. Levin Woolford, Henry Ennalls and John Hooper, Trustees for the Poor of Dorchester County, to Bartholomew Ennalls: Indenture of James Lankfit alias Woodards and Hartly Booth alias Keene to serve as apprentices until age 21 (Lankfit being now 12 years old and Booth 10 years old), to learn the occupation of farming. Witness: Thos. McKeel.

3 HD 565. October 24, 1791 - March 19, 1792. Commission to Richard Pattison, Benjamin Woodard, Ezekiel Vickars and Thomas Vickars of Dorchester County, Gent., to perpetuate bounds of land of James Ross called "Ross's Purchase," adj. "Daniels Choice," and Return. Deposition of John Causey, aged about 70 years, mentions John Stevens, grandfather of the present William Stevens, and William Ross, grandfather of the present James Ross, about 40 years ago. Deposition of Thomas Ross, aged about 57 years.

3 HD 568. March 17, 1792. John Owens of Dorchester County, planter, to William Phillips of the same county, planter: Negro slaves. Witnesses: David Smith, Jno. Muir. Acknowledged before David Smith, Justice.

3 HD 570. March 27, 1792. William Vaughan of Dorchester County to Negro slaves: Manumission. Witnesses: Tho. Jones, Moses LeCompte. Acknowledged before Moses LeCompte, Justice.

3 HD 571. February 15, 1791. Jno. Eccleston, Sheriff, to Daniel Nicols: Receipt for the purchase price of a Negro slave of Kenneth McKenney, sold by virtue of a Fieri Facias suit of Mrs. Muse. Witness: Thomas Ennalls.

3 HD 571. March 24, 1792.. John Woollen of Dorchester County, planter, to Thomas Jones Junr.: livestock, furniture, etc. Witnesses: John, Jones, William Jones. Acknowledged before Tho. Jones, Justice.

3 HD 572. May 10, 1787. Deposition of Andrew Robinson re bounder of "Boar Brook" set down by John Megraw, John Booth and Thomas Johnson, states that Reubin Andrews had offered deponant ten Pounds to prove it in another place. Witness: Henry Leak.

3 HD 573. April 2, 1792. Acknowledgment by Hetty Harper, wife of Joseph

Harper of Delaware, of a deed from said Joseph Harper to Isaac Bell of Dorchester County. Certified by Jno. Crapper and David Smith, Justices.

3 HD 573. August 25, 1787. James Booze of Dorchester County, planter, to Ezekiel Meekins, Thomas Barns, Thomas Macnamara and Wm. Keene of the same county: Bond to cut a ditch at Blackwater River and Coles Creek. Witnesses: John Mills, Jeene Merideth.

3 HD 575. April 27, 1792. Randolph Johnson of Dorchester County to James Steele of the same county: slaves and livestock, and a crop of wheat on the said Steele's farm on Chicamacomico River, now in the occupation of said Johnson. Witnesses: John Johnson, Joseph Jeams. Acknowledged before David Smith, Justice.

3 HD 577. May 3, 1792. George Ward, Levin Woolford and Henry Ennalls, Trustees of the Poor of Dorchester County, to Joseph Dodson of said county, shoemaker: Indenture of John King, a poor boy of said county, to serve the said Dodson as an apprentice until age 21, he being now about II years old, to learn the trade of shoemaker. Witness: Thomas McKeel, Clk.

3HD 578. March 9 1792. Nathan Harrington and Benjamin Collinson of Dorchester County, planters, to Joshua Willis of Caroline County, planter: bond to convey part of "Goodridges Choice" heretofore purchased by Harrington & Collinson from James Carter & wife. Witnesses: Benthall Stevens, Charles Willis.

3 ED 579. March 31, 1792. Nathan Harrington and Elizabeth his wife, Benjamin Collinson and Mary his wife, all of Dorchester County, to Joshua Willis of Caroline County: part of "Goodridges Choice" between Cabin Creek and Blinkhorns Creek, heretofore sold to said Harrington & Collinson by James Carter and Ann Ennalls Carter his wife, daughter of Ennalls Hooper deceased, containing 155 acres more or less. Witnesses: Jno. Eccleston, Jno. Stevens. Acknowledged before Jno. Eccleston and Jno. Stevens, Justices.

3 HD 58.3. May .3, 1792. George Ward, Levin Woolford and Henry Ennalls, Trustees of the Poor of Dorchester County, to James Douglass of said county, Tailor: Indenture of John Scot and David Morgan, poor boys of the same county, to serve Douglass as apprentices until age 21, to learn the trade of Tailor. Witness: Thos. McKeel, Clk.

3 HD 584. May 7, 1792. John Eccleston, Gent., late High Sheriff of Dorchester County, to Levin Keene (son of Benjamin Keene Esquire) of the same county, planter: part of "Pilgrimage," formerly the property of Thomas Hill Airey, sold by said Sheriff under Court Order for satisfaction of Airey's debts to Esther Green; 200 acres more or less hereby conveyed, on the main road from the Methodist Meeting House to John Pitt's plantation. Witnesses: Levin Woolford, Stanley Byus. Acknowledged before Levin Woolford and Stanley Byus, Justices. .

3 HD 589. December 31, 1791. Isaac Holland and Jane his wife of Annapolis to Ann Ennalls of Blackwater in Dorchester County, widow: "Murrays Friendship" and "Ennalls Outrange" on Blackwater River, adj. "Perth" and containing 108 acres. Witnesses: Jno. Brice, Jno. Edwards. Acknowledged before Jno. Brice and Robt. Couden, Justices for Ann Arundel County. Nich. Harwood, Clk.

3 HD 593. April 23, 1792. Robert Norris of Dorchester County, Miller, to Benjamin Kemp of Talbot County, planter: personal property. Witnesses: Peregrine Beaston, Thomas Abbett. .

3 HD 594. June 27, 1792. Valentine Peers of Prince William County, Virginia, to James Ritchie of Vienna, Maryland, Mcht.: Power of Attorney concerning business of Peers with Mr. Alexander Smoot of said town. Witnesses: Alexander Douglass, Jno. Hill.

3 HD 595. April 10, 1792. Absolum Willey of Dorchester County to his nephew Littleton Willey of the same county: part of "Venture" between Coles Creek and Worlds End Creek. Witnesses: Henry Lake, Jno. Keene. Acknowledged before Henry Lake and Jno. Keene, Justices.

3 HD 598. December 17, 1791. James Swiggett of Dorchester County and Femy his wife to William Murphy of the sarre county: "Third Purchase," adj. land of James Murphy and containing 100 acres more or less. Witnesses: E. Richardson, Jno. Crapper. Acknowledged before E. Richardson and Jno. Crapper, Justices.

3 HD 601. April 16, 1792. Peter Rea of Cambridge in Dorchester County, Mcht., to Charles Winrow of the sarre county, painter: lease of part of "Lockermans Regulation" near Cambridge . Witnesses: Thomas Abbett, Peregrine Beaston. Acknowledged before Jno. Stevens and Levin Woolford, Justices.

3 HD 604. January.6, 1792. Henry Ennalls of Dorchester County and Sarah his wife to George Ward of the same place: land on the road from Cambridge to the Poor House, on the road from Cambridge to Thomas Airey's, and containing 550 acres. Also all lands near Fishing Creek, in Cambridge or elsewhere now belonging to said Henry and Sarah in right of the said Sarah. Witnesses: Jno. Crapper, Jno. Stevens. Acknowledged before Jno. Crapper, and John Stevens, Justices.

3 HD 607. April 28, 1792. Edward Wheatley of Dorchester County to Negro slaves: Manumission. Acknowledged before Jno. Crapper, Justice.

3 HD 608. January 7, 1792. Henry Ennalls of Dorchester County and Sarah his wife to Thomas Brannock of the same county: part of "Harwoods Choice" on the west side of Geators Creek, containing 24 acres more or less. Witnesses: Jno. Stevens, Jno. Crapper, Soln. Birckhead. Acknowledged before Jno. Stevens and Jno. Crapper, Justices.

3 HD 611. January 7, 1792 George Ward of Dorchester County to Henry Ennalls and Sarah his wife: 550 acres and lands near Fishing Creek and in Cambridge, conveyed to said Ward by said Ennalls and wife January 6, 1792. Witnesses: Jno. Crapper and Jno. Stevens. Acknowledged before Jno. Crapper and Jno. Stevens, Justices.

3 HD 613. January 7, 1792. Henry Ennalls of Dorchester County and Sarah his wife to Mary Brannock and Philemon Brannock of the same county: in compliance with a verbal contract made by Robert Goldsborough deceased with Philemon Brannock deceased, father of the aforesaid Philemon Brannock, Ennalls and wife convey part of "Harwoods Choice" on a cove called Sloop Cove which issues out of Fishing Creek, to said Mary Brannock for her lifetime and at her death to said Philemon j Brannock. Witnesses: Jno. Stevens, Jno. Crapper. Acknowledged before Jno. Stevens and Jno. Crapper, Justices.

3 HD 617. August 27, 1776. Thomas Hodson Senr. of Dorchester County to George Bonwill and Charles Dean of the same county: Bond to convey part of "Maidens Forrest" on the east side of the main branch of Chicamacomico River, in accordance with Power of Attorney to said Thomas Hodson Senr. from Thomas Hodson of Boston Town in the Province of Massachusetts Bay. . Witnesses: John Maybury, Denwood Walter.

3 HD 619. May 14, 1792. Thomas Ratcliff of Dorchester County to William

Hayward of the same county: two parcels of a tract called "Ratcliffs Addition" on Castle Haven Creek, containing 10 acres and ½ acre respectively, the second part adj. "the first line of the original Tract of Land called Contention." Witnesses: Robt. Harrison, Moses LeCompte. Acknowledged before Robt. Harrison and Moses LeCompte, Justices.

3 HD 623. April 6, 1792. Aney Barns to Negro Saul: Manumission. Witnesses: Richd. Pattison, James Hooper. Acknowledged before Richd. Pattison, Justice.

3 HD 624. May 1, 1792. Roger Jones of Dorchester County to John Jones of the same county: part of "Addition to Joneses Chance," containing 11 acres more or less. Witnesses: Tho. Jones, John Keene. Acknowledged before Tho. Jones and John Keene, Justices.

4 HD 1. May 14, 1792. William Hayward of Dorchester County to Thomas Ratcliff of the same county: two parcels of "Ratcliffs Addition" on Castle Haven Creek, containing 1 ½ acres and 10 ½ acres more or less, respectively. Witnesses: Robt. Harrison, Moses LeCompte. Acknowledged before Moses LeCompte and Robt. Harrison, Justices.

4 HD 5. February 27, 1792. Henry Hodson, son of John, of Dorchester County, planter, to Levin LeCompte, son of John, of the same county, planter: "Smarts Inclosure" adj. "Pounds Third Addition" on the north side of Chicamacomico River, containing 163 acres more or less. Also "Pounds Third Addition" on the west side of Chicamacomico River near "Pounds Second Addition," containing 100 acres more or less. Also part of "Pounds Second Addition Corrected" (granted to John Hodson Senr. April 4, 1717) containing 237 acres more or less, excepting 30 ½ acres sold by said Henry Hodson to Anthony Manning February 7, 1791. Witnesses: Jno. Eccleston, David Smith. Acknowledged by Henry Hodson and Elizabeth his wife before Jno. . Eccleston and David Smith, Justices.

4 HD 9. March 22, 1792. James Steele Esq. of Dorchester County to Isaac Steele, Gent., of the same county: part of "Handsell" on the west side of Nanticoke River at Taylors Creek (otherwise Chickawan Creek), containing 484 acres more or less. Witnesses: Moses LeCompte, Henry Lake. Acknowledged by James Steele and Mary his wife before Moses LeCompte and Henry Lake, Justices.

4 HD 13. April 10, 1792. Absolem Willey of Dorchester County to Philip

Graham of the same county: "Nuners Discovery," near 'Worlds End" and "Affine Increase." Also part of "Venture," on the road to Coles Creek. 46 acres hereby conveyed, clear of elder surveys, in both of said tracts. Witnesses: Henry Lake, Jno. Keene. Acknowledged before Henry Lake and Jno. Keene, Justices.

4 HD 16. May 26, 1792. Matthew Jarrett and Jemima his wife and Rhoda Foxwell of Dorchester County to Roger Foxwell of the same county: "Foxwells Lott" on the west side of Charles Creek, containing 46 acres more or less. Witnesses: Henry Lake, Jno. Keene. Acknowledged before Henry Lake and Jno. Keene, Justices.

4 HD 19 May 30, 1792. William S. Bond of Dorchester County, Mcht., to James Birckhead of the same place, Mcht.: Negro man named Thomas. Witness: David Smith. Acknowledged before David Smith.

4 HD 21. May 31, 1792. James Birckhead of Dorchester County to William Norman of the same county: Negro man named Tom, about 35 years of age. Witness: David Smith. Acknowledged before David Smith, Justice.

4 HD 22. January 7, 1792. Henry Ennalls, John Stevens, Peter Gordon and Edward Wright of Dorchester County to Thomas Connerly of the same county: land on Northwest Fork called "Tryall," late the property of John Goslen deceased and conveyed by him to Henry Ennalls, John Stevens and Nathan Wright by deed dated May 20, 1789. Witnesses: E. Richardson, Jno. Crapper. Acknowledged before E. Richardson and Jno. Crapper, Justices. Sarah Ennalls is named as wife of Henry Ennalls, Frances Stevens, wife of John Stevens.

4 HD 25. December 8, 1791. James Smith of Dorchester County to Nancy Scoggins: Release of her indenture, "whereby she was bound to serve until her thirty first year." Witness: George Ward.

4, HD 25. February 7, 1792. Jesse Cannon of Dorchester County to Negro Plemmoth: Manumission. Acknowledged before Jno. Eccleston, Justice.

4 HD 26. June 11, 1792. Tristram Martin of Talbot County to Richard Martin of Dorchester County: part of "Darby" in accordance with Will of Thomas Martin deceased, adj. Joseph Martin's part of said tract. Also "Darbys Addition Enlarged." Witnesses: Richd. Pattison, Jno. Crapper. Acknowledged by Tristram Martin and Sally his wife before Richd. Pattison and Jno. Crapper, Justices.

4 HD 29. June 11, 1792. Tristram Martin of Talbot County to Joseph Martin of Talbot County: part of "Darby" in accordance with Will of Thomas Martin deceased. Witnesses: Jno. Crapper, Richd. Pattison. Acknowledged by Tristram Martin and Salley his wife before Jno. Crapper and Richd. Pattison, Justices.

4 HD 32. June 6, 1792. Richard Tubman of Dorchester Countl to Matthias Traverse of the same county: part of "Walnut Neck," containing 50 acres more or less. Witnesses: Moses LeCompte, Richard Pattison. Acknowledged before Moses LeCompte and Richd. Pattison, Justices.

4 HD 35. June 6, 1792. Matthias Travers and Letitia his wife of Dorchester County, planters, to Richard Tubman of the same county, planter: part of 3 tracts called "Pine Point," "Robson Pasture" and "Contention" on the road into Meekins Neck, on Hungar River, containing 74 acres more or less. Witnesses: Moses LeCompte, Richd. Pattison. Acknowledged before Moses LeCompte and Richd. Pattison, Justices.

4 ED 41. February 6, 1792. Thomas Colsten, Carpenter, of Dorchester County, Trustee for Thomas Kallender, to William Dail, Blacksmith, of the same county: part of "Tootles Venture" and part of "Busicks Range," adj. "Outlett" and containing 94 ½ acres. Witnesses: Tho. Jones, Jno. Stevens. Acknowledged before Tho. Jones and Jno. Stevens, Justices.

4 HD 43. December 24, 1791. James Sykes (Jr.) of Dover, Delaware and Elizabeth Sykes (formerly Elizabeth Goldsborough) his wife to William Goldsborough of Dorchester County: Elizabeth's 1/8 interest in a house and lot in Cambridge, devised by her father Robert Goldsborough to her brother Robert Goldsborough who has died intestate. Witness: Howes Goldsborough. Acknowledged before R. Goldsborough, one of the Judges of the General Court.

4 HD 47. June 20, 1792. George Ward, Levin Woolford and Henry Ennalls, Trustees of the Poor of Dorchester County, to Thomas McKeel of said county: Indenture of Hannah Huggins, a poor girl of said county, to serve as an apprentice until age 16, she being now 10 years of age, to learn the trade of spinster. Witness: Levin Travers.

4 HD 49. June 16, 1792. John Jones of Morgan, Morgan Jones, Hill Lockerman and Lovey his wife, and Edward Kilman of Dorchester County to Edward Woollen of Dorchester County: part of "Morgans Venture" near the head of St. Stevens Creek, containing 27 acres more or less. Witnesses: Tho. Jones, Moses

LeCompte. Acknowledged before Tho. Jones and Moses LeCompte, Justices. Lurana Jones is mentioned as wife of John Jones.

4 HD 54. June 16, 1792. Henry McCotter of Dorchester County to Edward Woollen of the same county: part of "Lockermans Regulation" near the head of St. Stevens Creek, adj. Henry Kilman's land and containing 10 acres more or less. Witnesses: Tho. Jones, Moses LeCompte. Acknowledged before Tho. Jones and Moses LeCompte, Justices.

4 HD 57. July 10, 1792. Michael Hall Bonwill of Dorchester County to Thomas Stevens of the same county: part of "Machthacutawakin" adj. "Eppin Forrest" and containing 2 1/4 acres more or less. Witnesses: Jno. Eacleston, Jno. Stevens. Acknowledged by Michael Hall Bonwill and Mary Bonwill his wife before Jno. Eacleston and Jno. Stevens, Justices.

4 HD 61. June 16, 1792. Thomas Kilman of Dorchester County to Henry McCotter of the same county: part of "Lockermans Regulation," containing 60 ½ acres. Witnesses: Tho. Jones, Moses LeCompte. Acknowledged by Thomas Killman and Reanace his wife before Tho. Jones and Moses LeCompte, Justices.

4 HD 65. March 21, 1792 - April 16, 1792. Commission to James Shaw, Robert Dennis, Richard Waters and David C. Smith of Dorchester County, Gent., to perpetuate bounds of James Steele's lands called "Daniels Helicon" and "Bacon Quarter," and Return. Deposition of John Dick, aged about 35 years, mentions Benjamin Bayly who lived about 12 years ago where John Macguire now resides. Deposition of Nathan Johnson, aged about 48 years, re bounder of "Daniels Helicon" shown by John Pike to William Tickle. Also mentions James Brown, Wm. Jones, David Tickle and Henry Hooper Qs., and "Bacon Quarter." Deposition of John Dick concerning "Bacon Quarter" mentions Levin Bestpitch and others named by Nathan Johnson, at a survey about 15-16 years ago. Also mentions a survey by George Bonnewell. Also mentions his father in law Levin Williams and Daniel Wilcocks, when deponant was a boy. Depositions taken in the presence of John Macguire, Capriel Callander, William Adly, Zepheniah Jones and two daughters, and Hooper Henly and William Meddis' two boys, "to hold the same in memory."

4 HD 69. June 18, 1792. John Aaron of Dorchester County to Negro Rachel: Manumission. Witnesses: Moses LeCompte, Nancy LeCompte. Acknowledged before Moses LeCompte, Justice.

4 HD 71. June 23, 1792. Mary Dawson of Dorchester County to Negro Amy: Manumission. Acknowledged before Jno. Stevens.

4 HD 72. July 16, 1792. Mary Pitt of Dorchester County to Negro Anthony: Manumission. Witnesses: Wm. Pitt, Moses LeCompte. Acknowledged before Moses LeCompte, Justice.

4 HD 73. July 16, 1792. John Pitt, William Pitt and Mary Pitt to Negro slaves: Manumission. Witness: Levin Woolford. Acknowledged before Moses LeCompte, Justice.

4 HD 74. May 26, 1792. John Barns of Dorchester County from John Mills and Betsey (Eliza- beth) his wife: "Little Creek Point" on the south side of Meekinses Creek which makes out of Blackwater River, near "Hogg Quarter," and containing 3 acres. Witnesses: Henry Lake, John Keene. Acknowledged before Henry Lake and John Keene, Justices.

4 HD 77. May 31, 1774. Elijah Tilghman of Dorchester County to George Bonwill of the same county: Bond to convey "Wet Work," on the east side of "Fishers Title' and near James Brown's plantation near Vienna, containing 50 acres, granted to John Wheeler deceased; and "Addition to Wet Work," containing 50 acres, also granted to said John Wheeler. Witnesses: James Shaw, Levin Kirkman.

4 HD 78. July 10, 1792. Charles Dean of Dorchester County, planter, to Michael Hall Bonwill of the same county: part of "Hickory Ridge Inlarged" on the main branch of Chicamacomico River, adj. "Maiden Forrest." Witnesses: Jno. Eccleston, Jno. Stevens. Acknowledged by Charles Dean and Allefare his wife before Jno. Eccleston and Jno. Stevens, Justices.

4 HD 81. July 19, 1792. Joseph Johnson and Annaritta Johnson and Peter Bramble of Dorchester County to William Hurley of the same county: Negro slaves. Witnesses: John McCkredey, Isaac Hurley.

4 HD 82. July 17, 1792. William Hollock of Dorchester County, Farmer, to Thomas Hollock, farmer, of the same county: Negro slaves. Witnesses: Dolley Williams, Thomas Roberts.

4 HD 83. April 3, 1792. Solomon Jones of Talbot County to Jeremiah Pattison of Dorchester County: part of "Edmondsons Regulation" on Slaughter Creek

and in Piney Neck, bought by said Jones from Pollard Edmondson, Talbot County. Witnesses: Tho. Jones, Richd. Pattison. Acknowledged before Tho. Jones and Richd. Pattison, Justices.

4 HD 85. July 14, 1792. John Henry to James Moore: lease of part of "Riders Forrest" where said Moore now resides, for the term of 7 years. Witness: Moses W. Nisbett.

4 HD 89. June 27, 1792. William Roberts and Rosanna McGraw of Dorchester County to William Howard of the same county: Negro girl named Dafney. Witnesses: Nathaniel Elliott, Nathal. Whitley.

4 HD 90. August 3, 1792. James Murray of Annapolis to James Dail of Dorchester County: parts of "Cornwell" and "Head Range" at the head of Fishing Creek, containing 74 acres more or less, agreeably to deed of August 15, 1753 between John Mace and Mary his wife and Jean Fishwick, daughter of William Fishwick. Witnesses: Nich. Carroll, Samuel Ridout. Acknowledged by James Murray and Sarah his wife before Nich. Carroll and Samuel Ridout, Justices for Ann Arundel County. Nich. Harwood, Clk.

4 HD 94. March 25, 1775. James Brown of Dorchester County, shipwright, to George Bonwill of the same county, joiner: Bond concerning lands called "Trump- about," "Browns Meadow," "Wet Work" and "Johns Industry" (between "Daniels Heliken " and "Bacon Quarter"). Witnesses: Jno. Tootell, John Langfitt. Assigned July 10, 1792 by Michael Hall Bonwill to John McGuire. Witness: Jno. Eccleston.

4 HD 97. July 10, 1792. Michael Hall Bonwill of Dorchester County to John Maguire of the same county: Bond to convey to James Brown, son of James, land called "Wet Work" on the east side of "Fishers Title," upon receiving a deed for said land from the heirs of Elijah Tilghman. Witnesses: Jno. Eccleston, Theo. Marshall.

4 ED 98. July 10, 1792. Michael Hall Bonwill of Dorchester County to John Maguire of the same county: part of "Bonwills Regulation on Halls Seat" adj. "Browns Meadows," also adj. "Fishers Title," "Trumpabout" and "Daniels Helicon" and containing 258 1/4 acres more or less. Also another part of the same tract, adj. "Fishwicks Adventure" and containing 5 3/4 acres more or less. Elizabeth White, formerly Elizabeth Bonwill, mother of said Michael Hall Bonwill, now resides on said land. Witnesses: Jno. Eccleston, Jno. Stevens.

Acknowledged by Michael Hall Bonwill and Mary his wife before Jno. Eccleston and Jno. Stevens, Justices.

4 HD 103. March 3, 1792. Ezekiel Fitchew of Dorchester County, planter, to Roger Jones of the same county: part of "Addition to Fitchews Range" on the east side of White Marsh, between "Fitchews Industry" and "Busicks Lott," containing 15 3/4 acres more or less. Witnesses: Tho. Jones, Moses LeCompte. Acknowledged before Tho. Jones and Moses LeCompte, Justices.

4 HD 106. August 8, 1792. George Ward, Levin Woolford and Henry Ennalls, Trustees of the Poor of Dorchester County, to Andrew Satchel of said county: Indenture of Thos. Crocket, a poor boy of said county, about 16 years old, as an apprentice until age 21 to learn the trade of farmer. Witness: Thos. McKeel, Clk.

4 HD 107. August 8, 1792. George Ward, Henry Ennalls and Levin Woolford, Trustees of the Poor of Dorchester County, to Ralph Paul of said county: Indenture of Caty Brewington, a poor girl of said county, supposed to be about 9 years old, to serve as apprentice until age 16 to learn the trade of spinster. Witness: Thos. McKeel, Clk.

4 HD 109. August 13, 1792. David Mills of Dorchester County to Stanley Byus of the same county: parts of "Mills's Security," "Mills's Choice" and "Mills's Course" (excepting that part of "Mills's Security sold by John Mills to William Taylor). Witnesses: Jno. Stevens, Levin Woolford. Acknowledged before Jno. Stevens and Levin Woolford, Justices.

4 HD 111. August 14, 1792. Jacob Wright of Dorchester County to Negro slaves: Manumission. Witnesses: Moses LeCompte, James LeCompte. Acknowledged before Moses LeCompte, Justice.

4 HD 113. August 6, 1792. Robert Ewing and Gustavus Scott to Patrick Kelly: two lots in Cambridge, purchased by Ewing from Adam Muir deceased and by Scott from Charles Crookshanks and Archibald Moncrieff, Trustees under Will of Archibald Patison deceased. Witnesses: Levin Woolford, Jno. Stevens. Acknowledged before Jno. Stevens and Levin Woolford, Justices. Margaret Scott is named as wife of Gustavus Scott.

4 HD 115. August 20, 1792. Ebenezer Newton of Dorchester County to Andrew McDonald of the same county: the lowermost parts of "Addition to Fishers Landing," "Weston," "Fishers Landing" and "St. Bartholomews," according to a

division between Edward White and John Leatherbury, being the parts of which Jolley Leatherbury died seised. Also a tract called "The Land of Promise." Witnesses: Robt. Harrison, Levin Woolford. Acknowledged before Robt. Harrison and Levin Woolford, Justices.

4 HD 118. August 20, 1792. James Douglass of Kent County, Delaware, Administrator of Samuel Shelton Sloss deceased; and Jehu Davies and Sarah his wife, formerly Sarah Carpenter, Administratrix of William Douglass deceased, of Kent County, Delaware, to Thomas Lockerman of Dorchester County: 20 acres of land formerly the property of Samuel Shelton Sloss and William Douglass deceased, at the head of Chicamacomico River, being 10 acres of "Luck by Chance" and 10 acres of "Bridge Neck" (per lease of confirmation granted to George Middleton, deceased, for a grist mill). The said James Douglass, as heir at law of William Douglass, who survived the said Samuel Shelton Sloss deceased, further conveys part of "Johns Industry" on the east side of Chicamacomico River, adj. "Sarah Land Addition" and containing 52 acres more or less. Witnesses: Jno. Eccleston, Jno. Stevens. Acknowledged before Jno. Eccleston and Jno. Stevens, Justices.

4 HD 125. August 11, 1792. Isaac Short to Arthur Bell: Receipt for the hire of a negro slave for the term of 12 years. Witnesses: Jno. Crapper, Benthal Fletcher.

4 HD 125. August 11, 1792. Isaac Short of Dorchester County, shoemaker, to Arthur Bell of the same county, planter: Negro slave called Tom, left by Ann Taylor the wife of the said Isaac Short. Witnesses: Jno. Crapper, Benthal Fletcher. Acknowledged before Jno. Crapper, Justice.

4 HD 126. August 24, 1792. Henry Hicks Travers of Sussex County, Delaware to Negro Harry: Manumission. Witnesses: Peggy Cox, George Ward. Acknowledged before Richd. Pattison, Justice.

4 HD 127. March 3, 1792. William Harrison LeCompte of Dorchester County, Gent., to John Ratcliff of the same county, planter: livestock and furniture. Witnesses: Wm. Hayward, Thos. Barnett.

4 HD 129. July 19, 1792. Richard Pattison, William Pattison and Thomas James Pattison of Dorchester County to Risdon Harriss of the same county: "Marshahope Regulated" (except part belonging to John Barnes Heirs); "Inlett"; "Cow Pasture"; and "Pattisons Beginning," all lying on Taylors Island, on Slaughter Creek and on Hogg Marsh. Witnesses: Moses LeCompte, Levin

Woolford. Acknowledged before Moses LeCompte and Levin Woolford, Justices. Mary and Margaret are named as wives of Richard and Thomas James Pattison.

4 HD 132. June 16, 1792. Henry McCotter of Dorchester County to Nathan Stevens of the same county: part of "Lockermans Regulation," adj. land bought by Edward Woollen from Henry McCotter and containing 1 ½ acres more or less. Witnesses: Tho. Jones, Moses LeCompte. Acknowledged before Tho. Jones and Moses LeCompte, Justices.

4 HD 135. June 16, 1792. Thomas Kilman of Dorchester County to John Jones, son of Morgan: part of "Lockermans Regulation" near the head of St. Stevens Creek, containing 9 acres more or less. Witnesses: Moses LeCompte, Tho. Jones. Acknowledged by Thomas Kilman and Reanace his wife before Moses LeCompte and Thos. Jones, Justices.

4 HD 138. June 16, 1792. John Jones of Morgan of Dorchester County to Morgan Jones of the same county: part of "Lockermans Regulation" near the head of St. Stevens Creek, containing 9 acres more or less. Witnesses: Tho. Jones, Moses LeCompte. Acknowledged by John Jones and Lurany his wife before Thos. Jones and Moses LeCompte, Justices.

4 HD 140. May 5, 1792. John Brohawn of Dorchester County, planter, and Mary his wife to Levin Phillips of the same county, planter: "Busicks Venture," on the east side of Slaughter Creek and on the north side of the road that leads from the main road to Patrick Brohawn's, containing 29 acres more or less. Also part of "Defiance" which is not deeded to James Edmondson, containing 78 acres more or less. Also the vacancy added to "Defiance," now called "Reliance."The entire tract with vacancy added adjoins lands called "Little Brittain" and "Robinsons Craft," and contains 94 ½ acres more or less. Witnesses: Tho. Jones, Jno. Keene. Acknowledged before Tho. Jones and Jno. Keene, Justices.

4 HD 144. July 20, 1792. John Geoghegan of Dorchester County to Negro Tom (alias Tie): Manumission. Witnesses: Moses LeCompte, Richd. Pattison. Acknowledged before Moses LeCompte.

4 HD 145. August 18, 1792. Rebecca North of Dorchester County to Richard Hayward of the same county: Negro woman named Daff, aged about 19 or 20 years. Witnesses: James Hubbard, Hugh Spedden, John Murray.

4 HD 146. January, 1792. Elizabeth Hammilton of Dorchester County to Negro Murray: Manumission. Witnesses: Joseph Dodson, James Coulter. Acknowledged September 8, 1792 before Robt. Harrison, Justice.

4 HD 147. August 20, 1792. Woolford Stewart of Dorchester County, Blacksmith, to Nehemiah Whiteley of the same county, planter: "Reeds Hazard" adj. "Turcells Neck" on the east side of Blackwater River, containing 98 acres more or less. Also "Stewarts Outrange" containing 388 acres more or less. Also "Stewarts Discovery," adj. "Jarrell Neck" and containing 4 3/8 acres more or less. Witnesses: Robt. Harrison, Levin Woolford. Acknowledged before Robt. Harrison and Levin Woolford, Justices.

4 HD 151. September 3, 1792. William Vans Murray and Charlotte his wife of Dorchester County to William Dail of the same county: part of "Murrays Settlement" on the east side of the main road from the meeting house towards Wright's store (at the head of Fishing Creek), adj. "Addition to Harwick" and containing 51 acres. Witnesses: Levin Woolford, Stanley Byus. Acknowledged before Levih Woolford and Stanley Byus, Justices.

4 HD 154. August 21, 1792. Thomas Colsten of Dorchester County, carpenter, to John Williams of the same county, Mcht.: part of "Priviledge," adj. "Outlett" and containing 14 ½ acres more or less (formerly deeded by said Thomas Colsten and Betsey his wife to the said John Williams, by the name of "Colstens Industry." Witnesses: Moses LeCompte, Richd. Pattison. Acknowledged before Moses LeCompte and Richd. Pattison.

4 HD 157. August 20, 1792. Jehu Davis and Sarah Davis his wife of Kent County, Delaware, Administratrix of William Douglass of Caroline County deceased, and James Douglass of Kent County, Delaware, heir of William Douglass and Executor of Samuel Shelton Sloss of Sussex County, Delaware, to Michael Hall Bonwill of Dorchester County: Release of a Mortgage from George Bonwill of Dorchester County to said William Douglass and Samuel Shelton Sloss, dated January 22 1778, "Bonwills Regulation on Halls Seat" and "Maidens Forrest." Witnesses: Jno. Eccleston, Jno. Stevens. Acknowledged before Jno. Eccleston and Jno. Stevens, Justices.

4 HD 160. October 5, 1785. Agreement between Thomas Thompson of Dorchester County, planter, and Archibald Patison of the same county, Mcht., concerning part of a tract called "Whitehaven" to be conveyed by said Thomas Thompson and Priscilla his wife to the said Archibald Patison, adj. land

conveyed May 14, 1784 by said Thompson and wife to Thomas Colsten, carpenter, 3 1/4 acres more or less, hereby conveyed. Witnesses: Daniel McDonnell, John Foulue.

4 HD 163. September 17, 1792. John Huffington of Dorchester County to Rhodes Riggen of the same county: all the "lands and tenements devised by Thomas White (of Edward) except the lots in the town of Vienna to the said John Huffington situated on Nanticoke River in said County." Witnesses: Levin Woolford, Stanley Byus. Acknowledged before Levin Woolford and Stanley Byus, Justices.

4 HD 165. July 25, 1792. Jacob Insley of Dorchester County to Levi Insley of the same county: part of "Andrews Fortune" "that my father James Insley willed to me," between "Betties Lott" and Goose Creek Swamp, supposed to be 53 acres, between Fox Creek and Firm Creek. Witnesses: Henry Lake, Jno. Keene. Acknowledged before Henry Lake and Jno. Keene, Justices.

4 HD 167. September 18, 1792. Levi Insley and Joice his wife of Dorchester County, planters, to William Insley of the same county; part of "Andrews Fortune" "that my father James Insley willed to me," between "Betties Lott" and Goose Creek Swamp, supposed to be 53 acres more or less, between Fox Creek and Firm Creek. Witnesses: Henry Lake, Jno. Keene. Acknowledged before Henry Lake and Jno. Keene, Justices.

4 HD 169. October 1, 1792. Francis Walker of Dorchester County, planter, to Thomas Perry of the same county, planter: Negro slave named Mynta, livestock, furniture and other personal property. Witnesses: Ellis Thomas, Hugh McColl.

4 HD 170. September 26, 1792. George Ward, Henry Ennalls and Levin Woolford, Trustees of the Poor of Dorchester County, Levy Hust of said county, Bricklayer: Indenture of Henry Campbell, a poor boy of said county, supposed to be about 8 years old, as an apprentice until age 21 to learn the trade of Bricklayer. Witness: Thos. McKeel, Clk.

4 HD 172. October 1, 1792 George Ward, Levin Woolrord and Col. John Eccleston, Trustees of the Poor of Dorchester County, to Thomas Lockerman of said county: Indenture of Amy Adams, a poor girl of said county, supposed to be about 6 yeers old, as apprentice until age 16 to learn the trade of spinster. Witness: Thos. McKeel, Clk.

4 HD 174. October 1, 1792. Randolph Johnson of Dorchester County to Samuel Abbott of Talbot County: household furniture. Witnesses: Jno. Stevens, Nathaniel Manning Junr. Acknowledged before Jno. Stevens, Justice.

4 HD 175. July 10, 1792. Michael Hall Bonwill of Dorchester County to Charles Dean of the same county: part of Maiden Forrest on the west side of the said Dean's dwelling plantation and between said plantation and the main branch of Chicamacomico River, adj. "Hickory Ridge Inlarged" and containing 9 3/4 acres more or less. Witnesses: Jno. Eccleston, Jno. Stevens. Acknowledged by Michael Hall Bonwill and Mary Bonwill his wife before Jno. Eccleston end Jno. Stevens, Justices.

4 HD 179. April 28, 1792. Anderton Brown and Betty his wife of Sussex County, Delaware and .John Turpin of Dorchester County to Charles Brown of Dorchester County: their part of lands lying part in Dorchester County and part of Caroline County, called "Hopewell," "Laytons Chance," "Crooked Ridge," "Scholarship" and "Scholarship Improved." Witnesses: Jno. Crapper, David Smith. Acknowledged by Anderton Brown and Betty his wife, John Turpin and Margaret his wife, before John Crapper and David Smith, Justices for Dorchester County.

4 HD 183. November 29, 1792. John Finley late of Cambridge in Dorchester County, "Dealer and Chapman," now residing in the City of Philadelphia, to Robert Henderson of the city aforesaid, Mcht. and Peter Ferguson of Cambridge, Mcht.: Power of Attorney. Witnesses: Edward Fox, Abram Woodside. Acknowledged before Edward Fox, Notary Public of Pennsylvania.

4 HD 185. 1792. Andrew Clow & Co., Alexander and William Cochran, Robert Smith, Miller & Abercrombe, Andrew Tybout and Thomas Dobson of Philadelphia, Mchts., Creditors of John Finlay of Cambridge, Maryland, Storekeeper, to Robert Henderson of Philadelphia, Mcht. and Peter Fergusson of Cambridge, Shop Keeper: Bond concerning property of John Finlay, who is stated to have become insane, although not so declared by process of law. Witnesses: Geo. Kemp, David Todd. John Finley consents to the measures taken by his creditors, stating that at the time of the execution of the above writing he was deprived of his reason but has since been restored thereto, although yet in a bad state of health. (November 29, 1792).

4 HD 189. September 8, 1792. Michael Hall Bonwill of Dorchester County to William Littleton of the same county: part of 2 tracts near said Bonwill's Mill,

called "Maidens Forrest" and "Hickory Ridge Inlarged," containing 97 ½ acres more or less. Witnesses: E. Richardson, Jno. Eccleston. Acknowledged by Michael Hall Bonwill and Mary his wife before E. Richardson and Jno. Eccleston, Justices.

4 HD 193. September 10, 1792. Philemon Simmons of Dorchester County to Thomas Jones Junr.: Schooner boat called the "Polly," 2 feather beds, furniture and other personal property. Witnesses: Tho. Jones, Wm. Ryan. Acknowledged before Tho. Jones, Justice.

4 HD 194. October 4, 1792. Michael 'Hall Bonwill to Negro slaves: Manumission. Acknowledged before Jno. Stevens, Justice. .

4 HD 196. September 29, 1792. Rebecca Budd and Thomas Tolley of Dorchester County to John Phillips of the same county: "Tuckers Folly," adj. "Poppelar Point" near Tar Bay and containing 20 acres more or less. Witnesses: Moses LeCompte, Richard Pattison. Acknowledged before Moses LeCompte and Richd. Pattison, Justices.

4 HD 199. October 17, 1792. Triphena Wingate of Dorchester County to James Wingate, Lovy Wingate, Henry Wingate, Dorothy Wingate and Nancy Wingate of the sarre county: personal property. Witness: Henry Lake. Acknowledged before Henry Lake, Justice.

4 HD 201. July 14, 1792. Willism Ennalls, Joseph Ennalls, John Ennalls, Elizabeth Ennalls and Ann Whittington, heirs of their brother Thomas Ennalls, son of Joseph Ennalls deceased (see Act of Assembly passed Nov. session 1786, entitled "An Act to direct descents"), to Edward Brodess of Dorchester County: part of "Ecclestons Regulation Rectified" on the west side of Transquakin River, containing 400 acres more or less, as described in a deed from Hugh Eccleston and Elizabeth his wife to Mary Trippe the mother of said Thomas Ennalls and the grantors above mentioned, dated September 4, 1764. Also part of "Ennalls Regulation" on the west side of Transquakin River, adj. "Taylors Delight" at a branch called Halls Branch, containing 42 acres more or less, as described in a deed from William Ennalls Hicks and wife to Joseph Ennalls the father of the said Thomas Ennalls and the grantors aforesaid. Witnesses: Jno. Stevens, Levin Woolford. Acknowledged before Jno. Stevens and Levin Woolford, Justices.

4 HD 208. May 26, 1792. Reubin Andrews of Dorchester County to Thomas McNemara of the same county: part of a tract called "Bourbourk," containing 20

acres more or less, "exclusive what land lies in Joseph Andrews." Witnesses: Henry Lake, Jno. Keene. Acknowledged by Reubin Andrews and Judah his wife before Henry Lake and John Keene, Justices.

4 HD 211. May 26, 1792. Roger Foxwell of Dorchester County to Isaac Woodland of the same county: part of a tract called "Foxwells Lott" on the west side of Charles Creek, on Seven Oaks Point, containing 2 ½ acres more or less. Witnesses: Henry Lake, Jno. Keene. Acknowledged before Roger Foxwell and Elizabeth his wife before Henry Lake and John Keene, Justices. .

4 HD 215. May 26, 1792. John McNemara Pritchett of Dorchester County to Solomon Tylor of the same county: part of "Cow Range" containing 2 ½ acres more or less. Witnesses: John Keene, Henry Lake. Acknowledged by John McNemara Pritchett and Elisabeth his wife before John Keene and Henry Lake, Justice.

4 HD 219. July 31, 1790. John Eccleston of Dorchester County to Thomas Ross Junr. of the same county: Bond to convey lot No.3, part of the Nanticoke Indian lands, containing 576 ½ acres more or less. Witnesses: Thomas Ross, Thomas Webster.

4 HD 220. May 26, 1792. Thomas Whitley and Solomon Tylor of Dorchester County to David it Tylor of the same county: part of "Worlds End" on the west side of Hungar River, containing 21 ½ acres more or less; part of "Project" containing 8 acres more or less; part of "Project" containing 42 ½ acres more or less; and "Tylors Stave Landing" containing 18 acres more or less. Witnesses: Henry Lake, John Keene. Acknowledged before Henry Lake and John Keene, Justices.

4 HD 224. February 16, 1793. William Vickars 2nd to the State of Maryland: Bond as Inspector of Tobacco, with Levin Woolford and Joseph Ennalls as sureties. Witnesses: Wm. Jones, Washington Jones. Proved by witnesses before Tho. Jones.

4 HD 225. March 18, 1793. Charles Hodson to the State of Maryland: Bond as High Sheriff of Dorchester County, with Levin Hodson and Thomas Smith as sureties. Witness: H. Dickinson.

4 HD 227. March 20, 1793. John Pitt to the State of Maryland: Bond as Inspector of Tobacco at Ennalls Warehouse, with Thos. Martin and William Pitt

as sureties. Witnesses: Anthony Boyle, Walter Roly. Proved by witnesses bofore Tho. Jones.

4 HD 229. April 15, 1792, . James Tregoe of Dorchester County, planter, to Levin Woolford of the same county: part of two tracts called "Williams Goodwill" and "Spite," beginning at a division between James Tregoe and William Tregoe. Also "Addition to Turkey Neck"; "Tregoes Division"; and part of two tracts called "Hazard" and "Addition to Outlett" beginning at a division post between James Tregoe and Levin Tregoe, containing 195 acres more or less in all. Witnesses: Tho. Jones, Moses LeCompte. Acknowledged by James Tregoe and William Tregoe before Tho. Jones and Moses LeCompte, Justices.

4 HD 232. October 24, 1792. Thomas Taylor of Caroline County to Thomas Kilman of Dorchester County: part of "Ross's Chance" on the north side of Little Choptank River, adj. "Jumps Point" and containing 92 acres more or less. Witnesses: Richd. Pattison, Levin Woolford. .Acknowledged by Thomas Taylor and Prudence his wife before Richd. Pattison and Levin Woolford, Justices.

4 HD 236. January 3, 1790. Cyrus Mitchell and Sarah his wife of Dorchester County to Abraham Lewis of the same county: Bond to convey part of a tract on the Northwest Fork River of Nanticoke, called "Norage," containing 31 3/4 acres more or less. Witnesses: Thos. Melloy, Sarah Melloy.

4 HD 238. October 29, 1792. Peter Ferguson of Cambridge, Dorchester County, Trustee and Agent for the affairs of John Findlay, to Thomas Colsten of Dorchester County: lands near Fishing Creek supposed to contain about 200 acres; and lots at the head of said creek purchased by Findlay at a vendue of the real estate of Archibald Patison deceased. The said Thomas Colsten agrees to pay the purchase money for said lands to Charles Crookshanks and Archibald Moncrieff of Baltimore Town or their assigns in accordance with bonds of the said Findlay. Witnesses: Robert Muir, Nathaniel Manning Junr.

4 HD 239. September 29, 1790. John Reed of Dorchester County to Noble Dean of said county: Bond for said Reed and Susanna his wife to convey to the said Dean all their claim to any real estate of Capt. John Ross deceased, and the saw or grist mill and utensils thereunto belonging. Witnesses: Theophilus Marshall, Ebenezer Newton.

4 HD 240. October 30, 1792. Gustavus Scott of Dorchester County to John Eccleston of the same county: part of a tract on Choptank River, adj. lands of

William Murray Robinson, called "Lockermans Regulation on the road from Cambridge to Hambrooks Point, containing 99 acres more or less. Witnesses: John Done, Robt. Harrison. . Acknowledged by Gustavus Scott and Margaret his wife before John Done and Robt. Harrison, Justices.

4 HD 244. October 29, 1792. Thomas Burn of Dorchester County, planter, to Moses Martin of the same county, planter: personal property. Witnesses: Saml. Sappington, Hugh McColl.

4 HD 246. October 31, 1792. Thomas Colsten, Carpenter, and Thomas Colsten Junr., both of Dorchester County, to Clement Walters of the same county: "Hoopers Delight" on the west side of the Northwest Branch of Blackwater River, containing 20 acres more or less. Witnesses: Moses LeCompte, Jno. Stevens. Acknowledged before Moses LeCompte and Jno. Stevens, Justices.

4 HD 249. April 16, 1793. John Ball to the State of Maryland: Bond as Inspector of Tobacco with Thomas Hodson and William Jones as Sureties. Witnesses: Rob Dennis, John Reed. Proved by witnesses before David Smith.

4 HD 251. October 19, 1792. William Madkin of Dorchester County to Richard Woodland of the same county: part of "Madkins Forrest" on the Northwest side of White Marsh Branch, exclusive of 15 acres laid off for Charles Thomas. Also "Talls Contrivance" containing 20 acres, and "Madkins Venture" containing 6 acres (90 acres in all). Witnesses: Moses LeCompte, Richd. Pattison. Acknowledged before Moses LeCompte and Richd. Pattison, Justices.

4 HD 255. July 16, 1792. John Pitt and Mary his wife of Dorchester County to Samuel Trego of the same county: part of "Pitts Desire" on a branch of Transquakin River, containing 14 ½ acres more or less. Witnesses: Jno. Stevens, Levin Woolford. Acknowledged before Jno. Stevens and Levin Woolford, Justices.

4 HD 259. October 23, 1792. Richard Goldsborough of Dorchester County to William Dail of the same county: part of a tract formerly called "Lee Grand" but now by resurvey called "Bell Field," on the main road from Cambridge to the head of Fishing Creek, adj. "Murrays Settlement" and containing 112 acres more or less. Witnesses: Henry Lake, Levin Woolford. Acknowledged before Henry Lake and Levin Woolford, Justices.

4 HD 263. May 26, 1792. Keziah Jones of Dorchester County to Solomon Tylor

of the same county: "Project" on the east side of Charles Creek. Witnesses: Henry Lake, Jno. Keene. Acknowledged before Henry Lake and Jno. Keene, Justices.

4 HD 266. June 13, 1792. Matthias Travers and Letitia his wife of Dorchester County to William Pattison Junr. of the same county: part of two tracts t near the head of Hungar River called "Surveyors Point" and "Piney Point," containing ½ acre more or less, with a windmill erected by said Matthias Travers and Capewell Keene. Witnesses: Moses LeCompte, Richd. Pattison. Acknowledged before Moses LeCompte and Richd. Pattison, Justices.

4 HD 269. November 10, 1792. William Pattison Junior of Dorchester County to Matthias Travers, and CapewelKeene of the same county: part of two tracts near the head of Hungar River called "Surveyors Point" and "Piney Point" containing ½ acre more or less, with windmill erected by Matthias Travers and Capewell Keene. Witnesses: Richd. Pattison, Moses LeCompte. Acknowledged before Richd. Pattison and Moses LeCompte.

4 HD 272. November 10, 1792. Jeremiah Pattison of Dorchester County to Richard Woodland of the same county: part of "Pattisons Priviledge" on Slaughter Creek, adj. David Sare's land and containing 8 acres more or less. Witnesses: Richd. Pattison, Moses LeCompte. Acknowledged before Richd. Pattison and Moses LeCompte.

4 HD 275. August 31, 1792. Thomas Thompson of Dorchester County, planter, to Edward Wright of the same county, Mcht.: part of "Addition to White Haven" on the road from the head of Church Creek to Cambridge, containing 3 3/4 acres more or less. Witnesses: Moses LeCompte, Richd. Pattison. Acknowledged by Thomas Thompson and Priscilla his wife before Moses LeCompte and Richd. Pattison, Justices.

4 HD 279. August 20, 1792. John Foxwell of Dorchester County to Isaac Woodland of the same county: part of "Foxwells Lott" on the east side of Hungar River near the mouth of Worlds End Creek, adj. Vachel Keene's plantation. Witnesses: Henry Lake, Jno. Keene. Acknowledged by John Foxwell and Sarah his wife before Henry Lake and Jno. Keene, Justices.

4 HD 283. August 20, 1792. John Foxwell of John of Dorchester County and Sarah his wife to Vachel Keene of the same county: part of "Foxwells Lott" at the mouth of Charles Creek on the east side of Hungar River, containing 28

acres more or less. Witnesses: Henry Lake, Jno. Keene. Acknowledged before Henry Lake and Jno. Keene, Justices.

4 HD 287. May 26, 1792. Abram Foxwell of Dorchester County to Roger Foxwell of the same county: part of "Morefields Addition" on the east side of Hungar IRiver at Worlds End Creek, beginning at a division between Abram Foxwell and Peter Kirwan, and containing 8 acres more or less. Witnesses: Henry Lake, Jno. Keene. Acknowledged before Jno. Keene and Henry Lake, Justices.

4 HD 291. August 20, 1792. Roger Foxwell of Dorchester County from John Tyler Kirwan and Betsy Kirwan, Administrator and Administratrix of Peter Kirwan deceased: part of "Morefields Addition" on the Northeast side of Hungar River, beginning at a division between Abraham Foxwell and Peter Kirwan and containing 8 acres more or less. Witnesses: Henry Lake, Jno. Keene. Acknowledged before Henry Lake and Jno. Keene, Justices.

4 HD 293. November 27, 1792. James Hodson of Dorchester County, farmer, to James Ayres of the same county, farmer: "Trippes Discovery" containing 168 ½ acres. "Trippes Marsh" containing 48 3/4 acres; and "Trippes Inclosure" containing 177 acres. Witnesses: Jno. Stevens, David Smith. Acknowledged by James Hodson and Catharine his wife before Jno. Stevens and David Smith, Justices.

4 HD 297. June 5, 1792. Ann Blackwell of Northumberland County, Virginia, to William Price of Dorchester County: land formerly known as "St. Johns Island" near Kadjers Straits, left to said Blackwell by her father Thomas Cottrell. Witnesses: Thomas Harcum, Richd. Hudnall, Wm. Harcum, John Price, Laban Price, Ephraim Price. Proved by John Price, Ephraim Price and Laban Price, three of the witnesses, before Levin Woolford, Justice.

4 HD 300. June 5, 1792. Ann Blackwell of Northumberland County, Virginia, to John Price of Dorchester County: land formerly called "Taylors Island" near Kedgers Straits, left to said Blackwell by her father Thomas Cottrell. Witnesses: Thomas Harcum, Richd. Hudnall, William Harcum, William Price, Laban Price, Ephraim Price. Proved by Laban Price, Ephraim Price and William Price, Witnesses, before Levin Woolford, Justice.

4 HD 303. December 3, 1792. Richard Martin of Dorchester County to Joseph Martin of Talbot County: part of "Darby's Addition Enlarged," adj. "Darby" and

containing 66 ½ acres more or less. Witnesses: Tho. Jones, Levin Woolford. Acknowledged by Richard Martin and Nancy his wife before Tho. Jones and Levin Woolford, Justices.

4 HD 307. November 12, 1792. John Windows of Dorchester County to Henry Hodson of the same county: part of "Batchelors Forrest," adj. "Maiden Forrest" and containing 30 acres more or less. Witnesses: Jno. Stevens, David Smith. Acknowledged before Jno. Stevens and David Smith, Justices.

4 HD 309. July 10, 1792. Michael Hall Bonwill of Dorchester County, Miller, to Levin .LeCompte Junr. of the same county: part of "Exchange," part of "Spring Valley" and part of "Security" on the main branch of Chicamacomico River, adj. "Sector," "Epping Forrest" and "Sarahs Delight Inlarged." Witnesses: Jno. Eccleston, Jno. Stevens. Acknowledged by Michael Hall Bonwill and Mary his wife before Jno. Eccleston and Jno. Stevens, Justices.

4 HD 314. December 3, 1792. Henry Edgar of Dorchester County to Joseph Robins of the same county: part of original "Callis" on the Southwest side of Blackwater River, containing 2 acres more or less. Witnesses: Jno. Keene, Henry Lake. Acknowledged by Henry Edgar and Keziah his wife before John Keene and Henry Lake, Justices.

4 HD 318. December 3, 1792. Thomas Barns of Dorchester County to Moses Barns of the same county: Part of "Buck Valley," part of "Last Vacancy" and part of "Moses' Liberty," adj. "Gift to My Daughter." Witnesses: Henry Lake, Jno. Keene. Acknowledged before Henry Lake and Jno. Keene, Justices.

4 HD 321. November 30, 1792. William Keene of Dorchester County, planter, to Aaron Wallace of the same county: part of "Brambles Delight' on the south side of Meekinses Creek, supposed to contain 6 1/4 acres more or less. Witnesses: Henry Lake, Jno. Keene. Acknowledged before Henry Lake and Jno. Keene, Justices.

4 HD 324. December 15, 1792. John McKeel of Dorchester County, Gent., to Solomon Frazier of the same county, Gent.: part of "Spocott" on Little Choptank River, conveyed by Charles LeCompte and Sarah his wife to Thomas McKeel deceased, father of said John McKeel, by deed dated May 9, 1759, beginning at a post on School house Cove fixed by Henry Ennalls, late Surveyor, as a division between said Thomas McKeel and Charles Powell. Also a piece of land which was supposed to lie within the bounds of "Spocott," but

surveyed by Stephen Warner and patented by William Warner, called "Warners Chance." .Mary is mentioned as wife of Thomas McKeel. Witnesses: Richd. Pattison, Levin Woolford. Acknowledged by John McKeel and Mary his wife before Richd. Pattison and Levin Woolford, Justices.

4 HD 330. October 10, 1792. Thomas Dare Junr. of Anne Arundel County to Levin Parker of the same county: "Shore Ditch" or "Shear Ditch" on the Northwest Branch of Nanticoke River, formerly laid out for Andrew Willson, containing 200 acre more or less. Witnesses: Sam Harrison, Thos. Tongue. Acknowledged by Thomas Dare Junr. and Ann his wife before Sam Harrison and Thos. Tongue, Justices for Anne Arundel County. Nich. Harwood, Clk.

4 HD 334. June 26, 1792. Mary Keene of Dorchester County to William Reed of the same county: "Honourable Division," being a resurvey of "Headrange" in Blackwater, devised to said Mary Keene in fee tail under the Will of her father Isaac Andrews, and now conveyed in fee simple in accordance with Act of Assembly. Witnesses: Richd. Pattison, John Keene. Acknowledged before Richd. Pattison and Jno. Keene, Justices.

4 HD 339. August 27, 1792. John McKeel of Dorchester County to Isaiah Brickell and Macall Brickell of the same county: part of "Muirs Inspection" in Town Point Neck, on Smiths Creek, containing 45 acres more or less. Witnesses: Stanley Byus, Richd. Pattison. Acknowledged before Stanley Byus and Richd. Pattison, Justices.

4 HD 343. August 11, 1789. Mary Jones (Relict of James Jones Junr.) and her eldest son John Jones, both of Dorchester County, to James Steele of the same county: part of "Friends Assistance" devised to James Jones by .his father Leonard Jones, sold by said James Jones to James Jones Junr., his son, and devised by the Will of said James Jones Junr., dated December 7, 1784, to be sold, containing 67 ½ acres at the least. Witnesses: D. Sulivane, Moses LeCompte. Acknowledged before D. Sulivane and Moses LeCompte, Justices.

4 HD 350. December 24, 1792. Richard Goldsborough to Gustavus Scott: part of "Clifton" on the road from Cambridge to the late Richard Glover's farm, adj. Scott's lands and containing 24 1/4 acres more or less. Witnesses: Levin Woolford, Stanley Byus. Acknowledged before Levin Woolford and Stanley Byus, Justices.

4 HD 353. July 25, 1792. Levi Insley of Dorchester County, planter, to William

Sothern of the same county, Mcht.: part of "Andrews Fortune," containing 5 3/4 acres more or less. Joyce Insley, wife of Levi Insley, joins in deed. Witnesses: Jno. Keene, Henry Lake. Acknowledged by Levi Insley and Joyce his wife before Jno. Keene and Henry Lake, Justices.

4 HD 357. December 24, 1792. Edward Dean of Dorchester County to Henry Corkrin of Caroline County: lease of "Exchange" for the term of 10 years. Witnesses: Ezekiel Henry, Sary Henry.

4 HD 359. March 19, 1792 - August 15, 1792. Commission to Moses LeCompte, Richard Pattison and Thomas Jones of Dorchester County to perpetuate bounds of land of Benjamin Keene, Jr., David Rogers, Joshua Hooper, Henry Meekins Junr., Peter Harrington, Mary Meekins, Job Wheatley and Mark Meekins called "Meekins Hope," and Return. Certificate mentions adjoining tracts called "Reserve," "Masons Vineyard," "Shambles," and "Stapleforts Recreation"; markers proved by Thomas Mace Meekins, David Rogers, Richard Gadd, John Pickron, Catherine Meekins, Joshua Meekins and Peter Harrington; and adjoining lands of Richard Meekins, John Meekins, the heir of George Fargusson, Benjamin Keene, the heirs of Abram Meekins, and Joshua Hooper. Land surveyed by Richd. Pattison as surveyor, with Ellet Phillips and Edward Ruark as chain carriers.

4 HD 367. January 14, 1790. John Elliott to Negro Leah: Manumission. Witnesses: Alexander Douglass, R. Stevens. Acknowledged before Jno. Smoot, Justice.

4 HD 369. December 7, 1792. Mary Payne, widow of Daniel Payne of Dorchester County, to Daniel Nicols of Dorchester County: Negro slaves, furniture and livestock. Witness: David Smith. Acknowledged before David Smith, Justice.

4 HD 371. December 3, 1792. William Hammond to Thos. Kallender and Thos. Colsten: Receipt for note concerning mortgage of Thomas Kallender's land. Witness: D. Sulivane.

4 HD 371. December 3, 1792. Thos. Barnes of Dorchester County to Daniel Barnes of the same county (son of said Thos.): ½ of "Priviledge" and other land on Blackwater Marsh, excepting "Gift to My Daughter." Witnesses: Henry Lake, Jno. Keene. Acknowledged before Henry Lake and John Keene, Justices.

4 HD 374. December 3, 1792. Thomas Barnes of Dorchester County to John Barnes son of said Thomas, of the same county: "Gift to My Daughter" containing 36 acres by patent. Witnesses: Henry Lake, Jno. Keene. Acknowledged before Henry Lake and Jno. Keene, Justices.

4 HD 377. January 4, 1793. Theophilus Marshall of Dorchester County to Robert Griffith: Bond concerning "Carthagenia," "Marshall Chance" and "New Market," all adj. each other in the neighborhood of New Market, formerly sold by Marshall to Charles Muir who has not complied with certain conditions. Witness: Jno. Stevens.

4 HD 379. January 3, 1793. Theophilus Marshall and Elizabeth his wife of Dorchester County to Robert Griffith of the same county: part of two tracts called "Marshalls Chance" and "Carthagenia," on a division line between John and Theophilus Marshall, on a branch of Secretary Creek, containing 27 acres clear of elder surveys. Witnesses: Jno. Stevens, David Smith. Acknowledged before Jno. Stevens and David Smith, Justices.

4 HD 383. January 7, 1793. Charles Hodson, Sheriff of Dorchester County, to Robert Leatherbury of Somerset County: "Promise" on Nanticoke River, containing 200 acres, sold by the said Sheriff under writ of Fieri Facias at the suit of said Robert Leatherbury, Executor of Jolley Leatherbury, against Samuel Muir, eldest son and heir of Charles Muir late of Dorchester County, deceased. Witnesses: Jno. Stevens, Levin Woolford. Acknowledged before Jno. Stevens and Levin Woolford, Justices.

4 HD 386. January 5, 1793. Isaac Canter of Dorchester County, Carpenter, to Thomas Wilcox of the same county, farmer: goods and household furniture. Witnesses: Mary N. Douglass, Catharine Kennedy, Jno. Crapper. Acknowledged before Jno. Crapper, Justice.

4 HD 388. December 24, 1792. Gustavus Scott to Richard Goldsborough: land on the road from Cambridge to the Chapel and Hills Point, adj. lands purchased by the late Robert Gold.sborough Esq. from said Scott, and containing 24 1/4 acres more or less. Witnesses: Levin Woolford, Stanley Byus. Acknowledged by Gustavus Scott and Margaret his wife before Levin Woolford and Stanley Byus, Justices.

4 HD 391. December 19, 1791. John Twyford of Dorchester County to Francis Turpin of Sussex County: Bond for conveyance by said John Twyford and Mary

his wife of "Hazard," containing 80 acres more or less. Witnesses: Thomas Chilcut, Cain Wright. Receipt for purchase money for part of "Hazard" outside the lines of "Red Oak Level ," which at this time belongs to John Turpin.

4 HD 393. April 1, 1778. Spencer Martrum Waters of Dorchester County to John Walker Senr. of the same place: Bond to convey 25 acres of "Brown Neglect," adj. said Walker's land. Witnesses: Isaac Reed, Beachamp Harper. Assigned November 20, 1781 by John Walker Senr. to his son John Walker Junr. Witnesses: John Reed, Thomas King Senr. Assigned September 3, 1783 by John Walker Junr. to Francis Turpin. Witnesses: Jno. Turpin Junr., Abel Tull.

4 HD 395. June 13, 1787. Edward Brown of Dorchester County, planter, to Ezekiel Reed of the same county, planter: Bond for conveyance by said Edward Brown and Betsey his wife of part of "Browns Meadows" (formerly the property of James Brown the Eldest) containing 382 acres more or less; and part of "Waterses Last Choice," containing 38 1/4 acres more or less, both tracts lying between the Northwest and Northeast Forks of Nanticoke River. Witnesses: Matthew Smith D.S.D.C., Elisabeth Smith.

4 HD 399. December 18, 1792. Pollard Edmondson and Elisabeth his wife of Dorchester County to Jeremiah Pattison of the same county: part of "Edmondsons Regulation" on Slaughter Creek, containing 40 acres more or less, deeded to John Pitt Airey, father of said Elisabeth, by Pollard Edmondson of Talbot County. Witnesses: Moses LeCompte, Richd. Pattison. Acknowledged before Moses Lecompte and Richd. Pattison.

4 HD 402. January 14, 1793. Charles Hodson Esq., Sheriff of Dorchester County, to John Eccleston Junr., Physician: "Pilgrimage" containing 440 acres more or less, where Thomas Hill Airey now lives, sold by the Sheriff under writ of Fieri Facias at suit of Edward Harris of Queen Anns County against said Thomas Hill Airey. Witnesses: Jno. Stevens, Levin Woolford. Acknowledged before Jno. Stevens and Levin Woolford, Justices.

4 HD 405. December 22, 1792. John Smoot of Dorchester County to Ezekiel Wall of the same county: part of "Conclusion" between the Northwest and Northeast Forks of Nanticoke River, adj. "Waters Lott" and containing 47 acres more or less. Witnesses: Jno. Stevens, Jno. Crapper. Acknowledged before Jno. Stevens and Jno. Crapper, Justices.

4 HD 409. January 14, 1793. Jonathan Patridge of Dorchester County to Richard Martin of the same county: 17 acres more or less, between the third line

of "Outlet" and the second course of "Derby." Witnesses: Levin Woolford, David Smith. Acknowledged before Levin Woolford and David Smith, Justices.

4HD 412. August 24, 1792. Archy Dannielly of Harford County, planter, to Jacob Wright of Dorchester County, planter: part of "Good Luck by Friendship" on the road from Cabin Creek to Hunting Creek, containing 33 acres .more or less. Witnesses: Jno. Eccleston, Jno. Stevens, Acknowledged before Jno. Eccleston and Jno. Stevens, Justices.

4 HD 416. January 26, 1793. William Moore of Dorchester County and Eba his wife to Charles Johnson of the same county: part of "Kings Chance," containing 50 acres more or less. Witnesses: Jno. Crapper, David Smith. Acknowledged before David Smith and Jno. Crapper, Justices.

4 HD 420. January 26, 1793. George Gale of Dorchester County to Stoughton Tull of the same county: part of "Browns Neglect," containing 142 acres more or less. Witnesses: Jno. Crapper, David Smith. Acknowledged before Jno. Crapper and David Smith.

4 HD 423. February 1, 1793. Moses LeCompte of Dorchester County to Elizabeth Woollen of the same county: "Woollens Possession" on Taylors Island, containing 41 ½ acres more or less. Witnesses: Richd. Pattison, Levin Woolford. Acknowledged before Richd. Pattison and Levin Woolford.

4 HD 425. January 19, 1793. William Pattison Junr. and James Pattison of Dorchester County to Moses Geoghegan and John Geoghegan of the same county: the interest of said William and James (under the Will of Jacob Pattison, deceased, father of William, and in consequence of the said James having intermarried with Sarah Pattison, widow of said Jacob Pattison) in part of "Armstrongs Folly" on James Island, in Kilmans Neck, containing 100 acres more or less. Witnesses: Moses LeCompte, Richd. Pattison. Acknowledged by William Pattison, James Pattison and Sarah, wife of said James, before Moses LeCompte and Richd. Pattison, Justices.

4 HD 428. August 22, 1792. Captain Levin Marshall and Mary his wife of Dorchester County to Benjamin Collinson of the same county, Planter: part of "Goodridges Choice" on the north side of Cabin Creek, containing 70 acres more or less. Witnesses: Jno. Eccleston, E. Richardson. Acknowledged before Jno. Eccleston and E. Richardson.

4 HD 431. February 11, 1793. Michael Hall Bonwill of Kent County, Dellaware

to Handy Handley Senr. of Dorchester County: part of "Friends Assistance," near "Handleys Regulation" and containing 40 acres more or less. Witness: Moses LeCompte. Acknowledged before Moses LeCompte and Jno. Stevens, Justices.

4 HD 435. February 18, 1793. Garner Bruffitt of Dorchester County to John McKeel of the same county: part of "Sharpes Point" sold by Da.niel Bruffitt, grandfather of said Garner, to a. certain Robert Wing, containing 50 acres more or less. Witnesses: Robt. Harrison, Jno. Stevens. Acknowledged before Robt. Harrison and Jno. Stevens, Justices.

4 HD 438. February 23, 1793. William Geoghegan of Dorchester County to Moses Geoghegan of the same county: part of "the Grove" on James Island, on Killmans Cove, adj. "Johns Venture" and containing 12 ½ acres more or less. Also "LeComptes Addition," containing 17 ½ acres more or less. Witnesses: Moses LeCompte, Richd. Pattison. Acknowledged by William Geoghegan and Rebecca. his wife before Moses LeCompte and Richd. Pattison.

4 HD 441. February 23, 1793. William Geoghegan of Dorchester County to John Bell of the same county: part of "the Grove" on James Island, on Killmans Cove, adj. "Johns Venture" and containing 20 acres more or less. Witnesses: Moses LeCompte, Richd. Pattison. Acknowledged by William Geoghegan and Rebecca his wife before Moses LeCompte and Richd. Pattison.

4 HD 444. February 23, 1793. William Geoghegan of Dorchester County to John Geoghegan of the same county: "Armstrongs Folly" on James Island, containing 100 acres more or less, excepting 15 ft. square where the father and mother of Thomas Pattison are buried, who sold the said land to a certain Edward Parker November 9, 1763, it also being the land the aforesaid John Geoghegan now lives on. Also part of "the Grove," containing 5 acres more or less. Witnesses: Moses LeCompte, Richd. Pattison. Acknowledged by William Geoghegan and Rebecca his wife before Moses LeCompte and Richd. Pattison.

4 HD 446. December 22, 1792. John Laing of Dorchester County to John Dean of Jno. of the same county: part of "Discovery" on the Southwest side of the Northwest Fork of Nanticoke River, on Bryans Branch, containing 92 1/4 acres more or less. Witnesses: Jno. Crapper, Jno. Stevens. Acknowledged by John Laing and Hosanna Laing his wife before Jno. Crapper and Jno. Stevens, Justices.

4 HD 451. February 14, 1793. Jeremiah Pattison of Dorchester County to John

Edmondson, James Edmondson, Samuel Edmondson and Moses Edmondson of the same county: part of "Pattisons Priviledge," adj. "Pleasant Grove Regulated' and "Gum Swamp" and containing 63 acres more or less. Witnesses: Moses LeCompte, Richd. Pattison. Acknowledged before Moses LeCompte and Richard Pattison, Justices.

4 HD 454. February 25, 1793. William Robertson of Cambridge, Gent., to Peter Rea of the sane town, Mcht.: part of "Lockermans Regulation" adj. the said town of Cambridge, adj. John Blair's enclosed lot. Witnesses: Richd. Pattison, Levin Woolford. Acknowledged before Richd. Pattison and Levin Woolford, Justices.

4 HD 456. March 8, 1793. James Muir of Dorchester County, Joiner, to Edwards Thompson of the same county, planter: part of "Discovery," containing 1 acre more or less. Witnesses: Jno. Stevens, David Smith. Acknowledged before Jno. Stevens and David Smith, Justices.

4 HD 459. September 27, 1792. John McWilliams and Hopkins Willen to Thomas Hingson, John Ellett, Jacob Wright and Joseph Douglass, "Trustees to the Independent Meetinghouse": part of "Armstrongs Venter" and part of "Dixons Discovery," containing 1 acre more or less. Witnesses: Jno. Crapper, David Smith. Acknowledged by John McWilliams and Rebecca his wife, Hopkins Willen and Sealey his wife before John Crapper and David Smith, Justices.

4 HD 463. March 20, 1793. Job Slacum of Dorchester County to John Barnes (of Thomas) of the same county: part of "Addition to Liberty," containing 10 acres more or less. Witnesses: Robt. Harrison, Tho. Jones. Acknowledged before Robt. Harrison and Tho. Jones, Justices.

4HD 466. October 18, 1792. James Maccubbin Lingan of Montgomery County to John Griffith of Dorchester County: "Chalmors Chance" granted to James Chalmers about July 16, 1761 and late the property of James Maccubbin deceased, adj. "White Oak Range," on the north side of Blackwater River, in Peters Neck and containing 342 ½ acres more or less. Witnesses: Tho. Turner, Joseph Hall. Acknowledged by James Maccubbin Lingan and Janet his wife before Tho. Turner and Joseph Hall, Justices for Montgomery County. Brooke Beall, Clk.

4 HD 470. December 3, 1792. Stephen Pearson of Dorchester County to William Lake of the same county: part of "Bansbury" adj. the Chapel land and

containing 3 1/4 acres more or less. Witnesses: Henry Lake, Jno. Keene. Acknowledged by Stephen Pearson and Lidia his wife before Henry Lake and John Keene, Justices.

4 HD 473. March 21, 1793. Levin Phillips of Dorchester County, planter, to Henry Meekins of the same county: "Busicks Defiance" now called "Relyance," adj. "Busicks Venture," "Little Brittain" and "Robinsons Craft" and containing 94 ½ acres more or less. Also "Busicks Venture" on the road from Henry Dean's to John Brohawn's plantation, containing 25 acres more or less. Witnesses: Stanley Byus, Richd. Pattison. Acknowledged before Stanley Byus and Richd. Pattison, Justices.

4 HD 477. March 7, 1793. John Muir of Dorchester County to Stevens Woolford of the same county: "Woolfords Content" on a cove of Fishing Creek called Broad Cove, adj. "Hackerin" and containing 56 acres more or less. Witnesses: Jno. Stevens, David Smith. Acknowledged before Jno. Stevens and David Smith.

4 HD 480. March 21, 1793. William Ennalls of Dorchester County to John Scott of the same county: part of "Partnership" on the road from Hall's Branch to Jonathan Bestpitch's lands. Witnesses: Jno. Stevens, Stanley Byus. Acknowledged before Jno. Stevens and Stanley Byus, Justices.

4 HD 483. October 24, 1792. Thomas Hicks and Sarah his wife of Dorchester County to John Scott of the same county: part of "Darley" on Hockadays Branch, adj. "Buckfield" and containing 193 1/4 acres more or less. Witnesses: Jno. Stevens, Jno. Crapper. Acknowledged before Jno. Stevens and Jno. Crapper, Justices.

4 HD 488. March 25, 1793. Jonathan Patridge of Dorchester County to William Pattison of the same county: 27 acres of "Patridges Regulation." Witnesses: Moses LeCompte, Levin Woolford. Acknowledged before Moses LeCompte and Levin Woolford, Justices.

4 HD 489. February 28, 1793. The State of Maryland by Alexander Contee Hanson Esq., Chancellor, to Gustavus Scott Esq. of Dorchester County: One Moyety of two tracts called "Marsh Pasture" and "Meadow," containing in the whole 280 acres, patented to Pritchet Willey. Witness: Henry Whetcroft.

4 HD 491. March 26, 1793. Archibald Gray of Dorchester County to Thomas Gray of the same county: part of "Black Walnut Island," containing 14 acres

more or less. Witnesses: Moses LeCompte, Levin Woolford. Acknowledged before Moses LeCompte and Levin Woolford, Justices.

4 HD 494. December 19, 1792. William McBryde and James Ritchie of Somerset County to James Birckhead of Dorchester County: lots in Vienna. Witnesses: Jno. Crapper, David Smith. Acknowledged before Jno. Crapper and David Smith, Justices. Acknowledged by Sarah McBryde, wife of William McBryde, before Will Stone and Saml. Smyly, Justices for Somerset County. Wm. Done, Clk.

4 HD 497. March 4, 1793. Peter Rea of the town of Cambridge, Mcht., to John Bradshaw of the same place, Carpenter and Joiner: lease of part of "Lockermans Regulation" adj. John Blair's enclosed lot, containing 1 acre and 9 square perches more or less, for the term of 99 years, renewable forever. Witnesses: Levin Woolford, Stanley Byus. Acknowledged before Levin Woolford and Stanley Byus, Justices.

4 HD 501. March 23, 1793. William Mediss of Dorchester County, planter, to Thomas Kallender of the same county: part of "Tootells Venture" containing 189 acres more or less, formerly conveyed to said William Mediss by William Kallender. Witnesses: Tho. Jones, Stanley Byus. Acknowledged before Tho. Jones and Stanley Byus, Justices.

4 HD 503. March 22, 1793. Joseph Meekins of Dorchester County to Thomas Kallender of the same county: "Chance" on the Northwest Branch of Blackwater River, containing 149 3/4 acres more or less. Witnesses: Jno. Stevens, Levin Woolford. Acknowledged before Jno. Stevens and Levin Woolford, Justices.

4 HD 506. April 9, 1793. George Roberts of Dorchester County, Schoolmaster, to Richard Tubman, planter: "Robearts Beginning" in Meekins Neck, on the road to Fishing Creek, near the house where Thomas Ruark lives, containing 20 acres more or less. Witnesses: Levin Woolford, David Smith. Acknowledged before Levin Woolford and David Smith, Justices.

4 HD 508. April 8, 1793. John Eccleston of Dorchester County, Gent. and late High Sheriff, to John Elder Gist of the same county, Mcht.: storehouse and lot of Joseph Dowson late of Dorchester County, Mcht., sold by said Sheriff under Court Order for payment of Dowson's debts to James DeDrusina, Julius Conrad Ridder and James Clerk; located in front of the jail (see lease from Justices to Dowson, 2 HD 19, etc.). Witnesses: Jno. Stevens, Levin Woolford.

Acknowledged before Jno. Stevens and Levin Woolford, Justices.

4 HD 513. April 8, 1793. Peter Rea of Cambridge, Mcht., to James Arnett of the same county, farmer: part of "Belfield," heretofore conveyed by Richard Goldsborough to said Peter Rea, adj. land of John Blair of Cambridge, on the road to Fishing Creek, adj. the Presbyterian Meeting House survey, adj. William Vickers' part of "Belfield" and containing 29 acres more or less. Witnesses: Jno. Stevens, Levin Woolford. Acknowledged by Peter Rea and Sarah his wife before Jno. Stevens and Levin Woolford, Justices.

4 HD 516. March 21, 1793. John Martin Baker of Dorchester County, planter, to Moses LeCompte of the same county, Esq.: lands in Meekins Neck called "Lancaster Lot," containing 144 acres; "Philadelphia Range" containing 77 acres more or less; "Bakers Marsh" containing 33 ½ acres more or less; and "Bakers Chance" containing 20 acres more or less. Witnesses: Levin Woolford, Richd. Pattison. Acknowledged before Levin Woolford and Richd. Pattison, Justices.

4 HD 520. April 9, 1793. Moses LeCompte of Dorchester County to Richard Tubman of the same county: lands in Meekins Neck called "Lancaster Lot" containing 144 acres; "Philadelphia Range" containing 77 acres; "Bakers Marsh" containing 33 ½ acres; and "Bakers Chance," containing 20 acres. Witnesses: Levin Woolford, David Smith. Acknowledged before Levin Woolford and David Smith, Justices.

4 HD 524. April 18, 1793. Thomas Smith Junr. of Dorchester County to Charles Hodson of the same county: "Smith Field" on Chicamacomico River, containing 400 acres more or less. Witnesses: Levin Woolford, Richd. Pattison. Acknowledged before Levin Woolford and Richd. Pattison, Justices.

4 HD 526. April 18, 1793. Charles Hodson of Dorchester County to Thomas Smith Junr. of the same county: "Smith Field" on Chicamacomico River, containing 400 acres more or less. Witnesses: Richd. Pattison, Levin Woolford. Acknowledged before Richd. Pattison and Levin Woolford, Justices.

4 HD 529. April 22, 1793. Thomas Hicks of Dorchester County to Levin Wall of the same county: part of "Darley." Witnesses: Jno. Stevens, Levin Woolford. Acknowledged before Jno. Stevens and Levin Woolford, Justices.

4 HD 531. April 29, 1793. Gustavus Scott of Cambridge and Margaret his wife to Peter Rea of the same place, Mcht.: part of Lockermans Regulation,"

containing 2 acres. Witnesses: Levin Woolford, Jno. Stevens. Acknowledged before Jno. Stevens and Levin Woolford, Justices.

4 HD 535. April 26, 1793. David Dean and Mary Dean his mother of Caroline County to Thomas Nicolls of Dorchester County: "Deans Beginning," beginning to the northward of Whiteleys Swamp and near John Andrews' cow path and containing 31 ½ acres more or less. Witnesses: Jno. Stevens, Jno. Gooding. Acknowledged before Jno. Stevens and Jno. Gooding, Justices.

4 HD 538. January 10, 1793. John Riddle of Vienna in Dorchester County, Surgeon, to Alexander Douglass and John Smoot of said county: furniture, medicine, etc. Witness: David Smith. Acknowledged before David Smith, Justice.

4 HD 540. January 12, 1793. List of Negro slaves acquired by Thomas White Junr. by marriage with Sarah Small, daughter of Richard Small of Delaware and removed January 2, 1793 to Dorchester County, Maryland.

4 HD 541. January 12, 1793. Owen Corkran of Dorchester County, planter, to his brother James Corkran of the same place, planter: all of grantor's right under his father's Will at the death of his mother Rachel Corkran, until said Owen shall pay to said James the sum of 65 Pounds specie. Witnesses: John Nash, Rachel Carrol.

4 HD 542. January 14, 1793. William Geoghegan and Capewell Keene to Negro Dominick: Manumission. Witnesses: Moses LeCompte, John Aaron. Acknowledged before Moses LeCompte. 4HD 544. January 21, 1793. Eleanor Jones of Dorchester County to Charles Stainton of the same county, planter: livestock, furniture, etc., and a tract of land called "Friends Assistance" where grantor now lives. Witnesses: Jno. Crapper, Arthur Pritchard. Acknowledged before Jno. Crapper, Justice.

4 HD 545. April 6, 1793. Thomas Hicks to William S. Bond and William Buchanan: Schooner "Thomas and Betsey" (Wm. Frazier, Master), built at Blackwater River in 1792. Witness: Levin Woolford. Acknowledged before Levin Woolford.

4 HD 548. October 22, 1792 - December 21, 1792. Commission to Daniel Sulivane, John Stevens, Theophilus Marshall and Charles LeCompte of Dorchester County, Gent., to perpetuate bounds of Thomas Hicks' land called "Crooked Billet," and Return. Deposition of John Hooper, aged about 62 years,

concerns survey of the said tract by Henry Ennalls, Surveyor, about 40 years ago. Deposition of Roger A. Hooper, aged about 55 years, concerning survey of "Exchange" about 16-17 years ago, mentions Willis Newton at that time, on the road from Cambridge to the Free School.

4 HD 552. July 22, 1793. Charles Hodson to the State of Maryland: Bond with John Eccleston Senr. and William Ennalls as Sureties. Witnesses: Saml. Brown', Arthur Pritchard. Proved by Samuel Brown and Arthur Pritchett, Witnesses, before Tho. Jones, Justice.

4 HD 553. January 24, 1793. John Shenton of Dorchester County to Thomas Wheeler Junr.: Negro slave, livestock, furniture and other personal property. Witnesses: Edwd. Chappell, Sarah Chappell.

4 HD 554. February 7, 1793. Susanna Keene of Dorchester County to Negro slaves: Manumission. Witnesses: Catherine Jones, George Ward. Acknowledged before Levin Woolford, Justice.

4 HD 555. February 23, 1793. Elizabeth Heron (widow of Robert) of Dorchester County to her daughter Susanna Heron: Negro slaves. Witness: Hy. Waggaman. Acknowledged before Jno. Stevens, Justice.

4 HD 556. March 1, 1793. Leven Stack of Dorchester County to his son Nuton Stack of the same county: livestock, etc. Witnesses: Elisabeth Stack, Samuel McGee.

4 HD 557. December 25, 1792. Clement Vickars of Dorchester County, planter, and Hugh Orem of Talbot County, planter, to John Coleson of Dorchester County, planter: Bond for conveyance by said Vickars of part of "South Preston" on the north side of Vickars Creek which makes out of the east side of Little Choptank River, to the said John Coleson ; when said Clement arrives at age 21 years. Witnesses: Elizabeth LeCompte, Hugh McColl.

4 HD 558. March 16, 1793. Charles Winrow of Dorchester County, planter, to Hugh McCall of the same county, Schoolmaster: One bay horse, saddle and bridle, one horse cart and harness. Witnesses: Joseph Williams, John Pattison.

4 HD 559. March 9, 1793. William C. Angell of Dorchester County to William Jones of the sarre county: Negro boy named Charles, aged about 11 years. Witness: David Smith.

4 HD 560. March 19, 1793. John Hollock of Sussex County, Delaware, to Negro slave named Rachel, lately removed to Dorchester County by James Hollock: Manumission. Witnesses: Ns. Hammond, Thos. Martin. Acknowledged before Moses LeCompte, Justice.

4 HD 561. October 1, 1792. Randolph Johnson of Dorchester County to John Price of Talbot County: Riding carriage, Negro slave named Fanny, etc. Witnesses: Levin Ball, John Johnson. Acknowledged before Jno. Stevens, Justice.

4 HD 562. March 18, 1793. Woolford Stewart of Dorchester County, Blacksmith, to Nehemiah Whiteley of the same county, planter: livestock, tools, etc. Witnesses: Nathaniel Walker, Hugh McColl.

4 HD 563. October 22, 1792 - December 14, 1792. Commission to Richard Pattison, William Stevens, Benjamin Woodard and Samuel Hooper of Dorchester County, Gent., to perpetuate bounds of land of Nathaniel Manning called "Pokety," and Return. Marked post and a stone bounder set down by agreement of Nathaniel Manning, William Trippe, Charles LeCompte and Edward Noel, who were present and said to be the only persons interested, near Wm. Palmer's blacksmith shop. A post was also put down to mark a division between Nathaniel Manning and William Trippe, at a bridge called Matthew Errexsons Bridge.

4 HD 566. August 5, 1793. Henry Dickinson of Dorchester County to Josiah Bayly of the same county: part of "Carthagenia" at the head of Secretary Creek, devised to said Henry Dickinson by Henry Trippe deceased by Last Will and Testament in tail, now conveyed in fee simple in accordance with Act of Assembly. Witnesses: Jno. Stevens, Levin Woolrord. Acknowledged before Jno. Stevens and Levin Woolford, Justices.

4 HD 568. August 8, 1793. Josiah Bayly of Dorchester County to Henry Dickinson of the same county: part of "Carthagena" at the head of Secretary Creek. Witnesses: Jno. Stevens, Levin Woolford. Acknowledged before Jno. Stevens and Levin Woolford, Justices.

4 HD 570. Levin Phillips of Dorchester County, planter, to Henry Meekins of the same county: personal property.

4 HD 571. March 25, 1793. Edward Riggin of Dorchester County, planter, to Ebenezer Kennard of the same county, planter: Negro slave named Dick.

Witnesses: Moses LeCompte, Hy. Waggaman. Acknowledged before Moses LeCompte.

4 HD 572. March 21, 1793. John Faunce of Dorchester County, shoemaker, to Henry Smoot of Dorchester County, planter: personal property. Witnesses: Thomas Mackey, Thos. Hengson. Acknowledged before Jno. Crapper, Justice.

4 HD 573. April 15, 1791. Agreement between Jonathan Bestpitch and John Eccleston of Dorchester County concerning the lines of "Ecclestons Regulation Rectified," on the path from Transquakin to Blackwater. Witnesses: Edwd. Brodess, Jabus Gootee. Sworn to by witnesses before Levin Woolford, Justices.

4 HD 574. March 19, 1792 - March 8, 1793. Commission to James Sulivane, Henry Hicks, Theophilus Marshall, Mitchell Russum and Jacob Wright of Dorchester County, Gent., to perpetuate bounds of Daniel Nicols' land called "Hamton" ("Hampton"), and Return. Deposition of James Coleman, aged about 40 years, mentions Isaac Nicolls about 1775. Deposition of Robert Hardikin, aged about 58 years, states "that in the year 1759 Thomas Andrew Guardian to Isaac Nicolls son of Jno. and Nehemiah Nicolls Guardian to Levin Nicolls son of Jno. and Mark Nicolls son of John did meet at the first boundary of the tract of land called "Hampton," to divide the tract according to the said John Nicolls' Last Will and Testament, with Joseph Ennalls as surveyor. The deposition mentions John Trice and Thomas Busick at the survey in 1759, and locates the land on the road from Hunting Creek to Cabin Creek. Witnesses: Elizabeth Nicolls, Benthal Stevens, William Parker. Chain carriers: John McCotter, Henry Anderson.

4 HD 580. July 26, 1781. John Shenton of Dorchester County, planter, to Richard Sprigg: Bond to convey land in Meekins Neck where Joseph Shenton now lives, containing by patent 200 acres, and other lands in Meekins Neck (excepting 9 acres called "Johns Adventure"). Witnesses: Benjamin Stevens, Jno. M. Anderson.

4 HD 581. March 26, 1793. Nathan McCollister to Levin Marshall of Dorchester County: livestock. Witnesses: Thos. Hingson, Thos. Insley. Acknowledged before Jno. Crapper, Justice.

4 HD 582. October 16, 1792. Valuation of land of Nathan Wright deceased, containing 120 acres, by John McCotter and Thos. Anderson (called "Trippes Desire"). Samuel Wright agrees to pay 25 shillings per acre for said land. Witness: Saml. Brown. The land called "Trippes Desire" adj. "Hamton" and

"Addition," on the road from Cabin Creek Mill to Hunting Creek.

4 HD 584. April 22, 1793. Levin Wall of Dorchester County to Thomas Hicks of the same county: Bond to convey part of "Darley" which said Hicks has this day deeded to said Levin Wall. Witnesses: Levin Woolford, Jno. Stevens.

4 HD 585. December 15, 1792. Agreement between Richard Tubman and Mark Meekins, both of Dorchester County, concerning a windmill and house erected by them jointly on a piece of property belonging to said Richard Tubman, near the lower bridge of Blackwater. Witnesses: Wm. Johnson, Joshua Meekins.

4 HD 587. August 12, 1793. Suspension of license of Thomas Abbet to retail spirituous liquors, by Robt. Harrison and Moses LeCompte, Justices. Abbet's license is said to have been granted by Peter Rea, whose license is also suspended. Henry Waggaman Esq., James Condon and Anthony Boyle are listed as "Informers." Daniel Parker Junr. delivered a copy of these documents to Thomas Abbott.

4 HD 589. April 22, 1793. William C. Angell of Dorchester County to James Layton of the same county: Negro slaves and furniture. Witness: David Smith. Acknowledged before David Smith, Justice.

4 HD 590. April 29, 1793. Gustavus Scott to Thomas Lockerman: part of "Lockermans Regulation" adj. the town of Cambridge, late the property of A. Patison deceased, containing 2 acres more or less. Witnesses: Jno. Stevens, Levin Woolford. Acknowledged by Gustavus Scott and Margaret his wife before Jno. Stevens and Levin Woolford, Justices.

4 HD 592. November 1, 1793. Theophilus Marshall of Dorchester County to Henry Dickinson of the same county: Indenture of William Marshall, son of said Theophilus, as an apprentice to the said Henry Dickinson to learn the business of County Clerk until September 30, 1800 when said William arrives at age 21. Witnesses: James Dickinson, Henry C. Kennedy.

4 HD 594. April 29, 1793. Gustavus Scott to John Blair: part of "Lockermans Regulation" containing 2 acres more or less, between the lots sold to William M. Robinson and Peter Rea of Cambridge. Witnesses: Levin Woolford, Jno. Stevens. Acknowledged by Gustavus Scott and Margaret his wife before Levin Woolford and Jno. Stevens, Justices.

4 HD 596. April 20, 1793. Bartholomew Fletcher of Dorchester County to

Thomas Webster of the same county: Negro slave. Witnesses: Thos. Hingson, Handa Stayton. Acknowledged before Jno. Crapper, Justice.

4 HD 597. April 29, 1793. Gustavus Scott to John Manning: part of "Loockermans Regulation" between the lot of Daniel Sulivane and the lands sold by Archibald Patison to Richard Glover, adj. the town of Cambridge and containing 1/4 acre. Witnesses: Jno. Stevens, Levin Woolford. Acknowledged by Gustavus Scott and Margaret his wife before Jno. Stevens and Levi Woolford, Justices.

4 HD 598. May I, 1793. Levin Woolford, John Hooper and Bartho. Ennalls, Trustees of the Poor of Dorchester County, to William B. Murphy of Dorchester County: Indenture of John Pritchett, a poor boy aged about 8 years, as apprentice until age 21 to learn the trade of farmer. Witness: Thos. McKeel, Clk.

4 HD 600. May 1, 1793. Levin Woolford, Henry Ennalls and John Hooper, Trustees of the Poor of Dorchester County, to Levin Travers of the said county: Indenture of Betsy Thompson, a poor girl aged about 12 years, as apprentice until age 16, to learn the trade of spinster. Witness: Thos. McKeel, Clk.

4 HD 601. May 7, 1793. Erasmus Chappell to Thomas Beard, planter: personal property. Witness: Elenor Seberry.

4 HD 601. April 27, 1793. Valentine Insley of Dorchester County to his sons Esau Insley and Valentine Insley Junr. of the same county: "Andrews Fortune' and "Hoopers Labour" on Jockeys Cabbin Branch and Farham Creek. Witnesses: Henry Lake, Jno. Keene. Acknowledged before Henry Lake and Jno. Keene.

4 HD 603. April 2, 1793. John Tripp of Talbot County to Henry Tripp of Dorchester County: "Dales Right" and "Dales Addition" in Cassons Neck. Witnesses: Tho. Jones, Stanley Byus. Acknowledged before Tho. Jones and Stanley Byus, Justices.

4 HD 605. May 2, 1793. Levin Keene of Dorchester County to Thomas Hill Airey of the same place: part of "Pilgrimage" containing 200 acres more or less, on the road from the Methodist Meeting House to John Pitt's plantation. Witnesses: Robt. Harrison, Levin Woolford. Acknowledged before Robt. Harrison and Levin Keene, Justices.

4 HD 607. September 8, 1792. Elizabeth Ennalls of Dorchester County, spinster,

to Garner Bruffitt of the same county, House Carpenter: lease of land on Hocady Creek in the occupation of William Warren. Signed by Joseph Daffin for Eliza. Ennalls. Witnesses: Wm. Piercy, Elijah Summers.

4 HD 609. May 1, 1793 Roger Foxwell of Dorchester County to Levi Foxwell of the same county: "Foxwells Endeavour," near Arthur Smith's house on Firm Creek, containing 30 acres more or less; "Strife" near Richard Hart's, on Cedar Creek, containing 30 acres more or less; and "Rogers Endeavour" adj. "Foxwells Endeavour" and containing 31 ½ acres. Witnesses: Henry Lake, Jno. Keene. Acknowledged before Henry Lake and Jno. Keene, Justices.

4 HD 611. December, 1793. Thomas Sears to David Bramble: lease of 50 acres of woodland adj. the land of Mr. Hollidays, in the Northwest Fork of Nanticoke River, for the term of 15 years. Witnesses: Jno. Crapper, John Smoot. Acknowledged before Jno. Crapper, Justice.

4 HD 612. October 22, 1792 - November 6, 1792. Commission to Richard Pattison, Matthias Travers, Jeremiah Pattison, John Braughan and Jacob Travers of Dorchester County, Gent., concerning Zebulon Whiteley's land, states that Thomas Hooper deceased died seized of lands called "Hoopers Conclusion," "the Pasture" and "Addition to Hoopers Pasture," which passed at his death intestate to his brother James Hooper and his sisters Mary and Nancy; that the said Zebulon Whiteley married the same Nancy Hooper, who is of full age, and that the said James and Nancy are still minors. It is found that the lands contain 71 acres (clear of elder surveys) in all, which would not admit of a division and the value is set at 17 shillings and 6 pence current money.

4 HD 616. May 10, 1793. Henry Macotter of Dorchester County to William Martain of the same county: part of "Lockermans Regulation" bought by said Macotter from Thomas Kilman except what is deeded to Edward Woollen and Nathan Stevens, located near the head of Parsons Creek. Witness: Tho. Jones, Richd. Pattison. Acknowledged by Henry Macotter and Sarah his wife before Tho. Jones and Richd. Pattison, Justices.

4HD 618. January 24, 1793. Benjamin Bright and Solomon Bright and Rhoda his wife of Dorchester and Caroline Counties, to Eccleston Brown of Dorchester County: 50 acres of "Windsor" (containing 350 acres) in Dorchester and Caroline Counties. Also "Sandy Hill" adj. "Windsor" and containing 100 acres. Witnesses: David Smith, Jno. Crapper. Acknowledged before Jno. Crapper and David Smith, Justices.

4 HD 623. May 20, 1793. Certificate of Charles Eccleston, Joseph Eccleston, Lemuel Beckwith and Jeremiah Beckwith, Freeholders, concerning the perpetuation of the first boundary of "Noels Regulation" belonging to Capt. Edward Noel.

4 HD 624. May 11, 1793. Priscilla Acworth of Somerset County to James Acworth: Negro slave named Jack. Witness: David Smith. Acknowledged before David Smith, Justice.

4 HD 625. May 11, 1793. John Riddle and Ann Riddle his wife of Dorchester County to James Birckhead of Dorchester County: Negro boy named Spencer. Witness: David Smith. Acknowledged before David Smith" Justice.

4 HD 626. May 11, 1793. James Birckhead of Dorchester County to Thomas Smith of Dorchester County: Negro boy named Spencer. Witness: David Smith. Acknowledged before David Smith, Justice.

4 HD 628. May 27, 1793. John Langfitt, son of John, of Dorchester County, to Michael Hall Bonwill of Kent County, Delaware: lease of part of "Bridge Neck" as in deed from John Langfit to George Bonwill dated March 13, 1782, containing 10 acres more or less. Witnesses: Jno. Stevens, Levin Woolford. Acknowledged before Jno. Stevens and Levin Woolford, Justices.

4 HD 630. June 21, 1793. Nancy Chapman of Dorchester County to Negro slaves: Manumission. Witnesses: Richard Pattison, Elizah Martin. Acknowledged before Richd. Pattison, Justice.

4 HD 631. May 25, 1793. Edward Pearson of Dorchester County to Laban Pearson of the same county, son of said Edward: part of "Addition to Anything" on Charles Creek which issues out of Hungar River" adj. "Stafford" and containing 86 acres more or less. Witnesses: Henry Lake, Moses LeCompte. Acknowledged before Henry Lake and Moses LeCompte, Justices.

6 HD 1. May 11, 1793. Nancy Chapman, Richard Keene and Lucrecy his wife and Catharine Chapman, all of Dorchester County, to Elijah Martin of the same county: parts of "the Four Sisters" (originally "Armstrongs Quarter") and "Dover," both on Taylors Island, adj. "Richards Discovery" and containing 70 acres more or less. Witnesses: Richard Pattison, John Keene. Acknowledged before Jno. Keene and Richd. Pattison.

6 HD 3. June 3, 1793. Levin Woolford, John Hooper and Dr. John Eccleston,

Trustees of the Poor of Dorchester County, to Thomas Corse of said county: Indenture of a poor girl of said county, about 8 years of age, as apprentice until age 16 to learn the trade of spinster. Witness: Thos. McKeel, Clk.

6 HD 5. May 25, 1793. Henry Travers Phillips and Nancy his wife of Dorchester County, planter, to Mark Meekins of the same county, planter: "Working Ridge," containing 60 acres more or less. Witnesses: Moses LeCompte, Jno. Keene. Acknowledged before Moses LeCompte and Jno. Keene, Justices.

6 HD 8. June 5, 1793. Thomas Linthicum of Dorchester County, planter, to his son Edward Linthicum: 6 Negro slaves. Witnesses: Thomas Jones, Stanley Byus. Acknowledged before Thomas Jones and Stanley Byus.

6 HD 10. May 25, 1793. John Riddell of Dorchester County to Thomas Walters and James Ackworth of the same county: Negro slave named Judah. Witness: Jno. Crapper. Acknowledged before Jno. Crapper, Justice.

6 HD 12. Edward King of Dorchester County to John Brierwood of the same county: Negro man named Charles. Witnesses: Jacob Todd, Thomas Breerwood. Acknowledged before Moses LeCompte, Justice.

6 HD 13. January 13, 1794. Thomas Hicks of Dorchester County to Daniel McDonnell of the same county, Mcht.: "Darley" and all other lands of the said Thomas Hicks (Mortgage). Witnesses: Jno. Stevens, Levin Woolford. Acknowledged by Thomas Hicks and Sarah his wife before Jno. Stevens and Levin Woolford, Justices.

6 HD 18. June 5, 1793. Thomas Linthicum of Dorchester County, planter, to his daughter Ann Linthicum: Five Negroes. Witnesses: Tho. Jones, Stanley Byus. Acknowledged before Tho. Jones and Stanley Byus, Justices.

6 HD 20. January 10, 1793. Gabriel Bramble of Dorchester County to John Breerwood: Negro man named Peter. Witnesses: Richard Batsey, Margaret Batsey.) Acknowledged before Moses LeCompte, Justice.

6 HD 22. June 12, 1793. John Breerwood of Dorchester County to Negro slaves: Manumission. Witnesses: Moses LeCompte, Levin Woolford. Acknowledged before Moses LeCompte, Justice.

6 HD 24. May 20, 1793. Edward Smith of Dorchester County to Alexander

Douglass of Dorchester County: all of the said Edward Smith's property, real, personal and mixed, in trust for the creditors of said Edward Smith, in accordance with order of Alexander Contee Hanson, Chancellor of Maryland, and Act of Assembly. Witnesses: Jno. Stevens, Jno. Gooding. Acknowledged before Jno. Gooding and Jno. Stevens, Justices.

6 HD 27. January 26, 1793. John Walker of Dorchester County to Charles Johnson of the same county: part of "Kings Chance," containing 25 acres more or less. Witnesses: Jno. Crapper, David Smith. Acknowledged by John Walker and Sarah his wife before Jno. Crapper and David Smith, Justices.

6 HD 31. April 2, 1793. Daniel Godwin of Dorchester County to Cyrus Mitchell of the same county: lot in the village of Newmarket purchased by said Godwin from Charles Daffin, who purchased from James Sulivane. Witnesses: Jno. Stevens, Jno. Gooding. Acknowledged by Daniel Godwin and Sarah his wife before Jno. Stevens and Jno. Gooding, Justices.

6 HD 35. May 10, 1793. Nathan Stevens of Dorchester County to Henry Kilman of the same county: part of "Lockermans Regulation" bought by said Stevens from Henry Macotter, containing 1 ½ acres, at the head of Parsons Creek. Witnesses: Richd. Pattison, Tho. Jones. Acknowledged before Richd. Pattison and Thos. Jones, Justices.

6 HD 37. June 14, 1793. Charles Crookshanks and Archibald Moncrieff of Baltimore Town, Executors of Archibald Pattison deceased to John McKeel of Dorchester County: "Boston," "Sharpes Point," "Addition to Sharps Point," "Pattisons Addition to Ennalls's Gift," "Rosses Purchase," "Medland" and "Arthurs Discovery," containing 477 ½ acres more or less in all. Witnesses: Jas. Calhoun, Thorowgd. Smith. Acknowledged before Jas. Calhoun and Thorowgd. Smith, Justices for Baltimore County. Wm. Gibson, Clk.

6 HD 41. July 16, 1793. Solomon Birckhead of Dorchester County, physician, to John Hooper (of Henry) of the same county, Gent.: Lot No. 66 in Cambridge, on the main street leading to the Church and Court House, near Thomas Stewart's Smith Shop. Witnesses: Richd. Pattison, Levin Woolford. Acknowledged by Solomon Birckhead and Jane Birckhead his wife before Richd. Pattison and Levin Woolford, Justices.

6 HD 46. May 11, 1793. James Hodson of Dorchester County to Anne Ennalls (relict of Thomas Ennalls) of the same county: part of "Ennalls's Friendship," containing 4 3/4 acres more or less. Witnesses: Levin Woolford, Jno. Stevens.

Acknowledged by James Hodson and Catharine Hodson his wife before Levin Woolford and Jno. Stevens, Justices.

6 HD 48. May 11, 1793. William Whittington of Dorchester County to Ann Ennalls (relict of Thomas Ennalls) of the same county: part of "Stewarts Third Beginning," containing 3 ½ acres more or less. Also "Whittingtons Adventure," adj. "McDaniels Desire" and containing 8 1/4 acres more or less. Witnesses: Jno. Stevens, Levin Woolford. Acknowledged by William Whittington and Anne Whittington his wife before Jno. Stevens and Levin Woolford, Justices.

6 HD 51. July 5, 1793. William Geoghegan to Negro slaves: Manumission. . Witnesses: Moses LeCompte, Nancy LeCompte. Acknowledged before Moses LeCompte, Justice.

6 HD 52. June 15, 1793. Rich Chance and Bethulia his wife of Caroline County to Thomas Williams of Dorchester County: "Boxalls Lott" on Cabin Creek, and "Huburtts Hazard" on a branch of Cabin Creek, containing 46 acres more or less. Witnesses: Jno. Stevens, Jno. Crapper. Acknowledged before Jno. Stevens and Jno. Crapper, Justices.

6 HD 55. July 22, 1793. Joseph Cator, with the consent of his father Levin Cator, to James Condon of Dorchester County, Tailor: Indenture as an apprentice to learn the trade of a tailor, for the term of 6 years from November 8 last. Witnesses: Moses LeCompte, Dan McDonnell. Acknowledged before Moses LeCompte, Justice.

6 HD 57. July 12, 1793. Eccleston Brown of Dorchester County to John Smoot of the same county: part of "Sandy Hill" on the upper side of North West Fork Bridge on the west side of the river, containing ½ acre more or less. Witnesses: Jno. Stevens, Jno. Crapper. Acknowledged before Jno. Stevens and Jno. Crapper, Justices.

6 HD 59. July 12, 1793. John Laing of Dorchester County to John Smoot of the same county: two parts of "Discovery" on the southwest side of the North West Fork, containing 275 ½ acres more or less in both parts. Witnesses: Jno. Stevens, Jno. Crapper. Acknowledged by John Laing and Rosana his wife before Jno. Stevens and Jno. Crapper, Justices.

6 HD 63. July 1, 1793. Henry Ennalls of Dorchester County and Sarah his wife to Thomas Coleson of the same place: land on the east side of Fishing Creek, adj. "Harwoods Choice" and containing 200 1/4 acres more or less. Witnesses:

Robt. Harrison, Levin Woolford. Acknowledged before Robert Harrison and Levin Woolford, Justices.

6 HD 65. July 20, 1793. William Butten of Dorchester County, planter, end Elizabeth his wife to John King of the same county: part of "Johns Delight" within the lines of "Phillips's Liberty." Witnesses: Richard Pattison, Jno. Keene. Acknowledged before Richd. Pattison and Jno. Keene, Justices.

6 HD 67. August 5, 1793. Ebenezer Kennard of Dorchester County to Negro slave Richard Grace: Manumission. Witnesses: Danl. McDonnell, George Ward. Acknowledged before Jno. Stevens, Justice.

6 HD 67. August 12, 1793. Bartholomew Ennalls and Mary Ennalls of Dorchester CountJ to Negro .slaves: Manumission. Witness.s: Moses LeCompte, Henry Trippe. Acknowledged before Moses LeCompte, Justice.

6 HD 68. May 25, 1793. Isaac Woodland of Dorchester County to Vachel Keene of the same county: part of "Foxwells Lot" at the mouth of Charles Creek, on Seven Oaks Point, containing 16 acres more or less. Witnesses: Moses LeCompte, Jno. Keene. Acknowledged by Isaac Woodland and Sarah his wife before Moses LeCompte and Jno. Keene, Justices.

6 HD 70. August 19, 1793. James Arnett of Dorchester County to Peter Rea of the same county: part of "Belfield" adj. lands of Dr. John Eccleston, John Blair and William Vickars and containing 11 acres. Witnesses: Richd. Pattison, .Levin Woolford. Acknowledged by James Arnett and Mary Arnett his wife before Richard Pattison and Levin Woolford, Justices.

6 HD 72. September 5, 1793. Henry Ennalls, John Eccleston and George Ward, Trustees of the Poor of Dorchester County, to Levin Hodson of said county: Indenture of Elizabeth McCray, a poor girl of said county supposed to be about 8 years old, as an apprentice until age 16 to learn the trade of spinster. Witness: Thos. McKeel, Clk.

6 HD 74. September 5, 1793. Henry Ennalls, John Eccleston and George Ward, Trustees of the Poor of Dorchester County, to Dr. John Tootle of the said county: Indenture of Nancy Welch, a poor girl of said county, supposed to be about 10 years of age, as an apprentice until age 16 to learn the trade of spinster. Witness: Thos. McKeel.

6 HD 75. July 20, 1793. William Button and Elizabeth his wife of Dorchester

County, planter, to Mark Meekins of the same county, planter: part of "Johns Delight," adj. "Johnsons Misfortune" and containing 14 acres more or less. Witnesses: Richd. Pattison, John Keene. Acknowledged before John Keene and Richd. Pattison, Justices.

6 HD 78. August 23, 1793. James Arnett and Mary Ann his wife to William Dail of Dorchester County: part of "Bellfield" on the road from the Meeting House to Arthur Wheatley's, adj. Wm. Vickars' part of "Bellfield" and John Blair's part of said tract and containing 18 acres more or less. Witnesses: Robt. Harrison, Levin Woolford. Acknowledged before Robt. Harrison and Levin Woolford. Justices.

6 HD 82. September 2, 1793. Henry Ennalls Esq. (son of Henry Ennalls Ferry) of Dorchester County, to Robert Harrison of the same county: part of "Ennalls Outrange" adj. said Harrison's field and dwelling house, adj. "Howells Regulation" on the Indian line and containing 5 ½ acres more or less. Witnesses: Jno. Stevens, Levin Woolford. Acknowledged before Jno. Stevens and Levin Woolford, Justices.

6 HD 84. July 8, 1793. Joseph Ennalls Junr. (son of Joseph) of Dorchester County to William Ennalls, brother of the said Joseph (Junr.): lands left to grantor by the Last Will and Testament of his father Joseph Ennalls deceased. Witnesses: Hy. Waggaman, Levin Woolford, R. Woolford, Jno. Stevens. Acknowledged before John Stevens and Levin Woolford, Justices.

6 HD 86. May 8, 1793. Capt. Levin Marshall and Mary his wife of Dorchester County to Thomas Hingson of the same county: part of "Upper Black Walnut Landing" on the road from Cratchers Ferry to New Market, near said ferry, adj. "Discovery" and containing 1 acre. Witnesses: Jno. Crapper. David Smith. Acknowledged before Jno. Crapper and David Smith, Justices.

6HD 89. June 10, 1793. Charles Crookshanks, Gent., and Archibald Moncrieff, Gent., of Baltimore Town, to Hugh McGuire of Dorchester County: land on Fishing Creek (lot No. 6), being part of "Whitehaven," adj. "Head Range" and containing 2 acres more or less. The said "Whitehaven" was mortgaged by Archibald Patison during his lifetime to said Archibald Moncrieff and is now sold under said Patison's Last Will and Testament. Witnesses: Thoroughgood Smith, Jas. Calhoun. Acknowledged before Thoroughgood Smith and Jas. Calhoun, Justices for Baltimore County. Wm. Gibson, Clk.

6 HD 93. September 21, 1793. Solomon Tyler of Dorchester County and Rachel

his wife to Job Tylor of the same county: part of "Kendals Chance" and part of "Safford" on the road from the Chapel towards Hooper Straits. Witnesses: Henry Lake, John Keene. Acknowledged before Henry Lake and Jno. Keene, Justices.

6 HD 96. August 17, 1793. Gustavus Scott of Baltimore County, Attorney at Law, to Thomas Hodson Senr. of Dorchester County, Farmer: "Scotts Purchase," being part of Nanticoke Manor, patented to said Scott February 27, 1793, on the road from Smiths Mills to Vienna, adj. "Jesseys Lot" and "Possump Ridge" and containing 103 1/4 acres. Witness: Samuel Chase. Acknowledged by Gustavus Scott and Margt. H. Scott his wife before Samuel Chase, Chief Justice of the State of Maryland.

6 HD 100. September 23, 1793. Morgan Jones of Morgan of Dorchester County to William Martin of the same county: part of "Lockermans Regulation" near the head of St. Stevens Creek, containing 9 acres more or less. Witnesses: Moses LeCompte, Thos. Jones. Acknowledged before Moses LeCompte and Tho. Jones, Justices.

6 HD 104. September 28, 1793. Richard Keene of Matthew of Dorchester County to James Smith Sullender of the same county: part of "Keenes Landing" adj. "Whiteleys Adventure," adj. land of Matthew Keene, brother of said Richard, and containing 115 acres more or less. Witnesses: Moses LeCompte, Jno. Keene. Acknowledged betore Moses LeCompte and Jno. Keene, Justices.

6 HD 107. September 2, 1793. Henry Ennalls of Dorchester County to Joseph Ennalls, Andrew Skinner Ennalls and Sarah Haskins, Executors of Joseph Haskins deceased: part of "Bartholomews Neck," "whereof Joseph Haskins afsd. in his lifetime was possessed and whereof his Executors afsd. have been and still are possessed since his decease." Witnesses: Levin Woolford, Jno. Stevens. Acknowledged before Levin Woolford and Jno. Stevens, Justices.

6 HD 110. September 21, 1793. John Meredith of Dorchester County to Thomas Meredith of the same county: part of "Tubs's Desire," between William Meredith senior and where William Meredith of John formerly lived." Witnesses: Henry Lake, Jno. Keene. Acknowledged betore Henry Lake and Jno. Keene, Justices.

6 HD 112. August 3, 1793. James Shaw and Ann his wife of Dorchester County to John Ball of the same county: "Browns Mistake" adj. Nantiooke Manor, adj. "Hicks Field" and containing 86 acres more or less. Witnesses: Jno. Crapper,

David Smith. Acknowledged before Jno. Crapper and David Smith, Justices.

6 HD 116. September 23, 1793. William Martin of Dorchester County to Morgan Jones of the same county: part of "Martins Beginning," containing 5 acres more or less. Witnesses: Moses LeCompte, Tho. Jones. Acknowledged before Moses LeCompte and Tho. Jones, Justices.

6 HD 118. November 1, 1793. Thomas Colsten of Dorchester County, Trustee of Thomas Kallender, to Abraham Neild of the same county, planter: part of "Tootles Venture" (part of Lott No. 3), containing 50 acres. Witnesses: Robt. Harrison, Jno. Stevens. Acknowledged before Robt. HarrIson and Jno. Stevens, Justices.

6 HD 121. October 23, 1793. Randolph Johnson of Dorchester County to William Jones of the same county: Negro man slave named Canterbury, aged about 45 years, and a negro girl slave named Leah, aged 9 years. Witness: David Smith, Justice.

6 HD 123. September 21, 1793. Henry Edgar of Dorchester County to Edmondson Bramble of the same county: part of "Callis," containing 60 acres more or less. Witnesses: Henry Lake, Jno. Keene. Acknowledged by Henry Edgar and Keziah his wife before Henry Lake and Jno. Keene, Justices.

6 HD 126. November 8, 1793. William Ennalls of Dorchester County, Gent., to John Eccleston Senr. of the same county, Physician: "Good Luck" on the west side of Transquakin River, left to said William by his father Col. Joseph Ennalls by will; and "Taylors Delight" adj. the aforesaid land. Witnesses: Levin Woolford, Thos. Barnett. Acknowledged before Levin Woolford and Thos. Barnett, Justices.

6 HD 129. October 16, 1793. Thomas Pritchett of Dorchester County to John Elliot of the same county: lease of ½ of the sawmill which formerly belonged to Daniel Payne deceased, on the southwest side of the Northwest Fork, for the term of five years. Witnesses: Thomas Hingson, Charles Stainton.

6 HD 132. October 30, 1793. Daniel Godwin of Kent County, Delaware and Sarah his wife to Williem M. Robertson of Dorchester County: lands between Hunting Creek and Blinkhorns Creek called "Goodridges Choice," "Walkers Lott" or "Chance" and "Chesmans Gore," containing in the whole 164 acres more or less. Witnesses: Jno. Stevens, Thos. Barnett. Acknowledged before Jno. Stevens and Thos. Barnett, JustIces.

91

6 HD 135. October 28, 1793. Thomas Hicks and Sarah his wife of Dorchester County to John Elder Gist of the same county: part of a tract formerly called "Ricarton," now called "Phillips Discovery," adj. John Manning's lot and Muir's land, on the street laid off by Archibald Patison leading to the .river, near the house of Dr. Daniel Sulivane, where Edward Cole now lives, containing 2 acres more or less. Witnesses: Levin Woolrord, Richd. Pattison. Acknowledged before Levin Woolford and Richd. Pattison, Justices.

6 HD 139. November 5, 1793. Thomas Colsten of Dorchester County, Trustee of Thomas Kallender, to James Dail of the same county, planter: part of "Tootles Venture" (lot No. 4), containing 89 ½ acres. Witnesses: Richd. Pattison, Thos. Jones. Acknowledged before Those Jones and Richd. Pattison, Justices.

6 HD 141. September 17, 1793. William Sothern of Dorchester County to Isaac Andrews of the same county: part of "Andrews Fortune" on the road from Firm Creek Bridge to the Straits, containing 5 3/4 acres more or less. Witnesses: Henry Lake, Jno. Keene. Acknowledged by William Sothem and Nancy his wife before Henry Lake and Jno. Keene, Justices.

6 HD 144. September 21, 1793. John Bramble of Dorchester County to Edmondson Bramble of the same county: "Liberty" on Bare Gardain Creek, containing 13 ½ acres more or less. Witnesses: Henry Lake, Jno. Keene. Acknowledged before Henry Lake and Jno. Keene, Justices.

6 HD 147. September 21, 1793. William Insley and Levi Insley of Dorchester County to Isaac Andrews of the same county: part of "Andrews Fortune," containing 7 acres more or less, in Goose Creek Swamp. Witnesses: Henry Lake, Jno. Keene. Acknowledged before Henry Lake and Jno. Keene, Justices.

6 HD 151. March 18, 1793 - June 1, 1793. Commission to Benjamin Todd, Naboth Hart, Levin Keene and Edward Griffith of Dorchester County, Gent., to perpetuate bounds of Levi Willen's land called "Willings Priviledge," formerly "Shapleys Rest," and Return. Deposition of John Rumbley, Straits, aged about 60 years, "saith that he hath been told by Edward Shores and his father William Rumbley and David Rumbley that the name of this Creek was formerly Hoplite, and by some saillers passing up the said Creek called it by the name of Tegious Creek." Deposition of Wm. Cannon aged 75 years states that this creek was called Hoplis Creek when he was a boy. Also mentions deponent's brother James Cannon. Deposition of Job Bramble.

6 HD 155. March 18, 1793 - October 23, 1793. Commission to Moses LeCompte, Richard Pattison and Thomas Jones of Dorchester County, Gent., to perpetuate bounds of John Lee's land called "Pollard's Choice," adj. land called "Patricks Wells" belonging to Sarah Stevens, orphan of Edward Stevens, and Return. Deposition of Nathan Stevens, aged 37 years, who was present about 20 years ago when Col. Thomas Jones surveyed the line of "Patricks Wells" between Wm. Pollard and Thomas Phillips. Deposition of Thomas Jones Esq., aged about 67 years, who surveyed said land about 20 years ago. Deposition of Thomas Navey, aged about 26 years, mentions William Lee Junr. about 5 years ago. James Fraizer and John Navey served as chain carriers at survey of this land by Richard Pattison, one of the Commissioners.

6 HD 162. December 30, 1793. John Murray of Dorchester County, Physician, to Peter Gordon and Samuel Brown of the same county, Merchants: land in Cambridge containing 1/4 acre more or less, bounded by Great Choptank River, by Archibald Patison's lot which he bought of Wm. Vans Murray, and by "a ditch dug during the contest between America and Great Britain as a fortification, the said ditch being between John Bradshaw's House and a granary which the said Gordon & Brown have erected upon the said lot." Witnesses: Jno. Stevens, Levin Woolford. Acknowledged before Jno. Stevens and Levin Woolford, Justices.

6 HD 164. September 21, 1793. Isaac Andrews of Dorchester County, planter, to William Insley of the same county: "Trouble Enough adj. "Insleys Folly," near the head of Cedar Creek, containing 40 acres more or less. Witnesses: Henry Lake, Jno. Keene. Acknowledged before Henry Lake and Jno. Keene, Justices.

6 HD 167. May 2, 1793. Thomas Hill Airey of Dorchester County to Robert Gilmore of Baltimore Town: part of "Pilgrimage" on the road from the Methodist Meeting House towards John Pitt's plantation, containing 200 acres more or less (Mortgage). Witnesses: Robt. Harrison, Levin Woolford. Acknowledged before Robt. Harrison and LevinWoolford.

6 HD 170. October 2, 1793. Randolph Johnson of Dorchester County to James Steele of Dorchester County: crops, in the possession of Ann Johnson. Witnesses: John McDaniel, Moses W. Nisbett, David Smith. Acknowledged before David Smith, Justice.

6 HD 172. December 8, 1792. Bartholomew Woolford of Dorchester County to Sarah Barron, heir by the Last Will and Testament of Joseph Barron deceased:

part of "Woolfords Purchase" at the head of Tobacco Stick Bay, containing 11 5/16 acres more or less. Witnesses: Tho. Jones, Moses LeCompte. Acknowledged by Bartholomew Woolford and Mary his wife before Tho. Jones and Moses LeCompte, Justices.

6 HD 175. November 14, 1793. Robert Wilson of Dorchester County, Merchant, to Thomas Jones of the same county: land formerly sold by Matthew Bright to said Wilson, called "Grove," on the north side of Blackwater River near Peters Neck, containing 40 ½ acres. Witnesses: Moses Lecompte, Richd. Pattison. Acknowledged before Moses Lecompte and Richd. Pattison, Justices.

6 HD 178. November 6, 1793. Thomas Colsten of Dorchester County, Trustee of Thomas Kallender, to John Mace of the same county, planter: part of "Tootles Venture" (lot No. 6), containing 5 3/4 acres. Witnesses: Tho. Jones, Jno. Stevens. Acknowledged before Thos. Jones and Jno. Stevens, Justices.

6 HD 181. November 8, 1793. David Dean and Mary Dean his mother, both of Caroline County, to James Payne of Dorchester County: part of "Deans Discovery" on the west side of the Northwest Fork of Nanticoke River, containing 21 ½ acres. Witnesses: Jno. Stevens, John Gooding. Acknowledged before Jno. Stevens and Jno. Gooding, Justices.

6 HD 184. November 11, 1793. Thomas Hicks and Sarah his wife of Dorchester County to Peter Rea and John Blair of the same county: part of a tract formerly called "Ricarton," now called "Phillips Discovery," adj. land of Richard Glover's heirs and land bought by said Peter Rea from Thomas Vickars, and containing 2 acres and 5 sq. perches more or less. Also "the street to be opened, called high street, which is now stopped up by the said Hicks's Dwelling House, and a street from said high street, two perches wide, to lead thro between said premises, and the Lott bought of Thomas Hicks, by John. E. Gist a few days ago." Witnesses: Jno. Stevsna, Levin Woolford. Acknowledged before Jno. Stevens and Levin Woolford, Justices.

6 HD 189. March 26, 1793 - July 25, 1793. Commission to Richard Pattison, John Keene, Levin Keene of Ben, Jacob Todd and Matthew Keene of Dorchester County, Gent., to divide land of Bedcar Gootee, John Gootee, Zebulon Gootee, Edward Gootee, Shadrach Gootee, Mary Gootee and Elizabeth Gootee, heirs of Capewell Gootee deceased (Edward and Shadrach are minors, the others of full age), called "Nuners Pasture Enlarged," and Return. The said land contains 235 acres clear of elder surveys, which the Commissioners consider would not admit of a division between the parties.

6 HD 195. March 18, 1793 - June 5, 1793. Commission to Robert Griffith, Henry Lake, John Griffith, Job Slacum Junr. and Levin Keene of Dorchester County, Gent., to divide land of Mary Kirwan (of full age, wife of Peter Kirwan and daughter of Thomas Edgar deceased) and Arnold Edgar (son of said Thomas Edgar, and now a minor), called "Edgars Beginning," "Pritchetts Forrest" and "Addition to Stave Landing," and Return. Nathaniel Elliott is mentioned as guardian of said Arnold Edgar.

6 HD 203. November 18, 1793. William Dail and Nancy his wife of Dorchester County to William Vans Murray of the same county: part of "Hayland" lately conveyed to said Dail by Charles Goldsborough, Executor of Robert, near Fishing Creek and the farm of James Patison, adj. "Hailes Choice" and containing 51 acres. Witnesses: Robt. Harrison, Levin Woolford. Acknowledged before Robt. Harrison and Levin Woolford, Justices.

6 HD 207. November 25, 1793. William Vans Murray and Charlotte his wife at Dorchester County to John Murray, Physician, of the same county: lots in Cambridge, at the intersection of the main street and the river. Witnesses: Jno. Stevens, Levin Woolford. Acknowledged before Jno. Stevens and Levin Woolford, Justices.

6 HD 210. November 25, 1793. William Vans Murray and Charlotte his wife of Dorchester County to John Murray, Physician, of the same county: lot in Cambridge adj. Dowson's lot, beginning near the house called the Shop, formerly the shop of Dr. H. Murray, adj. the lot of Charles Goldsborough Junr. and on the Creek, containing 1 acre more or less. Witnesses: Jno. Stevens, Levin Woolford. Acknowledged before Jno. Stevens and Levin Woolford, Justices.

6 HD 213. November 18, 1793. William Vans Murray and Charlotte his wife of Dorchester County to Thomas James Patison of the same county: part of "Hailes Choice," part of "Stokes Priviledge," part of "Stokes Adventure," part of "Addition to Skinners Choice" and part of the late resurvey called "Hayland" made by Robt. Goldsborough, conveyed by Charles Goldsborough, Executor of Robert, to William Dail and by said Dail conveyed to said Murray; located on Fishing Creek, adj. "Murrays Chance" and containing 200 acres. Witnesses: Robt. Harrison, Levin Woolford. Acknowledged before Robt. Harrison and Levin Woolford, Justices.

6 HD 219. December 30, 1793. John Murray of Dorchester County, Physician, to Peter Rea of the same place, Merchant: land in Cambridge, on Great Choptank River, adj. "Lockermans Regulation," adj. land this day conveyed by

said Murray to Peregrine Beaston, and containing 1 ½ acres more or less. Witnesses: Jno. Stevens. Levin Woolford. Acknowledged betore Jno. Stevens and Levin Woolford, Justices.

6 HD 223. November 6, 1793. Ann Muse to David Dean: Negro man named James. Witness: Moses LeCompte. Acknowledged before Moses LeCompte.

6 HD 224. January 13, 1792. Deposition of Samuel Evans, aged 60-odd years, who lived about 22 years ago as a tenant under Mr. John Scott. Deposition of William Mann, aged about 51 years, who was a cropper with Thomas Keene late of Dorchester County, mentions John Scott's land. .Deposition of Edward Stephens, aged about 33 years, touching the outlines of a tract called "Taylors Delight," mentions a bounder of "Buckfield" and Mr. John Scott's land. Deposition of John Bryerwood, aged about 40 years. Deposition of Jonathan Patridge, aged about 60 years, concerns survey of "Taylors Delight" about 24 years ago for Mr. John Scott by Henry Ennalls, son of Bartholomew. Charles Hodson, Sheriff.

6 HD 227. November 28, 1793. Division of land between John McKeel and James Ross, beginning at the first bounder of "Roses Purchase"; mentions a bounder of Williams Chance" which is also a division between said Ross and William Stevens; also mentions "Daniels Choice" and a division line made by old William Ross between his two sons John and William Ross. Witnesses: Richd. Pattison, Thomas Ross of Thos. Acknowledged before Richard Pattison, J. P.

6 HD 228. November 20, 1793. John Hooper, Bartholomew Ennalls, George Ward and Thos. Martin, Trustees of the Poor of Dorchester County, to Seth Sherman: Indenture of James Web, a poor boy about 14 years of age, to serve said Sherman as an apprentice until age 21 to learn the occupation of farming. Witness: Thomas White, Clk.

6 HD 230. December 2, 1793. John Greenwood to Richardson Gambrell: livestock, corn and household furniture. Witness: David Smith. Acknowledged before David Smith, J. P., John Long, William Long.

6 HD 233. December 14, 1793. Elizabeth Travers of Dorchester County to Vernon Creighton of the same county, her son: "Robsons Beginning" and "Edloes Purchase," both on Taylors Island. Witnesses: Moses LeCompte, Richd. Pattison. Acknowledged before Moses LeCompte and Richd. Pattison.

6 HD 235. November 19, 1793. John Jones of Morgan of Dorchester County to Thomas Loockerman of the same county, Gent.: part of "Loockermans Regulation," containing 38 acres. Witnesses: Moses LeCompte, Richd. Pattison. Acknowledged by John Jones and Luranah his wife before Moses LeCompte and Richd. Pattison.

6 HD 238. December 16, 1793. Robert Harrison of Dorchester County, planter, to Isaac Owens of the same county: part of "Loockermans Regulation" on the main road from Cambridge to the widow Glover's windmill, containing 2 acres. Witnesses: Levin Woolford, Jno. Stevens. Acknowledged before Levin Woolford and Jno. Stevens, Justices of the Peace.

6 HD 241. November 8, 1793. John McFarlin of Dorchester County to Isaac Charles of the same county: part of "Addition to Galloway" adj. land sold by said McFarlin to James Payne; 25 acres more or less, hereby conveyed. Witnesses: Jno. Stevens, Jno. Gooding. Acknowledged before Jno. Stevens and Jno. Gooding, Justices.

6 HD 245. December 9, 1793. Isaac Steele of Dorchester County, Gent., to Henry Steele of the same county, Gent.: part of "Partnership" at the head of Transquaking River, adj. lands of Thomas Stevens, Wm. Newton, and Roger A. Hooper and containing 363 acres more or lesse. Witnesses: Jno. Stevens, Levin Woolford. Acknowledged before Jno. Stevens and Levin Woolford, Justices of the Peace.

6 HD 249. December 9, 1793. Henry Steele of Dorchester County, Gent., to Isaac Steele of the same county, Gent.: part of "Handsell" on the west side of Nanticoke River at the mouth of Taylors Creek or Chickawan Creek, containing 484 acres more or less. Witnesses: Jno. Stevens, Levin Woolford. Acknowledged before Jno. Stevens and Levin Woolford, Justices of the Peace.

6 HD 254. March 18, 1793 - June 14, 1793. Commission to Moses Lecompte, Richard Pattison, Levin Woolford, Arthur Whiteley Junr. and Benjamin Woodard of Dorchester County, Gent., to perpetuate bounds of land of Richard Martin and Joseph Martin called "Darby," and Return. Deposition of Jonathan Patridge, aged about 61 years. Surveyed by William Barrow, Surveyor of Dorchester County, beginning at the first boundary of said tract as proved by Jonathan Patridge (with Gardner Bruffit and Elijah Pritchet, chain carriers).

6 HD 261. March 18, 1793 - September 20, 1793. Commission to Henry Lake, Benjamin Todd, Daniel Fallen and Naboth Hart of Dorchester County, Gent., to

perpetuate bounds of Gabriel Insley's land, part of "Andrews Fortune," and Return. Deposition of Jacob Insley, aged about 65 years. Deposition of Michael Todd, aged about 57 years, "sayeth that he saw Henry Ennalls the surveyor near forty years agoe run the divition line of Andrews Fortune between James Insley and Andrew Insley." Deposition of William Insley, aged about 45 years, who was present about 25 years ago when Jonathan Patridge ran the division line between Andrew Insley and Joseph Insley. Deposition of Benjamin Todd, aged about 50 years. Deposition of Valentine Insley, aged about 72 years, "sayeth that the pine that Jacob Insley sold to Robert Scott for a canoe stood to the northward of the divition line between Andrew Insley and his father James Insley." The above depositions were taken in the presence of Gabriel Insley, John Insley, Levi Insley and Whitington Johnson, parties concerned.

6 HD 266. December 14, 1793. William Hayward and Rebeckah his wife, John Ratcliff and Fanney his wife, all of Dorchester County, to Thomas Hubbard of the same county, planter: lands called "Indian Ridge," "Kilmons Folly" and "Addition to Kilmons Folly," all adj. each other on Stewarts Creek (mentions the first bounder of "Kilmons Folly or White Fryars"), containing 127 acres more or less, formerly sold March 5, 1792 to the said Thomas Hubbard by William LeCompte, son of Anthony Lecompte deceased, Hodson Cook and Elizabeth his wife. Witnesses: Stanley Byus, Thos. Barnett. Acknowledged before Stanley Byus and Thos. Barnett, Justices of the Peace.

6 HD 270. January 2, 1794. Certificate of Thomas Hubbard concerning the mark of his stock.

6 HD 271. December 30, 1793. John Murray of Dorchester County, Physician, to Peregrine Beaston of the same place land on t he main street of Cambridge, near Great Choptank River, adj. land sold to John Bradshaw by said John Murray and land this day conveyed by John Murray to Peter Rea. Witnesses: Levin Woolford, Jno. Stevens. Acknowledged before Levin Woolford and Jno. Stevens, Justices.

6 HD 274. October 21, 1793. Charles Hodson of Dorchester County, High Sheriff, and Ann Hodson his wife to Josiah Bayly of the same county, Attorney at Law: "Smith Field Composition," containing 300 acres more or less; "White s Friendship" containing 25 acres more or less; "Salsbury Plaine" containing 100 acres more or less; "Smiths Meadow" containing 7 3/4 acres more or less; "Smiths Discovery" containing 15 acres more or less; "Hogg Range" containing 40 acres more or less; "Ox Pasture" containing 5 acres more or less; "Billingsleys Chance" containing 655 acres more or less; "Hoopers Fortune"

containing 181 acres more or less; "Point Good Hope" containing 73 acres more or less; "Smith Field" containing 400 acres more or less; and "Cow Quarter." The said tracts were formerly owned by Thomas Smith late of Dorchester County who died intestate leaving the said Anne Hodson and Sophia Smith, his sisters, as his heirs at law. Witnesses: Jno. Stevens, Levin Woolford. Acknowledged before Jno. Stevens and Levin Woolford, Justices of the Peace.

6 HD 277. November 5, 1793. John McKeel of Dorchester County to Stanley Byus of the same county, farmer: part of "Boston" on the north side of Little Choptank River "or by some called Sharps Creek," beginning at the original boundary of "Berry Chance," adj. "Willmots Adventure" and containing about 13 1/4 acres. Witnesses: Moses Lecompte, Levin Woolford. Acknowledged before Moses LeCompte and Levin Woolford, Justices.

6 HD 279. January 6, 1794. Peter Gordon of Dorchester County, Merchant, to Negro Adam: Manumission, effective January 1, 1814. Witnesses: Stanley Byus, Saml. Brown. Acknowledged before Stanley Byus, J. P.

6 HD 280. January 6, 1794. Peter Gordon of Dorchester County, Mcht., to Edward Cole of the same county, bricklayer: Negro boy named Adam, until January 1, 1814, when the said boy is to be free. Witness: Stanley Byus. Acknowledged before Stanley Byus, J. P.

6 HD 281. December 20, 1793. Mary Ann Connolly of Dorchester County, widow, to Abraham Lewis of the same county, planter: "Security to Paint Point." Witnesses: E. Richardson, Jno. Gooding. Delivered twig and turf in the presence of E. Richardson, Jno. Gooding, Jno. Eacleston and Samuel McGee. Acknowledged before E. Richardson and Jno. Gooding, Justices.

6 HD 283. August 24, 1791. Daniel Nicols of Dorchester County to Samuel Wright of the same county: Bond to convey part of "Hampton" where said Nicolls formerly lived in Dorchester County near Hunting Creek, supposed to contain 78 acres more or less, "where Robert Hardican has lately shewed the sliped Trees." Also part of "Addition" adj. thereto, near land where James McCollister now lives, belonging to Nathan Wright; near the "Tan Yard" where John MoCotter lives; adj. "Addition to Britts Hope" and "Kings Misfortune," and containing 30 acres more or less. 'Witnesses: Theophilus Marshall, Jacob Wright.

6 HD 285. October 22, 1793. Josiah Bayly of Dorchester County, Attorney at Law, to Charles Hodson of the same county, High Sheriff: lands formerly

conveyed to said Josiah Bayly by said Charles Hodson and Anne his wife. Witnesses: Levin Woolford, Jno. Stevens. Acknowledged before Levin Woolford and Jno. Stevens, Justices of the Peace.

6 HD 286. December 1793. Jacob Loockerman of Dorchester County to Thomas Jones of the same County: one yoke of young oxen. Witnesses: John Nutterwell, Abey Busick.

6 HD 287. May 20, 1794. William Vickars 2nd. of Dorchester County to the State of Maryland: Bond as Inspector of Tobacco at White's Warehouse, with James Moore and John McGuire as sureties. Witnesses: Peregrine Beaston, Thomas Jones Junr. Proved by witnesses before Levin Woolford.

6 HD 288. March 24, 1794. John Pitt to the State of Maryland: Bond as Inspector of Tobacco at Ennalls Ferry Warehouse, with Thos. Hicks and Wm. Pitt as sureties. Witnesses: James Trippe Junr., Obadiah Jones. Proved by witnesses before Jno. Stevens.

6 HD 289. April 26, 1794. John Smith to the State of Maryland: Bond as Inspector of Tobacco with William Jones and Alexander Smith as sureties. Witnesses: John Reed, David Smith, James Shaw, Thomas Walters. Sworn to before John Reed.

6 HD 291. January 4, 1794. John Hooper, John Eccleston, and Bartholomew Ennalls, Trustees of the Poor of Dorchester County, to James McCotter of the said County: Indenture of PhIllip McCotter, about 3 years of age, as an apprentice until age 21 to learn the trade of Blacksmith. Witness: Thos. White.

6 HD 292. December 23, 1793. List of Negroes of Francis Turpin which "became my property by Marying Ann Reed."

6 HD 292. June 21, 1787. Ezekiel Reed of Dorchester County to Laben Jones of the same county: Bond for conveyance by said Ezekiel Reed and Nancy his wife of part of "Reeds Chance" on the west side of the main road from Cratchers Ferry to Fork Chapel; and a small tract called "Hickory Point," adj. thereto. Witnesses: Edwd. Wheatley, Joseph Wheatley.

6 HD 293. January 10, 1794. David Mills of Dorchester County to Negro man named Noker: Manumission. Witnesses: George Ward, Levin Woolford. Acknowledged before Levin Woolford, J. P.

6 HD 294. January 13, 1794. William Pitt of Dorchester County to Negro Shadrach, aged 24 years: Manumission. Witnesses: Moses LeCompte, Saml. Brown. Acknowledged before Moses LeCompte, Justice.

6 HD 295. January 13, 1794. John Pitt of Dorchester County to Negro Harry, aged 22 years: .Manumission. Witnesses: Moses LeCompte, Saml. Brown. Acknowledged before Moses LeCompte, Justice.

6 HD 296. January 23, 1794. Jno. M. Stevens to Ezekiel Keene: Receipt for purchase price of a Negro man named York. Witness: Pamela Stevens.

6 HD 296. January 11, 1794. Stanley Matkins and William Matkins, both of Dorchester County, to Henry Macotter of the same county: part of "Phillips Discovery," containing 11 3/4 acres. Also part of "Beaverdam Addition," excepting 11 3/4 acres conveyed to Richard Woodland, the remaining part containing 12 3/4 acres. Witnesses: Moses LeCompte, Richd. Pattison. Acknowledged by Stanley Matkins and William Matkins and by Elizabeth Matkins, wife of said Stanley, before Moses LeCompte and Richd. Pattison, Justices of the Peace.

6 HD 298. January 11, 1794. Stanley Matkins of Dorchester County to Richard Woodland of the same county: part of "Beaverdam Addition," containing 11 3/4 acres more or less. Witnesses: Moses LeCompte, Richd. Pattison. Acknowledged by Stanley Matkins and Elizabeth his wife before Moses LeCompte and Richd. Pattison.

6 HD 300. December 20, 1793. David Harper of Kent County, Delaware, to Samuel Smoot of Dorchester County: "Fishing Lot" on the southwest side of the Northwest Fork of Nanticoke River, containing 3 acres. Witnesses: Jno. Crapper, David Smith. Acknowledged before Jno. Crapper and David Smith, Justices.

6 HD 303. September 21, 1793. Henry Edgar of Dorchester County to Joseph Andrews of the same county: part of "Callis" adj. Edmondson Bramble's land. Witnesses: Jno. Keene, Henry Lake. Acknowledged by Henry Edgar and Keziah his wife before Henry Lake and Jno. Keene, Justices of the Peace.

6 HD 305. September 21, 1793. Joseph Andrews of Dorchester County to Henry Edgar of the same county: part of "Callis" adj. "Gootees Defiance." Witnesses: Henry Lake, Jno. Keene. Acknowledged by Joseph Andrews and Elizabeth his wife before Henry Lake and Jno. Keene, Justices.

6 HD 307. September 21, 1793. Reubin Andrews of Dorchester County to John Meredith of the same county: part of two tracts called "Resurvey Callis" and "Gootees Defiance" on the south side of Blackwater River, containing 11 ½ acres more or less. Witnesses: Henry Lake, Jno. Keene. Acknowledged before Henry Lake and Jno. Keene, Justices.

6 HD 310. January 28, 1794. Thomas Lee and Abraham Lee of Dorchester County to Elijah Marshall and Andrew Marshall of the same county: Negro man named James. Witness: Thomas Barnett. Acknowledged before Thomas Barnett, J. P.

6 HD 312. January 25, 1794. James Vinson of Dorchester County, Carpenter, to William Hayward of the same county, Mcht.: livestock and furniture. Witness: Thomas Barnett. Acknowledged before Thomas Barnett, J. P.

6 HD 313. January 23, 1794. William Hayward Senr. of Dorchester County to John Green of the same county: Negro man named Stephen. Witness: John Noble. Acknowledged before Jno. Stevens, J. P.

6 HD 314. January 17, 1794. John Ascum Traverse of Dorchester County to Henry Matney of the same county: part of "Williams Lott" on Hoopers Island, on Tobacco House Cove, containing 25* ½ acres more or less. Witnesses: Moses LeCompte, Richd. Pattison. Acknowledged by John Ascum Traverse and Priscilla his wife before Moses LeCompte and Richd. Pattison, Justices of the Peace.

6 HD 317. January 17, 1794. Henry Hooper of Dorchester County, planter, to Joseph Meekins of the same county, trader: part of a tract called "Hoopers Island" on Hoopers Island, on the south side of Back Creek and Hungar River, containing 15 acres more or less. Witnesses: Moses LeCompte, Richd. Pattison. Acknowledged before Moses LeCompte and Richd. Pattison, Justices of the Peace.

6 HD 320. January 17, 1794. Traverse Tolly of Dorchester County to Thomas Traverse of the same county: "Tuckers Lott" near "Plymouth," containing ½ acre more or less. Witnesses: Moses Lecompte, Richd. Pattison. Acknowledged by Travers Tolly and Anne his wife before Moses Lecompte and Richd. Pattison.

6 HD 322. January 17, 1794. John Ascum Travers of Dorchester County, planter, to Travers Tolly of the same county, planter: part of "Williams Lott" on

Hoopers Island, containing 57 3/4 acres more or less. Witnesses: Moses LeCompte, Richd. Pattison. Acknowledged by John Askum Travers and Priscilla his wife before Moses Lecompte and Richd. Pattison, Justices of the Peace.

6 HD 326. January 17, 1794. John Creaton of Dorchester County, trader, to John Ruark of the same county, trader: part of "Williams Lott" on Hoopers Island, on the east side of Back Creek, containing 12 ½ acres. Nancy Creaton, wife of said John Creaton (Creighton), joins in deed. Witness: Moses Lecompte. Acknowledged before Moses Lecompte and Richd. Pattison, Justices of the Peace.

6 HD 328. January 28, 1794. Sarah Aaron to Negro slaves Chloe, aged about 20 years, and Rhoda, aged about 13 years: Manumission. Witnesses: Moses Lecompte. Capewell Keene. Acknowledged before Moses Lecompte, Justice.

6 HD 329. April 12, 1794. Thomas Kallender and Thos. Colsten of Dorchester County to James Chisum of the same county: part of "Addition to White Haven" near the head of Fishing Creek, on the road from Fishing Creek to Cambridge. adj. the Methodist Meeting House land and containing 5 1/4 acres of land. adj. part of "White Haven" sold by the Executors of Archibald Pattison to Richard Keene. Witnesses: Thomas Jones, Richd. Pattison. Acknowledged by Thomas Kallender and Catharine his wife and by Thomas Colsten before Thos. Jones and Richd. Pattison.

6 HD 332. October 24, 1788. John Kennedy and Priscilla his wife of Somerset County, Zebulon Wingate and Ann his wife and Sarah Taylor of Dorchester County to James Steele of said county: lands on the Northwest Fork of Nanticoke River, being part of "Leinster" devised by John Dyer to his grandson Thomas Williams Junr. and by said Thos. Williams Junr. sold to the late Thomas Taylor by deed dated December 5, 1750, adj. land of Dyer Williams and containing 171 acres; part of "Taylors Neglect" adj. thereto, sold to said Thomas Taylor by Thomas Connerly by deed dated August 17, 1754, containing 19 1/4 acres more or less; and "Addition to Leinster" granted by the Lord Proprietarto Thomas Taylor August 10, 1753, containing 78 3/4 acres at the least. The said Priscilla, Ann and Sarah are daughters and coheirs of said Thomas Taylor. Witnesses: James Shaw, Levin Kirkman. Acknowledged before James Shaw and Levin Kirkman, Justices of the Peace.

6 HD 338. January 17, 1794. Travers Tolly of Dorchester County to Thomas Parker of the same county: part of "Range" on Hoopers Island, containing 5

acres more or less. Ann, wife of said Travers Tolly. joins in deed. Witnesses: Moses Lecompte, Richd. Pattison. Acknowledged before Moses Lecompte and Richd. Pattison, Justices of the Peace.

6 HD 341. February 8, 1794. John Hicks Stainton of Dorchester County to William Thompson of the same county: "Outlet." Surveyed April 3, 1765 for Charles Stainton for 7 3/4 acres, excepting 3/4 acre included in the lines of an elder survey called "Neighbourly Kindness." Witnesses: Jno. Stevens. Jno. Gooding. Acknowledged before Jno. Stevens and Jno. Gooding, Justices of the Peace.

6 HD 344. February 15, 1794. Peter Rea and John Blair of Dorchester County to Josiah Bayly of the same county: part of a tract conveyed to said Rea and Blair by Thomas Hicks and Sarah his wife by deed dated November 11, 1793. Witnesses: Jno. Stevens, Levin Woolford. Acknowledged before Jno. Stevens and Levin Woolford, Justices of the Peace.

6 HD 346. February 17, 1794. Josiah Bayly of Dorchester County to Peter Rea and John Blair of the same county: land formerly conveyed by Thomas Hicks and Sarah his wife to said Rea and Blair and by them to the said Josiah Bayly. Witnesses: Jno. Stevens, Levin Woolford. Acknowledged before Jno. Stevens and Levin Woolford, Justices of the Peace.

6 HD 348. February 6, 1794. Charles Crookshanks and Archibald Moncrieff of the Town of Baltimore to William Stevens of Dorchester County: "Good Intent" near the head waters of Little Choptank River, containing 23 ½ acres more or less, mortgaged to said Moncrieff byArchlbald Patison during his lifetime and now sold by said Patison's Executors as provided in his Will. Witnesses: Wm. Russell, Thorowgd. Smith. Acknowledged before Wm. Russell and Thorowgd. Smith, Justice s of the Peace for Baltimore County. Wllliam Gibson, Clk.

6 HD 352. February 13, 1794. Edward Dean of Dorchester County to Francis Rowins of the same county: part of "Exchange" on a branch of Herring Run Branch, on the south side of Hunting Creek, containing 112 ½ acres more or less. Witnesses: Jno. Gooding, Jno. Stevens. Acknowledged before Jno. Gooding and Jno. Stevens, Justices of the Peace.

6 HD 356. November 8, 1793. Edward Adams of Dorchester County to Job Williams of the same county: part of "Addition to the End of Strife" between the Northwest and Northeast Forks of Nanticoke River, containing 9 acres more or less. Witnesses: Jno. Gooding, Jno. Stevens. Acknowledged before Jno.

Gooding and Jno. Stevens, Justices of the Peace.

6 ED 359. February 15, 1794. William Trego of Dorchester County to Bruffett Tall of the same county: part of two tracts called "Williams Goodwill" and "Trego's Spite" on a branch of Blackwater River, containing 60 acres. Witnesses: Moses LeCompte, Richd. Pattison. Acknowledged before Moses Lecompte and Richd. Pattison.

6 ED 361. September 21, 1793. Reubin Andrews of Dorchester County, Blacksmith, to George Dean of the same county: part of "Bourbburk" on the south side of Coles Creek which issues out of Blackwater River, adj. "Georges Priviledge" and containing 5 acres more or less. Witnesses: Henry Lake, Jno. Keene. Acknowledged before Henry Lake and Jno. Keene, Justices of the Peace.

6 HD 363. December 3, 1793. Lydia Melvill of Dorchester County to John Smith of the same county: "Thames Street," containing 100 acres more or less. Witnesses: Jno. Gooding, David Smith. Acknowledged before Jno. Gooding and David Smith, Justices.

6 ED 366. March 18, 1794. John Smith of Dorchester County to Lydia Melvill of the same county: "Thames Street," containing 100 acres more or less. Witnesses: Jno. Stevens, David Smith. Acknowledged before Jno. Stevens and David Smith, Justices of the Peace.

6 HD 368. March 22, 1794. William Stevens of Dorchester County to John McKeel of the same county: part of "Daniels Choice" near the head of Sharps Creek, beginning near James Rosse's house, adj. "Rosses Purchase" and containing between 20 and 30 acres more or less. Witnesses: Richd. Pattison, Levin Woolford. Acknowledged before Richd. Pattison and Levin Woolford.

6 HD 371. March 6, 1794. Henry Ennalls, John Stevens and Edward Wright and Peter Gordon, Executors of Nathan Wright deceased, all of Dorchester County, to Hubird Frampton of the same county: part of a tract on ths Northwest Fork of Nanticoke River called "The End of Strife," containing 123 acres more or less. Witnesses: Levin Woolford, Jno. Gooding. Acknowledged before Levin Woolford and Jno. Gooding, Justices.

6 HD 373. March 25, 1794. Benjamin Keene of Dorchester County, Gent., to his son Levin Keene of the same county: part of "Mount Pleasant" on the road from Hungar River to Staplefors Creek, containing 400 acres more or less. Also part of "Skillington" at the head of Hungar River, containing 10 acres more or less.

Witnesses: Jno. Stevens, Levin Woolford. Acknowledged before Jno. Stevens and Levin Woolford.

6 HD 374. December 7, 1793. William Savory and Rosanah his wife of Baltimore County to Elijah Martin of Dorchester County: part of two tracts called "the Four Sisters" and "Dover," on Taylors Island, near ."Richards Discovery" and containing about 77 acres, laid off for Catherine Chapman and Sarah Martin. Witnesses: Geo. Salmon, George Gouldth. Presbury. Acknowledged before George Salmon and George Gouldsmith Presbury, Justices for Baltimore County. Wm. Gibson, Clk.

6 HD 377. February 14, 1794. Thomas Ennalls of Dorchester County to Arthur Pritchard of the same county: part of "Taylors Kindness," containing 15 ½ acres more or less. Witnesses: Jno. Stevens, Jno. Gooding. Acknowledged before Jno. Stevens and Jno. Gooding, Justices for Dorchester County.

6 HD 379. March 26, 1794. Thomas Vickars Senr. of Dorchester County, planter, to Arthur Whiteley of the same county: "Vickarses Priviledge" near the head of Fishing Creek, adj. "Anthonys Priviledge" and containing 12 ½ acres more or less (4 acres of which the said Thomas Vickars Senr. in a prior deed conveyed to Arthur Whiteley Senr. before his decease). Witnesses: Tho. Jones, Levin Woolford. Acknowledged before Tho. Jones and Levin Woolford, Justices.

6 HD 381. March 31, 1794. Thomas Thompson and Priscilla his wife of Dorchester County to Thomas Kallender of the same county: part of two tracts called "White Haven" and "Addition to White Haven," containing 105 acres, more or less, on Church Creek. Witnesses: Moses Lecoropte, Richard Pattison. Acknowledged before Moses LeCoropte and Richard Pattison.

6 HD 385. March 31, 1794. Thomas Thompson of Dorchester County to Thomas Jones of the same county: "Thompsons Range" (except that part before sold to the Phillipses, and now in the possession of Murray's heirs) on the east side of Thompson Branch. and "Taylors Good Will" on the north side of the aforesaid "Range," containing 123 acres more or less in both tracts. Witnesses: Moses LeCompte, Richd. Pattison. Acknowledged before Moses LeCompte and Richd. Pattison, Justices, by Thomas Thompson and Priscilla his wife.

6 HD 387. March 31, 1794. James Pattison of Annarundle County to James Pattison of Dorchester County: part of "Armstrongs Hog Pen Regulated" on James Island, on Davis Point, containing 3 ½ acres more or less. Witnesses:

Moses Lecompte, Richd. Pattison. Acknowledged before Moses Leoompte and Richd. Pattison.

6 HD 389. January 28, 1794. Gabriel Insley of Dorchester County, planter, to William Insley of the same county: "Mulbery Island" on the southwest side of Fishing Bay, below a tract called "Insleys Purchase," containing 19 3/4 acres more or less. Witnesses: Henry Lake, Jno. Keene. Acknowledged before Henry Lake and Jno. Keene, Justices of the Peace.

6 HD 391. March 19, 1794. John Henry to William Bradley: lease of part of "Riders Forrest" where said William Bradley now lives, tor the term of 15 years from January 1, next. Witness: Levin H. Campbell.

6 HD 394. April 14, 1794. Jacob Travers of Dorchester County to John Hooper of James of the same county: part of "Pilgrims Rest" on Slaughter Creek, containing 4 acres more or less. Witnesses: Moses Lecompte, Richd. Pattison. Acknowledged before Moses Lecompte and Richd. Pattison.

6 HD 396. April 19, 1794. Jacobus White and Elizabeth (Betty) his wife of Dorchester County to John Maguire of the same county: the life estate of the said Elizabeth (Betty) White in "Bonwills Regulation on Halls Seat," conveyed to her as Elizabeth (Betty) Bonwill for her lifetime by Michael Hall Bonwill by deed dated June 11, 1785; the fee simple interest in said land (after said life estate) having been conveyed by Michael Hall Bonwill July 10, 1792 to the said John Maguire. Witnesses: John Reed, David Smith. Acknowledged before John Reed and David Smith, Justices of the Peace.

6 HD 399. April 14, 1794. Levin Cator of Dorchester County from Jacob Traverse of the same county: part of "Pilgrims Rest" containing 14 3/4 acres more or less, adj. that part sold to John Hooper. Witnesses: Moses Lecompte, Richd. Pattison. Acknowledged before Moses Lecompte and Richd. Pattison, Justices.

6 HD 401. Fe bruary 17, 1794. Mary Ennalls to Negro slaves: Manumission. Witnesses: Jno. Stevens, Peter Gordon. Acknowledged before Jno. Stevens, J. P.

6 HD 402 February 15, 1794. Ralph Paul of Dorchester County to Tristram Thomas of the same county: livestock and other personal property. Witnesses: Nathan Williams, Peter Sarde. Acknowledged before Jno. Stevens, J. P.

6 HD 403. February 13, 1794. Daniel Carroll of Dorchester County to Daniel

Nicols of the same county: Negro slaves. Witnesses: Jno. Stevens, Samuel Wright.

6 HD 405. October 22, 1792 - February 15, 1794. Commission to Robert Dennis, Richard Waters, Isaac Steele and John Reed to perpetuate bounds of AndrewMcDonaldls lands called "St. Bartholomew," "Fishers Landing," " Addition to Fishers Landing" and "Weston," and Return. Deposition of Jonathan Patridge, aged 61 years, re survey about 1770 by deponent and William Haskins for Messrs. Smith and Steele. Deposition of George Brown, aged 59 years in June next.

6 HD 407. January 15, 1785. John Ross of Dorchester County, Gent. to Isaac Reed of the same county: Bond for conveyance by said John Ross and Elizabeth his wife to said Isaac Reed of part of "Hogg Range." Witnesses: Matthew Smith, Ezekiel Reed. Assigned by Isaac Reed of Sussex County, Delaware, Taylor, to Thomas Insley of Dorchester County, planter, May 20, 1791. Witnesses: Tho. Jones, Geo. Brown.

6 HD 409. February 15, 1794. Joseph Meekins of Dorchester County to Thomas Jones of the same county: livestock. Witnesses: Solomon Jonas, Thos. Thompson of Wm. Acknowledged before Thomas Jones, J. P.

6 HD 410. February 15, 1794. Jacob Tucker of Dorchester County to Thomas Jones of the same county: livestock and other personal property. Witnesses: John Tall, John Woollen. Acknowledged before Thomas Jones, Justice.

6 HD 411. November 26, 1793 . Division of "Maidens Lott" and "Wottles Desire" between Robert Wingate and Shadrach Wingate. both of Dorchester County. Witnesses: William Wingate. Levin McNamara.

6 HD 412. March 18. 1793 - March 13. 1794. Commission to Thomas Jones. Col. Richard Pattison. John Braughan. Jeremiah Pattison and Pollard Edmondson of Dorchester County. Gent., to perpetuate bounds of Moses Geoghegan's land called "Taylors Inheritance," and Return. Deposition of John Aaron, of full age. Certificate states that the said land has been surveyed by Richard Pattison, one of the Commissioners. and a marked post put down in the presence of all the parties interested. to wit. Moses Geoghegan, Henry Keene and Wm. Keene.

6 HD 415. August 12, 1794. Henry Maynadier of Anne Arundel County to Phillip Barton Key of Anne Arundel County: "Addition to Stewarts Marsh" in

Dorchester County, containing 25 acres more or less. patented to Daniel Maynadier June 7, 1770. Also part of "Cullenses Interest"; part of "Murrays Friendship"; and all of "Stewarts Marsh" as described in deed from John Stewart and Betty Stewart to Rev. Daniel Maynadier dated May 29, 1766. Also part of "Mannings Marsh" conveyed by John Stewart end Betty Stewart to Daniel Maynadier and entailed by the Will of said Daniel Maynadier on his son Henry Maynadier. Witness: J. Toy. Chase. Acknowledged by Henry Maynadier and Elizabeth his wife before J. Toy. Chase, one of the Judges of the General Court.

6 HD 418. August 14. 1794. Phillip Barton Key of Anne Arundel County to Henry Maynadier of Anne Arundel County: "Addition to Stewarts Marsh" in Dorchester County, containing 25 acres more or less, patented June 7, 1770 to Daniel Maynadier. Also part of "Cullenses Interest," part of "Murrays Friendship" and all of "Stewarts Marsh" as described in deed from John Stewart and Betty Stewart to Rev. Daniel Maynadier dated May 29, 1766. Also part of "Mannings Marsh" conveyed by John Stewart and Betty Stewart to Daniel Maynadier, and entailed by the Will of said Daniel Maynadier on his son Henry Maynadier. Witness: John Ross Key. Acknowledged by Phillip Barton Key and Ann his wife before J. Toy. Chase, one of the Judges of the General Court.

6 HD 420. March 18, 1793 - January 25, 1794. Commission to John Keene, Richard Tubman, Jacob Todd and Matthew Keene of Dorchester County, Gent. to perpetuate bounds of Thomas Dunnock's lands called "Discovery," "Addition," "Pasture Point," "Hawhill Security" and "Masons Vineyard," and Return. Deposition of Thomas Meekins, aged about 54 years, re division of lands of John Meekins and William Dunnock, mentions a bounded tree shown to deponent about 32 years ago by said John Meekins. Deposition of Edward Ruark, aged about 45 years, re surveyabout 25 years ago by Capt. Henry Keene. Deposition of John Meekins, aged about 19 years, mentions Theophilus Marshall, Edward Ruark and Peter Harrington about 20 days ago. Deposition of William Brooks, aged about 34 years, mentions his father Robert Brooks. Deposition of Thomas M. Meekins, aged about 55 years, re bounder shown him about 23 years ago by Matthew Meekins, now deceased. Deposition of Joshua Meekins, aged about 53 years. Deposition of Catherine Meekins, aged about 70 years, mentions her husband John Meekins, deceased, who showed her a bounded tree about 37 years ago.

6 HD 425. October 28, 1793 - February 8, 1794. Commission to Thomas Jones, Jeremiah Pattison, Pollard Edmondson and William Barnes of Dorchester County, Gent., to perpetuate bounds of Jacob Travers' land, part of "Pilgrims Rest," and Return. Deposition of Joseph Treves, of full age, mentions Mr.

Richard Patterson and Thomas Woollen about 8 years ago. Deposition of Henry H. Pagan, of full age. Deposition of Moses Lecompte, of full age, mentions John Pagan about 14-15 years ago when said John Pagan was the proprietor of "Pilgrims Rest." Certificate mentions Jacob Traverse and John Hooper as parties concerned.

6 HD 428. February 16, 1792. George Standly of Dorchester County to Negro slaves: Manumission. Witnesses: George Ward, John Fountain. Acknowledged before Levin Woolford, J. P.

6 HD 429. March 19, 1794. Abraham Gambrell of Dorchester County to Levin Layton and Richardson Gambrell of the same county: personal property. Witnesses: John Noble, Nathan Williams. Acknowledged before Jno. Stevens, J. P.

6 HD 430. March 19, 1794. Thomas Hicks to Negro Job: Manumission. Witnesses: Saml. W. Pitt, Denwood Hicks. . Acknowledged before Jno. Stevens, J. P.

6 HD 431. March 19, 1794. Pheby Moore of Dorchester County to James Moore of the same county: personal property. Witness: John Bromwell. Acknowledged before Henry Lake, J. P.

6 HD 432. March 20, 1794. John Riddle of Dorchester County to Thomas Walters: one sorrel horse. Witnesses: John Ennalls, Hugh McColl.

6 HD 432. March 31, 1794. James Acworth of Dorchester County to John Smith of Dorchester County: Negro boy named Jacob. Witness: David Smith. Acknowledged before David Smith, J. P.

6 HD 433. April 19, 1794. Henry H. Hicks of Dorchester County to Hooper Elliott of the same county: Negro slaves. Witness: John Reed. Acknowledged before John Reed, J. P.

6 HD 435. May 26, 1794. Henry Waggaman of Dorchester County, Attorney-at-Law, to Negro Fortune: Manumission. Witnesses: Richd. Pattison, Chas. Hodson. Acknowledged before Richd. Pattison, J. P.

6 HD 436. May 23, 1794. Sarah Taylor of Dorchester County to Negro slaves: Manumission. Witnesses: Charles K. Bryan, Elizabeth Bryan. Acknowledged before Levin Woolford, J. P.

6 HD 431. July 21, 1794. Solomon Martin of Talbot County to Edward Cole: Mulatto man called Henry (alias Henry Jinkins), formerly the property of Thomas Jinkins of Talbot County. Witnesses: Saml. Brown, Thomas Marshall. Acknowledged before Richd. Pattison, J. P.

6 HD 438. July 21, 1794. Edward Cole to Negro Henry (alias Henry Jinkins): Manumission. Witnesses: Saml. Brown, Thomas Marshall.

6 HD 439. March 27, 1794. Award by Ns. Hammond in a dispute between John Elder Gist and James Trippe, Representative of Mr. John Trippe deceased, concerning the ownership of a Negro slave.

6 HD 439. July 10, 1794. Thomas Kallender of Dorchester County, ship carpenter, to William Buchanan and William S. Bond of Talbot County, Merchants: "the ship which I am now building upon Fishing Creek." Witness: Robt. Harrison. Acknowledged before Robt. Harrison, one of the associate Justices of Dorchester County Court.

6 HD 440. August 4, 1794. John Rogers of Dorchester County to Negro Richard Holliday, aged about 32-33 years: Manumission. Witness: Wm. Marshall.

6 HD 441. July 26, 1794. William Geoghegan of Dorchester County to Negro slaves George and Tom: Manumission. Witnesses: Moses Lecompte, Matthias Traverse. Acknowledged before Moses Lecompte.

6 HD 442. July 26, 1794. William Geoghegan and Capewell Keene, both of Dorchester County, to Negro Dominico: Manumission. Witness: Richd. Pattison. Acknowledged before Moses Lecompte.

6 HD 443. March 28, 1785. Thomas Thompson of Dorchester County, planter, to Charles Shinton of the same county: Bond to convey "Thompsons Chance." Witnesses: John King, Elizabeth King. Proved by John King, one of the witnesses, before Tho. Jones, J. P.

6 HD 445. August 22, 1794. James Tucker of Dorchester County to Charles Adams: two mares. Witnesses: Henry Adams, John Vaughan. Acknowledged before John Reed, J. P.

6 HD 446. August 18, 1794. James Tucker of Dorchester County to George Gale, in consideration of 12 Pounds 10 Shillings paid by said George Gale to Joseph Douglass, Executor of Capt. John Smoot late of Dorchester County:

livestock. Witness: Charles Adams. Acknowledged before John Reed, J. P.

6 HD 447. August 22, 1794. John Vaughan of Dorchester County to Charles Adams: personal property. Witnesses: Henry Adams, James Tucker. Acknowledged before John Reed, J. P.

6 HD 448. March 27, 1794. George Slacom of Dorchester County to William Bramble of said county: Negro wench named Love. Witnesses: Wm. Sothen, Frederick Willey. Acknowledged before Henry Lake.

6 HD 450. April 4, 1794. John Kirwan of Dorchester County to George Slacum of the same county: Bond to convey "Todds Point" on the east side of Fern Creek. Witnesses: Wm. Sotherin, David Tyler. Assigned by George Slacum to William Sotherin August 7, 1794. Witnesses: Wm. Bramble, Frederick Willey. Proved by witnesses before Henry Lake.

6 HD 451. August 6, 1794. George Slacum of Dorchester County, Gent., to William Sotherin of the same county, planter: Bond. Witnesses: Frederick Willey, William Bramble. Proved by witnesses before Henry Lake.

6 HD 453. August 8, 1794. George Slacum of Dorchester County, Gent., to William Sotherin of the same county: Negro slaves. Witnesses: Frederick Willey, Wm. Bramble. Proved by witnesses before Henry Lake.

6 HD 454. August 26, 1794. Henry Trippe of Dorchester County to Negro Thomas Grace, aged 36 years: Manumission. Witnesses: Levin Woolrord, Daniel Akers. Acknowledged before Levin Woolford, J. P.

6 HD 455. April 12, 1794. Thomas Colsten of Dorchester County and Elizabeth his wife to Edmond Brannock of the same county: 116 acres on the east side of Fishing Creek, adj. "Harwoods Choice." Witnesses: Tho. Jones, Richd. Pattison. Acknowledged before Tho. Jones and Richd. Pattison, Justices.

6 HD 457. April 7, 1794. Benjamin Keene of Dorchester County to his son Benjamin Keene of the same county: part of three tracts called "Exchange," "Laybrook" and "Laybrook Regulated" (mentions codicil to the Last Will and Testament of Wm. Stephens, deceased). Witnesses: Tho. Jones, Levin Woolford. Acknowledged before Tho. Jones and Levin Woolford.

6 HD 459. April 26, 1794. Robson Barnes of Dorchester County, planter, to Mace Barnes of the same county, planter: lands conveyed to said Robson Barnes

by his father William Barnes by deed dated April 9, 1787, containing 150 acres more or less, on Taylors Island. Witnesses: Henry Lake, Richd. Pattison. Acknowledged by Robson Barnes and Elizabeth his wife before Lake and Richd. Pattison, Justices.

6 HD 462. April 26, 1794. Robson Barnes of Dorchester County to Mace Barnes of the county: "Johns Beginning" on Taylors Island, containing 32 1/4 acres. Witnesses: Henry Lake, Richd. Pattison. Acknowledged by Robson Barnes and Elizabeth his wife before Lake and Richd. Pattison, Justices.

6 HD 464. April 29, 1794. William K. Vass and Elizabeth (Betsey) his wife of Dorchester County to Ayres Busick and Mary his wife of the same county: "Robsons Chance" on the east side of Blackwater River." Witnesses: Richd. Pattison, Jno. Keene. Acknowledged before Richd. Pattison and Jno. Keene, Justices.

6 HD 466. April 29, 1794. Richard Tubman Junr. of Dorchester County to Frederick Bennett of the same county: part of "Shintons Addition" on Shintons Point, containing 2 acres more or less. Witnesses: Jno. Keene, Richd. Pattison. Acknowledged before Jno. Keene and Richd. Pattison, Justices.

6 HD 468. March 28, 1794. John Hooper and Elizabeth his wife of Sussex County Delaware to Isaac Creighton of Dorchester County: "Ferry Point" on Taylors Island, containing by patent 13 acres more or less. Witnesses: Jno. Crapper, David Smith. Acknowledged before Jno. Crapper and David Smith, Justices.

6 HD 470. April 2, 1794. Elizabeth Travers of Dorchester County to her son Vernon Creighton of the same county: "Edloes Purchase" on Taylors Island where said Elizabeth Travers now lives" heretofore conveyed to her by a certain Isaac Creighton. Witnesses: Richd. Pattison, Moses Lecompte. Acknowledged before Richd. Pattison and Moses Lecompte.

6 HD 471. May 2, 1794. Isaac Creighton of Dorchester County to Elizabeth Travers of the same county: part of "Edloes Purchase" on Taylors Island, containing 66 ½ acres. Witnesses: Moses Lecompte, Richd. Pattison. Acknowledged by Isaac Creighton and Lilly his wife before Moses Lecompte and Richd. Pattison.

6 HD 473. May 12, 1794. Joseph Trippe of Dorchester County to William Trippe of the same county: "Trippes Inclosure" containing 178 acres more or

less. Witnesses: Tho. Jones, Jno. Stevens. Acknowledged before Tho. Jones and Jno. Stevens, Justices.

6 HD 475. May 17, 1794. Thomas Tailor of Caroline County to George Applegarth of Talbot County: 'Deep Water Point" containing 16 acres; also part of two other tracts, one called "Rosses Chance" containing 30 acres and the other "The Addition to Rosses Chance" containing 151 acres, all adj. each other, on Hudsons Creek, adj. land of Ralf Smith. Witnesses: Tho. Jones, Thomas Barnett. Acknowledged by Thomas Taylor and Prudence his wife before Thos. Jones and Thos. Barnett, Justices.

6 HD 478. April 12, 1794. Thomas Kallender and Thomas Coleston of Dorchester County to Richard Keene Junr. of the same county: part of "Addition to White Haven" near the head of Fishing Creek, containing 1 3/4 acres. Witnesses: Richd. Pattison, Tho. Jones. Acknowledged by Thomas Kallender and Catherine his wife and Thomas Colsten before Richd. Pattison and Tho. Jones.

6 HD 481. January 2, 1771. John Smoot youngest of Charles County to Edward Smoot of the same county: Bond concerning division of two tracts of land in Dorchester County bought by said John and Edward Smoot from Col. Phillip Ludle Lee, on the east side of the Northwest Fork. Witnesses: John Bruce, Andrew Minitree. Edward Smoot assigns his interest in the above to his son Henry Smoot April 22, 1794. Witnesses: Neale H. Shaw, Burford Cottrell.

6 HD 482. April 22, 1794. Edward Smoot of Charles County to his son Henry Smoot of Dorchester County: Bond to convey his interest in lands purchased with John Smoot from Col. Phillip Ludle Lee. Witnesses: Burford Cottrell, Neale H. Shaw.

6 HD 483. June 6, 1794. Thomas Vickers 3rd of Dorchester County and Ann his wife to John Elder Gist of the town of Cambridge: 1/4 acre in Cambridge, adj. the Prison lot. Witnesses: Tho. Jones, Richd. Pattison. Acknowledged before Tho. Jones and Richd. Pattison, Justices.

6 HD 486. June 5, 1794. Thomas Vickars of Dorchester County and Ann his wife to Peter Rea of the Town of Cambridge: land in Cambridge containing 1 1/4 acre more or less, part of the land divided by a Jury in 1790 between William Stewart and Sarah Stewart. Witnesses: Tho. Jones, Richd. Pattison. Acknowledged before Tho. Jones, Richd. Pattison, Justices.

6 HD 489. May 30, 1794. John Langfitt of Dorchester County, Mcht., to William Jones, son of Wm., of the same county, Mcht.: part of "Bridge Neck" on the road from Lockerman's Mills to Vienna; also part of "Coxes Addition to Bridge Neck" Also part of "Sams Neglect" and part of "Johns Industry." All of said lands are on the east side of Chicamacomico River. Witnesses: John Reed, David Smith. Acknowledged before John Reed and David Smith, Justices.

6 HD 493. April 29, 1794. Ayrs Busick and Mary his wife of Dorchester County to William K. Vass and Betsy his wife of the. same county: "Robsons Range" on the west side of Blackwater River, containing 50 acres more or less. Witnesses: Richd. Pattison, Jno. Keene. Acknowledged before Richd. Pattison and John Keene, Justices.

6 HD 495. June 11, 1794. Horatio Hideout of Annapolis, Attorney-at-Law" and Rachel his wife, one of the daughters of Robert Goldsborough late of Cambridge, deceased, to Howes Goldsborough the younger, son of said Robert Goldsborough: the interest of said Hideout and wife in lands devised by said Robert Goldsborough deceased to his sons John and Howes as tenants in common and not as joint tenants; the said John having died a minor, intestate and without issue, whereby his interest passed to the testator's nine surviving children, viz., Rebecca (wife of Howes Goldsborough of Talbot County), Sarah (wife of Henry Ennalls of Dorchester County), Elizabeth (wife of Doctor James Sykes of Dover, Delaware), Charles, William, Robert, Richard, the aforesaid Rachel (wife of Horatio Hideout), and the aforesaid Howes Goldsborough the younger; and Robert, one of the children of said Robert the Testator, also having died intestate and without issue and his part of said lands having descended to his eight surviving brothers and sisters. The lands involved are several tracts near the head of Hungar River purchased by said testator from Lewis Griffith Paul; a tract purchased by testator from Jacob Goutee; and a tract called "Robins Defiance" purchased by testator from Nathaniel Elliot and wife, containing in the whole about 100 acres; and lands called "Town Point" and "Thomsons Island" (or "Hopkins ' s Island") . Witnesses: R. Goldsborough, Henry Dickinson. Acknowledged before. R. Goldsborough, one of the Judges of the General Court.

6 HD 499. March 21, 1794. Richard Keene Junr. of Dorchester County to Charles Shenton of the same county: "Keenes Timber Yard" containing 50 acres more or less; and "Addition to Keenes Timber Yard" adj. thereto, containing 59 acres. Witnesses: Tho. Jones, Henry Lake. Acknowledged by Richard Keene and Sarah his wife before Henry Lake ; and Tho. Jones.

6 HD 502. November 6, 1794. John Tootell to the State of Maryland: Bond as High Sheriff of Dorchester County with Charles Hodson, Peter Rea and Roger A. Hooper as sureties. Witnesses: Moses Lecompte, Jno. Eccleston.

6 ED 503. May 10, 1794. Ayrs Busick of Dorchester County and Mary his wife to Major Phillips of the same county: "Robsons Chance" in Blackwater, containing 100 acres more or less. Witnesses: Henry Lake, Jno. Keene. Acknowledged before Henry Lake and Jno. Keene, Justices.

6 HD 507. May 10, 1794. Benjamin Woollen and Keziah his wife to Charles Shinton of Dorchester County: part of "Johnsons Last Purchase" adj. "Richards Delight" and "Johnsons Plane." Witnesses: Henry Lake, Jno. Keene. Acknowledged before Henry Lake and Jno. Keene, Justices.

6 HD 509. April 24, 1794. Jeremiah Spicer of Dorchester County to Robson Barns of the same county: "Johns Beginning" on Taylors Island, containing 32 1/4 acres more or less. Witnesses: Moses Lecompte, Richd. Pattison. Acknowledged by Jeremiah Spicer and Lucrecy his wife before Moses LeCompte and Richd. Pattison.

6 HD 511. April 26, 1794. Moses Barns and Mary his wife of Dorchester County to Robson Barns of the sarre county: part of "Buck Valley" on the west side of Blackwater River, containing 35 acres more or less; part of "Last Vacancy" adj. thereto, containing 45 acres more or less; and part of "Moses Liberty" on said River and Coles Creek. Witnesses: Henry Lake, Richd. Pattison. Acknowledged before Henry Lake and Richard Pattison, Justic.s.

6 HD 515. June 3, 1793. Gustavus Scott of Baltimore Town to William Barrow of Cambridge: 38 3/4 acres between Cambridge and Hambrooks Point, adj. lands of the late Col. James Murray and the late Archibald Pattison; and 77 3/4 acres on the road from the cross roads to John Goldsborough's plantation. Witness: Samuel Chase. Acknowledged by Gustavus Scott and Margaret his wife before Samuel Chase, Chief Justice of the State of Maryland.

6 HD 519. July 14, 1794. Daniel McDonnell of Dorchester County, Mcht., to Thomas Hicks of the same county, Mcht.: "Darley" and other lands mortgaged by said Hicks to said McDonnell January 13, 1794. Witnesses: Levin Woolford, Jno. Stevens. Acknowledged before Levin Woolford and Jno. Stevens, Justices.

6 HD 521. July 14, 1794. Levin Wall of Dorchester County, planter, to Thomas Hicks of the same county, Mcht.: "Daley," conveyed by said Hicks to said Levin

Wall April 22, 1793. Witnesses: Jno. Stevens, Levin Woolford. Acknowledged before Jno. Stevens and Levin Woolford, Justices.

6 HD 523. January 28, 1794. Gabriel Insley and William Insley, both of Dorchester County, planters, to Whittington Johnson of the same county: part of "Andrews Fortune," adj. said Johnson's land and adj. lands of John Wingate ("Bettys Lot") and James Dean. Witnesses: Henry Lake, Jno. Keene. Acknowledged before Henry Lake and Jno. Keene, Justices of the Peace.

6 HD 525. July 21, 1794. Thomas Hicks of Dorchester County and Sarah his wife to Samuel W. Pitt of the same county: part of "Darley" on the east side of Blackwater River, granted and released to said Thomas Hicks by his brother William Ennalls Hicks pursuant to the Last Will and Testament of their father John Hicks, containing 414 acres more or less, adj. John Scott's part of "Darley." Witnesses: Jno. Stevens, Levin Woolford. Acknowledged before Jno. Stevens and Levin Woolford, Justices.

6 HD 529. July 16, 1794. David Hayward of Dorchester County to James Sullender of the same county: part of a tract called "All Three of Us," but by late resurvey called "Wallaces Addition," containing 12 ½ acres more or less. Witnesses: Moses LeCompte, John Keene. Acknowledged before Moses LeCompte and John Keene, Justices.

6 HD 532. June 20, 1794. Richard Wallace of Dorchester County to James Sullender Senr. of the same county: part of a tract originally called "All Three of Us" but by late resurvey called "Wallaces Addition," containing 12 ½ acres more or less. Witnesses: Moses LeCompte, Jno. Keene. Acknowledged before Moses LeCompte and Jno. Keene, Justices.

6 HD 534. March 28, 1794. Agreement between Richard Wallace and James Sullender Senr. concerning division by Capt. Benjamin Keene and Jacob Todd of a tract called "All Three of Us," which was obtained by Law from Elloner McGraw." Witnesses: Levin Todd, John Griffith. Proved by John Griffith before John Keene, Justicee.

6 HD 536. April 1, 1794. Award by Benjamin Keene and Jacob Todd in a dispute concerning a bond given by John Wallace deceased to Alin Hayward deceased in the year 1780, to convey part of a tract originally called "All Three of Us," but now called "Wallaces Addition," "at which time lay in dispute between the afsd. John Wallace and Elleanor McGraw."

6 HD 537. May 3, 1794. Charles Hodson Esq., High Sheriff of Dorchester County to William Campbell and Gabriel Duvall of Anne Arundel County: "Town Hill" adj. the Town of Vienna, formerly belonging to Clement Holliday and sold by the Sheriff under writ of Fieri Facias for satisfaction of judgments obtained in the General Court of the Western Shore by David Kerr against said Holliday. Witness: Danl. McDonnell. Acknowledged before Jno. Stevens and Levin Woolford, Justices.

6 HD 540. December 17, 1787. Daniel Payne of Dorchester County to William Paddison of the same county, Mariner: Bond to convey part of "Coles Gift" and "Coles Regulation," containing 40 acres. Witnesses: Moses Passapae, Amasa Robinson.

6 HD 541. March 13, 1794. Levin Stack and Nancy his wife of Dorchester County to Richard Cannon of the same county: part of "Priviledge," adj. "Taylors Neglect" and containing 63 acres more or less. Witnesses: Jno. Stevens, Jno. Crapper. Acknowledged before Jno. Stevens and Jno. Crapper, Justices.

6 HD 544. October 9, 1794. William Harrison LeCompte of Dorchester County, Farmer, to Thomas Hubbard of the same county: Negro girl called Phebe. Witness: Jno. Stevens. Acknowledged before Jno. Stevens, Justice.

6 HD 546. July 12, 1794. John Bromwell of Dorchester County to John Harrington of the same county: lease of part of "Bromwells Adventure" at the head of Tobacco Stick Bay, adj. "Woolfords Purchase." Witnesses: Tho. Jones, Moses LeCompte. Acknowledged before Tho. Jones and Moses LeCompte, Justices.

6 HD 549. July 26, 1794. John Langfitt of Dorchester County to William Jones of the same county: lands on the south side of the road from Thomas Lockerman's Mills to the Town of Vienna, on the east side of Chicamacomico River, called "Bridge Neck," "Cox Addition to Bridge Neck," "Sams Neglect" and "Johns Industry." Witnesses: John Reed, David Smith. Acknowledged before John Reed and David Smith.

6 HD 552. August 12, 1794. Hugh McGuire of Dorchester County to Charles Beacham of the same county: part of a tract on the south side of the road from Fishing Creek Church to Cambridge near Edward Wright's store, adj. Lot No. 6 of "White Haven," adj. "Head Range" and containing one acre more or less. Witnesses: Jno. Crapper, Jno. Stevens. Acknowledged before Jno. Crapper and

Jno. Stevens, Justices.

6 HD 555. September 15, 1794. Joseph Cantwell of Dorchester County, Farmer, to William Harrison LeCompte of the same county, Farmer: "all his right, Title, Interest & claim to one third of a Tract of land possessed by him in consequence of his Intermarriage with the widow of James Sewars deceased, called "Piney Point," on Phillips's Creek, containing in the whole tract 75 acres more or less. Witnesses: Jno. Stevens, Levin Woolford. Acknowledged before Jno. Stevens and Levin Woolford, Justices.

6 HD 557. August 12, 1794. Charles Beacham of Dorchester County to Joseph Benson of the same county: land on the south side of the main road from Fishing Creek Church to Cambridge, containing ½ acre more or less. Witnesses: Jno. Stevens, Jno. Crapper. Acknowledged before Jno. Stevens and Jno. Crapper, Justices.

6 HD 560. August 6, 1794. Arthur Pritchard of Dorchester County to James Muir of the same county: part of "Hard Fortune" and part of "Pritchards Lot," adj. "Discovery," on the road from New Market to Crotchers Ferry, containing 1 1/4 acres more or less. Witnesses: Jno. Stevens, Jno. Crapper. Acknowledged by Arthur Pritchard and Sally his wife before Jno. Stevens and Jno. Crapper, Justices.

6 HD 563. October 2, 1794. Sarah Eccleston to William Hurlook: Bill of Sale for a Negro girl called Susannah. Witnesses: Wm. W. Eccleston, Wm. Thomas. Acknowledged before Jno. Gooding, Justice.

6 HD 564. August 6, 1794. James Muir of Dorchester County and Charity his wife to Arthur Pritchard of Dorohester County: part of "Hope," adj. Mr. Waggaman's part of "Taylors Kindness" and containing 11 acres more or less. Witnesses: Jno. Crapper, Jno. Stevens. Acknowledged before Jno. Crapper and Jno. Stevens, Magistrates.

6 HD 567. September 11, 1794. Robert White of Dorchester County to Thomas Walters and Henry Hodson of the same county: Bill of sale for a Negro slave and other personal property. Witness: John Reed. Acknowledged before John Reed, Justice.

6 HD 569. September 2, 1794. John McKeel and Mary his wife of Dorchester County to Stanley Byus of the same county: part of "Partnership" on Smiths Creek which issues out of Little Choptank River, on the road from Fishing

Creek to Town Point, containing 183 1/4 acres more or less. Witnesses: Levin Woolford, Richd. Pattison. Acknowledged before Levin Woolford and Richd. Pattison, Justices.

6 HD 574. September 8, 1794. Joseph Daffin of Dorchester County to William Bonner of the same county: "Widows Purchase," containing 232 ½ acres more or less. Witnesses: John Stevens, Levin Woolford. Acknowledged before Jno. Stevens and Levin Woolford, Justices.

6 HD 576. September 15, 1794. William Vans Murray and Charlotte his wife of Dorchester County to William Goldsborough of the same county: part of "Ennalls's Outrange," adj. the town of Cambridge and containing 6 acres.) Witnesses: Jno. Stevens, Levin Woolford. Acknowledged before Jno. Stevens and Levin Woolford, Justices.

6 HD 579. September 6, 1794. Tristram Thomas and Eleanor his wife of Dorchester County to William Jones of the same county: land on the south side of the road from Thomas Lockermans Mills to the Town of Vienna, called "Johns Industry." Witnesses: John Reed, David Smith. Acknowledged before John Reed and David Smith, Justices.

6 HD 582. September 22, 1794. Stevens Woolford to Baptists: part of "Woolfords Content" on the road from Taylors Island to Cambridge, adj. "Hackaram" and containing 3/4 acre. Witnesses: Jno. Stevens, Stanley Byus. Acknowledged before Jno. Stevens and Stanley Byus, Justices.

6 HD 584. May 10, 1794. Rosanna McGraw and Sophia Roberts of Dorchester County to William Hayward and Mary his wife: part of "Lott" adj. "Wallaces Addition" and containing 4 acres more or less; and part of "Eloner McGraw Desire," containing 1 1/4 acre more or less. Witnesses: Henry Lake, Jno. Keene. Acknowledged before Henry Lake and Jno. Keene, Justices.

6 HD 587. May 10, 1794. Rosanna McGraw and Sophia Roberts of Dorchester County to William Hayward and Mary his wife of the same county: part of "McGraws Outlett" on the east side of Hunger River and containing 6 1/4 acres more or less. Witnesses: Henry Lake, Jno. Keene. Acknowledged before Henry Lake and Jno. Keene, Justices.

6 HD 590. May 3, 1794. Richard Tubman of Dorchester County, planter, to William Donnack of the same county: "Roberts Lott' in Meekins Neck, containing 16 ½ acres more or less. Witnesses: Moses LeCompte, Richd.

Pattison. Acknowledged before Moses LeCompte and Richd. Pattison, Justices.

6 HD 592. August 27, 1794. Edward Killman of Dorchester County to Anthony Thompson of the same county: part of "Morgins Venture" or "Timber Yard," bequeathed by Morgan Jones to his daughter, the wife of said Edward Killman, containing 25 3/4 acres more or less. Witnesses: Tho. Jones, Levin Woolford. Acknowledged before Thos. Jones and Levin Woolford, Justices.

6 HD 595. May 10, 1794. William Hayward and Mary his wife and Sophia Roberts, all of Dorchester County, to Rosanna McGraw of the same county: part of "McGraws Outlett" on the east side of Hungar River, containing 6 1/4 acres more or less. Witnesses: Henry Lake, Jno. Keene. Acknowledged before Henry Lake and Jno. Keene, Justices.

6 HD 598. May 10, 1794. William Hayward and Mary his wife and Rosanna McGraw of Dorchester .County to Sophia Roberts of the same county: part of "McGraws Outlett" on the east side of Hungar River, containing 6 1/4 acres more or less. Witnesses: Henry Lake, Jno. Keene. Acknowledged before Henry Lake and Jno. Keene, Justices.

6 HD 601. September 25, 1794. William Meredith of Dorchester County to Thomas Meredith of the same county: "Merediths Inclosure" except what is already sold to James Barkly, on Worlds End Creek and containing 394 acres more or less. Witnesses: Henry Lake, Jno. Keene. Acknowledged before Henry Lake and Jno. Keene, Justices.

6 HD 603. September 9, 1794. David Ramsey of Dorchester County, planter, to Joseph LeCompte, Junr. of the same county: livestock, furniture, etc. Witnesses: Fanny Wheeler, James McCall, Hugh McCall.

6 HD 604. July 30, 1792. Thomas Willin to his brother John Willin: Power of Attorney. Witnesses: Shadrack Allen, Stephen Brook. (Pitt County, North Carolina).

6 HD 606. June 28, 1794. Thomas Willin of Pitt County, North Carolina, Farmer, to Levi Willin of Dorchester County, Maryland, Farmer: Bond concerning land sold by said Thomas to the said Levi. Witnesses: Benjamin Todd Junr., Robert Evans.

6 HD 607. October 14, 1794. Elizabeth Caile of Dorchester County to Vestry of Great Choptank Parish: in consideration of 5 Shillings current money and a deed

of release of part of the said land, Elizabeth Caile surrenders her interest in land formerly leased by the Rector and Vestry of Great Choptank Parish to John Caile by Indenture dated July 3, 1750. The said land, lying in the town of Cambridge, was leased to said John Caile for the term of the natural lives of Rebecca Caile, Hall Caile and Margaret Caile; was devised by the Last Will and Testament of said John Caile to his nephew John Hall Caile and by the Last Will and Testament of said John Hall Caile to his mother Elizabeth Caile for her lifetime with remainder to Hall Harrison. Witnesses: Jno. Stevens, Levin Woolford. Acknowledged before Jno. Stevens and Levin Woolford, Justices.

6 HD 609. October 14, 1794. Vestry of Great Choptank Parish to Elizabeth Caile: part of a tract of land in Cambridge. Signed by Wm. Worthington Davis, Charles Goldsborough, Richd. Golds- borough and Wm. Goldsborough in the presence of Jno. Stevens and Levin Woolford. Acknowledged before Jno. Stevens and Levin Woolford, Justices.

6 HD 612. October 17, 1794. James Chizum of Dorchester County to John K. Fookes of the same county: part of "Addition to White Haven" near the head of Fishing Creek, adj. the Methodist Meeting House land, adj. Lot No. 10 of "White Haven" and containing 5 1/4 acres. Witnesses: Tho. Jones, Levin Woolford. Acknowledged before Tho. Jones and Levin Woolford, Justices.

6 HD 615. October 20, 1794. John K. Fookes of Dorchester. County to Levin Porter of the same county: part of "Addition to White Haven" near the head of Fishing Creek, containing 2 acres. Witnesses: Levin Woolford, Thos. Barnett. Acknowledged before Levin Woolford and Thos. Barnett, Justices.

6 HD 617. May 11, 1793. Ezekiel Mace and Angell Mace of Orange County, North Carolina, to Edmund Brannock of Dorchester County: Power of Attorney to convey to Alexander Robbs of Orange County, North Carolina, a tract called "Grass Reading" on St. Stephens Creek in Dorchester County, "belonging to us by the last will and Testament of our father Josias Mace, containing 60 acres more or less. Witnesses: Hardy Hurdle, J. P.; John Walker, J. P. Abner B. Bruce, Clerk of Court, Orange County, N. C.

6 HD 620. June 20, 1794. Edmund Brannock of Dorchester County, Attorney for Ezekiel Mace and Angell Mace of Orange County, North Carolina, to Alexander Robbs of Orange County, North Carolina: Part of "Grass Reading" on the south side of Little Choptank River, on St. Stephens Creek, formerly purchased by Josias Mace from Levin Woolford, containing 60 acres more or less. Witnesses: Richd. Pattison, Tho. Jones. Acknowledged before Richd.

Pattison and Tho. Jones, Justices.

6 HD 624. June 24, 1794. Alexander Robbs of Orange County, North Carolina, to George Brannock of Dorchester County: part of "Grass Reading" on St. Stevens's Creek, containing 60 acres. Witnesses: Tho. Jones, Richd. Pattison. Acknowledged before Tho. Jones and Richd. Pattison, Justices.

6 HD 627. May 13, 1794. Howes Goldsborough of Talbot County and Rebecca his wife to William Goldsborough of Dorchester County: their interest in lands devised by Robert Goldsborough, deceased, father of said Rebecca and Wm., to his son Robert who has since died intestate and without issue. Witness: R. Goldsborough. Acknowledged before R. Goldsborough, one of the Judges of the General Court of Maryland.

6 HD 630. September 24, 1794. Robert Dennis to Negro James: Manumission. Witnesses: Peter H. Waters, Anne H. Waters.

6 HD 630. October 25, 1794. James Tregoe of Dorchester County to Levin Woolford of the same county: part of two tracts called "Williams Good Will" and "Spite"; all of "Addition to Turkey Neck"; all of "Tregoes Division"; and part of two tracts called "Hazard" and "Addition to Outlett," adj. land of Levin Tregoe. 195 acres more or less in all, hereby conveyed. Witnesses: Moses LeCompte, Tho. Jones. Acknowledged before Moses LeCompte and Tho. Jones, Justices.

6 HD 633. October 23, 1794. Thomas Walters and James Ackworth of Dorchester County to John Riddle of Dorchester County: Negro woman slave called Judah. witness: John Reed. Acknowledged before John Reed, Justice.

8 HD 1. October 28, 1794. Thomas Woolford of Dorchester County, planter, to Richard Linchacombe of the same county, planter: part of "Woolfords Foresight" on the road from the head of Fishing Creek to Taylors Island, containing 18 1/4 acres. Witnesses: Jno. Stevens, Levin Woolford. Acknowledged before Jno. Stevens and Levin Woolford, Justices.

8 HD 4. March 17, 1794 - July 12, 1794. Commission to Moses LeCompte, Richard Pattison, John Keene and Richard Tubman of Dorchester County, Gent., to perpetuate bounds of John Denwood Meekins. land. called "Meekins's Hope," and Return. Deposition of John Shenton, aged about 58 years, re bounded tree shown deponent by Richard Meekins about 45 years ago. Deposition of Anne Shenton, aged about 60 years, mentions her father Richard

Meekins.

8 HD 8. July 12, 1794. Award in favor of Andrew McDonald against Dorchester County for work done on the Court House, signed by Tho. Jones, John Reed and Thos. Colston.

8 HD 8. March 17, 1794 - April 30, 1794. Commission to Thomas Jones, Richard Pattison, Jeremiah Pattison, William Pattison and John Jones, Capt., of Dorchester County, Gent., to divide "Lakes Discovery," land of Henry Navey, late of Dorchester County, who recently died leaving Briggs Navey, Thomas Navey, Richard Navey, Sarah Navey and Elizabeth Tall, wife of William, his brothers and sisters, and Mary and Elizabeth Hill, daughters of James Hill by his wife Mary the sister of said Henry Navey as his heirs at law (Moses LeCompte, guardian of Mary and Elizabeth Hill), and Return. The said land contains 96 acres clear of elder surveys, which the Commissioners consider would not admit of a division.

8 HD 12. March 17, 1794 - October 27, 1794. Commission to Solomon Frazier, Nathaniel Manning, Charles Eccleston, Joseph Eccleston and Samuel Hubbert of Dorchester County, Gent., to divide "Piny Point," land of James Sewers late of Dorchester County, who has died leaving Elizabeth, wife of Wm. Harrison LeCompte, and Mary, Rosannah, Deborah and Esther Sewers, sisters of said Elizabeth, his children and heirs at law, and Return. Jeremiah Beckwith is named as Guardian of the said Mary, Rosannah, Deborah and Esther, who are minors. The said land contains 79 3/4 acres, which the Commissioners consider would not admit of a division without injury to the parties.

8 HD 16. April 5, 1794 - June 10, 1794. Commission to Levin Woolford, Ezekiel Vickars, Arthur Whiteley and Benjamin Woodard of Dorchester County, Gent., to perpetuate bounds of William LeCompte's land called "Willoughbys Purchase" and "Willoughbys Purchase Resurveyed," and Return. Deposition of Charles LeCompte, aged about 72 years, mentions his father John LcCompte, now deceased, who showed deponent a bounded marker of said land about 40-50 years ago. Deposition of John LeCompte Senr., aged about 50 years, mentions his father John LeCompte, deceased. Deposition of William Pennington, aged about 68 years, mentions Paul Ingrum, a tenant on Charles Goldsborough's land about 30-40 years ago, and a boundary post said to have been burned by John Brannon and John Googe. Deposition of William Boyus, aged about 30 years, mentions Windsmore LeCompte about 15-16 years ago, and a marked pine at the head of Johns Creek which issues out of Great Choptank River.

8 HD 22. October 22, 1792 - June 21, 1794. Commission to John Eccleston, Cyrus Mitchell, James Sulivane, Jonathan Pinkney and Jacob Wright of Dorchester County, Gent., to perpetuate bounds of land of Levin Marshall, Nathan Harrington, Benjamin Collison and William Withgott called "Goodridges Choice," and Return. Deposition of Richd. Alford, aged 70 years, re division line of "Goodridges Choice" formerly run between the late Henry Withgott dec'd. and the late Gen. Henry Hooper, mentions a bounded tree shown to deponent by said Henry Withgott and by Mark Littleton and John Dannelly. Deposition of Joseph Withgott, aged 38 years, son of henry Withgott deceased, re bounded tree shown him about 20 years ago by his said father as a bounder between land of said Henry Withgott and land of Henry Hooper, son of Ennalls, now the property of Mr. Williss. Deposition of Thomas Hooper, aged 26 years, re land sold by him to Mr Joshua Williss, mentions a marked tree shown him about 12-13 years ago by his father James Hooper "who told him it was the Division Tree of the land as left him by his uncles Henry Hooper and the land then in possession of Genl. Hooper" Also mentions Kenneth McKinny about 7 years ago. Also mentions a corner tree between lands of James Mowbray, James Hooper and Edward Bromwell. Deposition of Christopher Connolly, aged about 30 years, mentions his father Dennis Connolly who lived about 11-12 years ago on the land of James Mowbray; and a division tree between James Mowbray, James Hooper and Benj. Collison. Deposition of John Nash, aged 50 years, who kept school near this place about 20-23 years ago, mentions Mr. James Hooper deceased, who asked this deponent about 9 years ago to buy some land for him, lying within the said Hooper's plantation and belonging to the heirs of John Richardson of Caroline County. Also mentions Hooper's wife, her son Tom, and Hooper's son James who died shortly after the time in question (about 9 years ago). Deposition of Dennis Connolly, aged about 60 years, who lived about 11 years ago on land of James Mobery, mentions a bounded tree of Mobery, Hooper and Wm. Jones. Deposition of Robert Hardican, aged about 60 years, mentions James Hooper, Richard Vinton and Kenneth McKinny about 25 years ago, when looking for timber to build the house where Joshua Willis now lives, and mentions Wm. Jones who lived where Benjamin Collison now lives. Deposition of Henry Hicks, aged about 33 years, mentions land marked by Edward Bromwell with the letter "E. B.." Deposition of Mrs. Ann Carter, aged about 50 years, mentions her uncle, Gen. Henry Hooper; lands in Cabin Creek Neck; her husband James Hooper; and a certain John Richardson. Gen. Hooper advised her shortly after the death of her husband James Hooper that Richardson had no claim to land left to her by her grandfather between her house and an old orchard formerly called "Richardsons Orchard." Also mentions a certain John Thomas who was a tenant to deponent's grandfather. Also mentions boundary of Bromwell's land, shown her about 12

years ago by her husband James Hooper. Deposition of Edward Grainger, aged about 48 years, mentions John Thomas and Peter Corkran, tenants under Col. Hooper. Deposition of John Thomas, aged about 56 years, who rented a place from Col. Henry Hooper on Blinkhorn Creek in Cabin Creek Neck and lived there six years until the death of the said Col. Henry Hooper. "This Deponent further sayeth that after the death of Col. Henry Hooper he paid his rent to Henry Hooper son of the said Col. Henry Hooper but that he the said Deponent never rented of the said Henry Hooper son of Henry afsd. Question asked by the Commrs. if he ever heard of Genl. Henry Hooper son of the former claiming any part of the Plantation whereon he the said Deponent lived this Deponent answered he never did." The said land called "Goodridges Choice" is divided by the Commissioners between Wm. Withgott, Levin Marshall (the part formerly held by Gen. Henry Hooper is now the part of Levin Marshall), Benjamin Collison and Nathan Harrington after survey by Theophilus Marshall, Surveyor.

8 HD 52. March 17, 1794 - June 14, 1794. Commission to Thomas Jones, Richard Pattison, Jeremiah Pattison and John Jones of Thos. of Dorchester County, Gent., to perpetuate bounds of Samuel Phillips' land called "Ragged Point," arid Return. Deposition of Henry Killman, aged about 37 years, re bounded tree on Little Choptank shown him about 30 years ago in the presence of Robert Willson. Deposition of William Ross, aged about 50 years, re second bounder of said land, identified by old John Killman and by John Clarriage de ce ase d. Deposition of Thomas Willis of full age, mentions William Steele who in his lifetime was proprietor of said land. Deposition of Sally Soward, aged about 40 years, daughter of Arabella Tunis, re bounded tree between Robert Willson and William Steele. The Commissioners set down a post on Bruckses Creek at the place shown by deponents.

8 HD 56. March 17, 1794 - August 20, 1794. Commission to William W. Davis, Jonathan Patridge, Levin Woolford (of John), Ezekiel Vickars and Solomon Frazier of Dorchester County, Gent., to perpetuate bounds of Wm. Stevens' lands called "Clift," "Stevens's Regulation," "Daniels Choice" and "Daniels Choice Resurveyed," and Return. Deposition of Thomas Vickars, aged about 60 years, re bounder between "Clift" and "Horn" shown to him about 35-40 years ago by Jonathan Holt and Joseph Parks, "the former overseer for Charles Goldsborough deceased, the latter overseer for John Stevens deceased." Also mentions marker shown him about 20 years ago by Peter Edmondson. William Stevens, Charles Goldsborough are named in the Return of the Commissioners as parties concerned. Lines surveyed by Wm. Barrow Esq., Surveyor, with Daniel Marshall and John Morris as chain carriers.

8HD 63. June 6, 1794. Award by Richard Pattison, Jacob Todd and John Griffith, Arbitrators, in an Action of Waste in Dorchester County Court between Vachel Keene, Plaintiff, and Ezekiel Keene, Defendant.

8 HD 64. "To the Honble John Done Esq. Chief Justice and his Associates We the Subscribers members of the Baptist Churches in Dorchester County, Pray to have the following Houses Recorded as places of Religious & Social Worship -
No. 1 Chicknicomico Meetg. House near the Draw Bridge
No. 2 Mill Meeting House near Thomas Lockermans Mills.
   3 Woolfords Meeting House near the head of Fishing Creek
    4 Streights meeting House near Lightwood Knott Chappel
J. E. Gist Tristram Thomas William Jones 3d Novr. 1794."

8 HD 65. "To the Honble John Done Esquire and his Associates, We the Subscribers members of the Methodist Episcopal Church, Pray to have the following Houses in Dorchester County recorded as places of Religious Worship - No. 1 Aireys Chapple; No.2 Bartholomew Ennalls Chapple; No. 3 Johnsons Chapple ; 4. Todds Chapple; 5. Taylors Island Chapple; 6. Church Creek Chapple ; 7. Beckwithith Chapple.
Hy. Ennalls Chas. K. Bryan November 6th 1794."

8 HD 65. August 18, 1794. Medford Andrews of Dorchester County to William Reed of the same county: "Honourable Division," being a resurvey on a tract called "Head Range" on Blackwater, devised to said Medford Andrews in fee tail under the will of his grandfather Isaac Andrews and now conveyed in fee simple in accordance with Act of Assembly of 1782-83. Witnesses: Those Jones, Levin Woolford. Acknowledged by Medford Andrews and Sarah his wife before Thos. Jones and Levin Woolford, Justices.

8 HD 69. August 8, 1794. George Slacum of Dorchester County, Gent., to William Sotherin of the same county: Negro slaves. Witnesses: Frederick Willey, William Bramble. Proved by witnesses before Hy. Lake. Assigned by Wm. Sotherin to Nathan Levering, by Levering to Henry Lake and by Henry Lake to Naboth Hart. Witnesses: Richard Dean, Jno. Keene, Wm. Lake.

8 HD 71. August 4, 1794. James Sulivene of Dorchester County to Edwards Thompson and Daniel Sulivane of the same county, Trustees of New Market Episcopal Chapel: part of a tract called "New Markett" on the east side of the main road from Cambridge to Cabin Creek Mills, containing 60 sq. perches more or less. Witnesses: Jno. Stevens, David Smith. Acknowledged before Jno. Stevens and David Smith, Justices.

8 HD 74. October 15, 1794. Charles Wheatley of Dorchester County to James Willson of the same county, planter: part of a tract called "Levertons Chance" within the lines of "Wateres Last Choice" that the said James Willson bought of one Robinson Stevens. Witnesses: Jno. Stevens, Jno. Gooding. Acknowledged before Jno. Stevens and Jno. Gooding, Justices.

8 HD 77. November 1, 1794. Henry Councell and Sally his wife of Queen Anns County to Richard Tubman of Dorchester County: "Shentons Advantage" near "Phillips Liberty" on the west side of the Northwest Fork of Blackwater, containing 20 acres more or less. Also "Addition to Shentons Advantage," containing 30 acres more or less. Witnesses: Henry Lake, Jno. Keene. Acknowledged before Henry Lake and Jno. Keene, Justices.

8 HD 80. September 4, 1794. John Windows of Dorchester County to John Long of the same county: "Bachelors Forrest," devised to said John Windows by the Last Will and Testament of his father Charles Windows late of Dorchester County, deceased. Witnesses: John Reed, David Smith. Acknowledged before Jno. Reed and David Smith, Justices.

8 HD 82. August 27, 1794. Edward Pritchett of Craven County, North Carolina, to Thomas Kallender of Dorchester County: parts of "Hereford" and "Pritchetts Regulation Regulated" not heretofore conveyed to James Moore and Moses Barns, on Hodson Branch, containing 10 acres more or less. Witnesses: Levin Woolford, Richd. Pattison. Acknowledged before Levin Woolford and Richd. Pattison, Justices.

8 HD 84. October 29, 1794. Theophilus Marshall of Dorchester County to Joseph Roberts of the same county: part of "Marshalls Chance," containing one acre. Witnesses: Jno. Stevens, Jno. Gooding. Acknowledged before Jno. Stevens and Jno. Gooding, Justices.

8 HD 87. November 8, 1794. Elizabeth Sparks of Dorchester County, spinster, to Peter Rea of the same county, Merchant: Bond, "Whereas the said Peter Rea has sold Negro Abraham's wife called Abigale to the said Elizabeth Sparks as a slave, and whereas the said Elizabeth Sparks has agreed to sell the said Negro Abigale again to any person whom she makes choice or to be sold to or to anyone whom she can pursuade to purchase her for thirty seven pounds ten shillings Current Money whom she may think more agreeable than the sd. Elizabeth Sparks And whereas the said Elizabeth Sparks hath further agreed not to sell the said Negro to any person living from or off the Eastern Shore of Maryland or remove the said Abigale from the same." Witnesses: Peregrine

Beaston, Thomas Abbett. Proved by Thomas Abbett, one of the witnesses, before Levin Woolford, Justice of the Peace.

8 HD 88. September 9, 1794. Order in Chancery appointing Thomas Kirwan Trustee for the benefit of the Creditors of Wm. Keene, Insolvent Debtor. Samuel H. Howard, Regr. Cur. Can.

8 HD 89. November 17, 1794. William Keene to Thomas Kirwan, Trustee: All of said William Keene's property, for the benefit of his creditors. Witnesses: Henry Lake, John Keene. Acknowledged before Henry Lake and Jno. Keene, Justices.

8 HD 91. October 10, 1794. Henry Ennalls to Joseph Ennalls: lease of land adj. lands of the said Joseph Ennalls and Henry Arnett. Witnesses: Henry Haskins, Geo. Ward. Acknowledged before Jno. Stevens and Levin Woolford, Justices.

8 HD 92. October 16, 1794. Harriot Hayward of Talbot County in the town of Easton to John Reed of Dorchester County: Negro woman named Caroline, about 17-18 years old. Witness: James Price. Acknowledged before James Price, Justice for Talbot County. Wm. S. Bond, Clk.

8 HD 94. November 17, 1794. Polley Skinner Vinson, James Vinson and John LeCompte, son of John deceased, all of Dorchester County, to Nathaniel Manning of the same county, planter: Bond for conveyance of part of a tract called "Deavors Choice," adj. land purchased by said Nathaniel Manning from David Peterkin and wife, and containing 96 acres more or less. The said land is sold to said Manning by Polley Skinner Vinson, who is now between 16 and 21 years of age, with the consent of the said James Vinson her uncle and guardian. Witness: Thos. Barnett.

8 HD 96. November 11, 1794. James Vinson of Dorchester County, shipwright, to Nathaniel Manning of the same county, planter: part of "Deavors Choice" on Great Choptank River, containing 96 acres more or less. Witnesses: Levin Woolford, Thos. Barnett. Acknowledged before Levin Woolford and Thos. Barnett, Justices.

8 HD 99. November 11, 1794. Depositions of James Vinson and John LeCompte state that Polley Skinner Vinson is 16 years of age (in October last). Taken before Thos. Barnett, Justice.

8 HD 100. October 17, 1794. Philemon Brannock of Dorchester County to

James Cooper of the same county: part of "Harwoods Choice" on the north side of Church Creek or the southern branch of Fishing Creek, on Sloop Cove, containing 20 acres more or less. Witnesses: Moses LeCompte, Thos. Jones. Acknowledged by Philemon Brannock and Ann his wife before Moses LeCompte and Tho. Jones.

8 HD 104. August 6, 1794. George Slacum to William Sotherin: Bond re lease of land, livestock and slaves. Witnesses: Frederick Willey, Wm. Bramble. Proved by witnesses before Henry Lake. Assigned by Wm. Sotherin to Gabriel Slacum. Witness: Henry Lake.

8 HD 106. April 4, 1794. John Kirwan of Dorchester County to George Slacum of the same county: Bond to convey "Todds Point" on the east side of Fern Creek. Witnesses: Wm. Sotherin, David Tyler. Assigned by George Slacum to Wm. Sotherin. Witnesses: Wm. Bramble, Frederick Willey. Assignment proved by Wm. Bramble and Frederick Willey, witnesses, before Henry Lake.

8 HD 108. November 25, 1794. William Sotherin of Dorchester County to Gabriel Slacum of Worcester County: Crops and livestock. Witnesses: Isaac Andrews, Edwd. Staplefort. Acknowledged before Henry Lake, Justice.

8 HD 109. July 29, 1794. William Weems of Ann Arundel County to Levi Willen of Dorchester County: Part of a tract on Hoopers Strait called "Arthur and Betty," containing 229 acres more or less. Witnesses: Saml. Harrison, Thos. Tongue. Acknowledged by Wm. Weems and Rachel his wife before Saml. Harrison and Thos. Tongue, Justices for Ann Arundel County. Nich. Harwood, Clk.

8 HD 112. Decembe r 9, 1794. Levin Ross to Negro Ben and others: Manumission. Witnesses: Edwd. Pritchett, George Lake. Acknowledged before Henry Lake, Justice.

8 HD 113. December 15, 1794. Thomas Vickars of Dorchester County to Negro Sidney: Manumission. Witness: Levin Woolford. Acknowledged before Levin Woolford, Justice.

8 HD 114. July 24, 1794. Jonathan Brodess to William Scott: Receipt for purchase money for a Negro lad slave named Ezekiel, now in the service of Jonathan Bestpitch. Witness: Joseph Brodess.

8 HD 114. August 7, 1794. Henry Hooper Qs. of Dorchester County to William

Scott of the same county: lease of the dwelling plantation of said Henry Hooper, consisting of part of a tract called "Addition to Outlet" and a tract called "Porpeigham," with buildings. Betty is mentioned as wife of the said Hooper. Witnesses: Levin Ball, Richard Brodess.

8 HD 119. October 15, 1794. Francis Hayward of Dorchester County to John Elliott of the same county: "Utophia," according to patent. Witnesses: Jno. Stevens, Jno. Gooding. Acknowledged before Jno. Stevens and Jno. Gooding, Justices.

8 HD 121. June 24, 1794. George Brannock of Dorchester County to Philemon Brannock of the same county: part of "Harwoods Choice" on the north side of Church Creek, containing 33 acres more or less; and "Brannocks Point" adj. thereto, containing 2 3/4 acres by patent. Also "Timber Neck" or "Brannocks Regulation." Witnesses: Thos. Jones, Richd. Pattison. Acknowledged by George Brannock and Sidney his wife before Tho. Jones and Richd. Pattison.

8 HD 124. May 24, 1794. Ezekiel Mace, John Dorris and Angell his wife, all of Orange County, North Carolina, (the said Ezekiel and Angell being the only surviving children and heirs of Josias Mace late of Dorchester County, deceased), to "our uncle" Alexander Robbs of Orange County, planter: Power of Attorney re land on Blackwater called "Buttons Intent" and " Addition to Buttons Intent." Witnesses: Hardy Hurdle, Stephen Mureign, Jacob Morton. Wm. McCauley, Esq., one of the Justices of the County Court of Pleas and Quarter Sessions of Orange County, North Carolina. A. B. Bruce, Clk.

8 ED 126. June 28, 1794. Alexander Robbs of Orange County, North Carolina, Planter, Attorney for Ezekiel Mace, John Dorris and Angel his wife, to John King of Dorchester County, planter: "Buttons Intent," adj. "Cow Pasture" and containing 163 acres more or less. Witnesses: Tho. Jones, Jno. Keene. Acknowledged before Tho. Jones and John Keene, Justices.

8 HD 128. March 6, 1795. Levin Stevens of Dorchester County to Stanley Byus of the same county: Power of Attorney. Witnesses: Wm. B. Martin, Wm. Lockerman.

8 ED 130. September 5, 1794. Phillip LeCompte, Thomas LeCompte, Daniel LeCompte and Isaiah LeCompte of Dorchester County to Negro Jim: Manumission. Witness: Tho. Jones. Acknowledged before Tho. Jones, Justices.

8 HD 131. November 28, 1794. John Geoghegan to Negro slaves:

Manumission. Witnesses: Moses LeCompte, Nancy LeCompte. Acknowledged before Moses LeCompte.

8 HD 132. November 16, 1794. Standley Matkin of Dorchester County to David Sares of the same county: part of "Matkins Forrest" on the south side of White Marsh Branch, containing 110 acres more or less. Witnesses: Moses LeCompte, Richd. Pattison. Acknowledged by Standley Matkin and Elizabeth his wife before Richd. Pattison and Moses LeCompte.

8 HD 134. December 24, 1794. Charles Goldsborough Senr. of Dorchester County to Thomas Woolford of the same county: "Teverton" on Fishing Creek, containing 250 acres more. or less. Also "Addition to Teverton," containing 342 acres more or less. Also "Greens Adventure" and "Addition to Greens Adventure," also on Fishing Creek containing 14 acres more or less; and all other lands of the said Charles on Fishing Creek. Witnesses: Levin Woolford, Stanley Byus. Acknowledged by Charles Goldsborough and Elizabeth his wife before Levin Woolford and Stanley Byus, Justices.

8 HD 137. December 11, 1794. Abraham Lee to John Chairs: Receipt for purchase price of Mulatto man David. Witness: John Hubbard.

8 HD 137. December 11, 1794. John Chairs of Queen Anna County to Negro David: Manumission. Witnesses: Edward White Junr., Peter Webb. Acknowledged before Thomas Barnett, Justice.

8 HD 138. December 12, 1794. Thos. Corse to Negro Jacob: Manumission.

8 HD 139. October 11, 1794. John Dawson of Dorchester County, planter, to Charles LeCompte (son of Philemon) of the same county: part of "Dawsons Lott," containing 120 3/4 acres more or less. Also "Dawsons Security," containing 27 3/4 acres more or less. Also "Gift," containing 12 1/4 acres more or less. Witnesses: Jno. Stevens, Levin Woolford. Acknowledged by Jno. Dawson and Elizabeth his wife before Jno. Stevens and Levin Woolford, Justices.

8 HD 142. August 20, 1766. Risdon Bozman of Dorchester County, shipwright, to John Macnemara of the same county, planter: bond for conveyance by Bozman and his wife Betsey of a tract called "Bozmans Beginning" near the head of Coles Creek on Blackwater River, containing 12 ½ acres. Witnesses: John Cole, George Cole. Assigned December 11, 1779 by Jno. Macnemara to Thomas McNamara. Assigned June 24, 1794 by Thomas McNamara to Joseph

Andrews.

8 HD 143. August 10, 1794. Charles Shinton of Dorchester County to Nicey Lewis of the same county: Bond to convey unto his son George Lewis two tracts which he bought of Absolom Goostree and Benjamin Woollen, containing 114 acres more or less; and to convey to his other sons Raymond and Joseph Lewis and Dennis Booze all his other lands. Dezilla and Mary Lewis are sisters of Raymond and Joseph, and Teresa is sister of Dennis. Witnesses: Frederick Bennett, Richd. Tubman.

8 HD 145. July 6, 1793. James Busick to Thomas Fitchu and Sarah his wife: receipt for purchase price of 2 Negro slaves. Witnesses: Thos. Colsten, Job Slacum Junr.

8 HD 145. December 19, 1794. James Stoaks of Dorchester County to Robert Dennis and Thomas Hingson of the same county: livestock and furniture. Witnesses: Smith Goslen, Jacob Jacobs. Acknowledged before Jno. Crapper, Justice.

8 HD 147. January 6, 1795. John M. Stevens, Administrator of James Rule Stevens late of Dorchester County, deceased, to John Goldsborough of the same county: land in Cambridge, on the main street, adj. lands of Anne Muse and Robert Harrison, as described in deed from Nicholas Hammond to James Rule Stevens. Witnesses: Moses LeCompte, Levin Woolford. Acknowledged before Moses LeCompte and Levin Woolford, Justices.

8 HD 149. December 13, 1794. Daniel Harper of Dorchester County to Daniel Nicols of the same county: livestock, furniture, etc. Witnesses: Bartholo. Fletcher, James Sulivane. Acknowledged before Jno. Stevens, Justice.

8 HD 150. January 12, 1795. Thomas Stewart of Dorchester County, Weaver, to John Cook Stewart of the same county, planter: Furniture and tools. Witnesses: Levin Woolford, Thos. Stanford.

8 HD 151. January 12, 1795. Mary Trippe of Dorchester County to Negro slaves: Manumission. Witnesses: Jas. Kemp, J. E. Gist. Acknowledged before Levin Woolford, Justice.

8 HD 152. January 12, 1795. Ann Ennalls (Blackwater) of Dorchester County to Robert Harrison of the same county, Gent.: parts of "Murrays Friendship" and "Ennalls's Outrange" on a branch of Blackwater River, adj. "Perth" . Witnesses:

133

Jno. Stevens, Levin Woolford. Acknowledged before Jno. Stevens and Levin Woolford, Justices.

8 HD 155. January 12, 1795. Robert Harrison of Dorchester County, Gent., to Ann Ennalls, daughter of Ann Ennalls of Blackwater: parts of two tracts called "Murrays Friendship" and "Ennalls's Outrange" on a branch of Blackwater adj. "Perth" and containing 61 ½ acres. Witnesses: Jno. Stevens, Levin Woolford. Acknowledged before Jno. Stevens and Levin Woolford, Justices.

8 HD 157. January 19, 1795. Edward Wright to Negro Jack: Manumission, effective January 1, 1810 when Jack arrives at age 31. Witnesses: Richd. Pattison, Thomas Parrott. Acknowledged before Moses LeCompte, Justice.

8 HD 158. January 19, 1795. Edward Stephens and Thomas Stephens of Dorchester County to Levin Stephens of the same county: "Labrook Regulated," formerly granted to a certain Edward Stephens by patent; "Roopers Outlett"; a tract called "the Outlett" formerly granted to William Stephens by patent; "LaBrook"; part of "Exchange" not devised by Edward Stephens deceased, father of the parties to these presents, "except that part which lies in the prong of the branch that runs toward Henry Hoopers Qs. & that lies between Benjamin Keene and Edward Stephens afores'd."; also part of "Good Luck" on Cooleys Branch, containing 126 acres. Witnesses: Levin Woolford, Richd. Pattison. Acknowledged before Levin Woolford and Richd. Pattison.

8 HD 161. January 19, 1795. Edward Stephens and Levin Stephens of Dorchester County, planters, to Thomas Stephens of the same county, planter: part of 'Good Luck" on Cooleys Branch, adj. "Johns Labour" and containing 292 acres. Witnesses: Richd. Pattison, Levin Woolford. Acknowledged before Richd. Pattison and Levin Woolford, Justices.

8 HD 163. January 19, 1795. Levin Stephens and Thomas Stephens, both of Dorchester County, planters, to Edward Stephens of the same county, planter: "Chiltenham" on Transquakin River, formerly granted to Edward Stephens by patent; a tract called "Pauls"; part of a tract called "Good Luck" containing 75 acres; and part of "the Exchange" not devised by the late Edward Stephens, "lying in the North prong of Beaver branch which runs towards Henry Hooper Qs. and between Edward Stephens party to these presents and Benjamin Keene." Witnesses: Levin Woolford, Richd. Pattison. Acknowledged before Levin Woolford and Richd. Pattison, Justices.

8 HD 165. January 22, 1795. Certificate of Levin Woolford concerning a black

horse taken up by George Ward Esq. as a stray.

8 HD 166. January 26, 1795. Daniel Paul of Dorchester County to Nehemiah Lingrell of the same county: livestock, furniture, etc. Witnesses: Jno. Stevens, Thomas Marshall. Acknowledged before Jno. Stevens, Justice.

8 HD 167. December 17, 1794. Henry Steele of Dorchester County to Samuel Rust: Negro girl named Cloe, aged about 14 years. Witness: Isaac Steele.

8 HD 168. Certificate of John Twyford re Negro girl named Leah, devised by John Crockett of Sussex County, Delaware by Last Will and Testament dated June 24, 1780 and recorded January 2, 1780 to his wife Mary, who has since intermarried with John Twyford of Maryland.

8 HD 169. February 2, 1795. John Maguire of Dorchester County to James Steele and Mary his wife: "Exchange," resurveyed May 1, 1794 for the said John Maguire adj. "Daniels Hellicon," "Sarah Land," "Fishwicks Adventure" and "Johns Industry" and containing 34 acres. Witnesses: Jno. Stevens, Levin Woolford. Acknowledged by John Maguire and Sarah his wife to Mary Steele, wife of James Steele, before Jno. Stevens and Levin Woolford, Justices.

8 HD 171. January 21, 1795. John Griffith of Dorchester County to Richard Dean of the same county: Bond re title to three Negro slaves. Witnesses: Gabriel Slacum, Edward Griffith.

8 HD 172. January 21, 1795. Richard Dean of Dorchester County to John Griffith of the same county: Bond re title to three Negro slaves. Witnesses: Gabriel Slacum, Edward Griffith.

8 HD 173. August 8, 1794. George Slacum of Dorchester County to William Sotherin of the same county: Negro slaves. Witnesses: Frederick Willey, William Bramble. Proved by witnesses before Henry Lake. Assigned by William Sotherin to Nathan Levering, by Nathan Levering to Henry Lake, by Henry Lake to Naboth Hart and by Naboth Hart to John Griffith.

8 HD 176. February 3, 1795. Levi Robinson of Dorchester County to Negro slaves Jim and Lydia, both of whom formerly belonged to Henry Hooper Qs.: Manumission. Witnesses: George Ward, Peggy Cox. Acknowledged before Moses LeCompte, Justice.

8 HD 176. October 22, 1792. William Bond and John Eccleston of Dorchester

County to James Steele: Bond. Witnesses: Thos. Smith, Robt. Sulivane.

8 HD 177. February 7, 1795. Nathan Stevens of Dorchester County to Ezekiel Vickars Junr. of the same county: "Stevens's Venture," adj. "Deans Chance" and containing 18 3/4 acres more or less. Witnesses: Moses LeCompte, Richd. Pattison. Acknowledged before Moses LeCompte and Richd. Pattison.

8 HD 179. January 27, 1795. Levin Hodson and Hannah his wife of Dorchester County to John Giffin of the same county: land left to said Hannah Hodson by her father William Hayward by his Last Will and Testament. Witnesses: Jno. Stevens, Jno. Gooding. Acknowledged before Jno. Stevens and Jno. Gooding, Justices.

8 HD 181. February 10, 1795. Thomas Corse to John Giffin: Negro slave, livestock, furniture, etc. Witnesses: Jno. Stevens, Jno. Crapper. Acknowledged before Jno. Crapper and Jno. Stevens, Justices.

8 HD 182. December 26, 1794. Richard Wallace of Dorchester County, Gent., to Matthew Turnbull of the same county: part of "Wallaces Addition" containing 6 acres more or less. Witnesses: Moses LeCompte, Henry Lake. Acknowledged before Moses LeCompte and Henry Lake, Justices.

8 HD 185. December 26, 1794. Matthew Turnbull of Dorchester County to Levin Keene of the same county: part of "Wallaces Addition," containing ½ acre more or less. This deed and receipt for purchase money are signed by Levin Keene. Witnesses: Moses LeCompte, Henry Lake. Acknowledged by Matthew Turnbull before Moses LeCompte and Henry Lake, Justices.

8 HD 188. December 27, 1794. Levin Keene of Dorchester County to Matthew Turnbull of the same county: part of "Keenes Regulation," containing 2 3/4 acres more or less. This deed and receipt for purchase money are signed by Matthew Turnbull. Witnesses: Moses LeCompte, Henry Lake. Acknowledged by Levin Keene before Moses LeCompte and Henry Lake, Justices.

8 HD 191. October 8, 1794. Thomas Nicols of Caroline County, Mcht., to Mark Noble of Dorchester County: part of "Addition to Rawley," containing 42 1/4 acres more or less. Witnesses: Joseph Douglass, Joseph Nicols. Acknowledged before Joseph Douglass and Joseph Nicols, Justices for Caroline County. Tho. Richardson, Clk.

8 HD 194. March 18, 1795. William Vickars 2nd to the State of Maryland:

Bond as Inspector of Tobacco at White's Warehouse, with Henry Lake and Edward Stephens as sureties. Witnesses: Edward Smith, Wm. LeCompte Junr. Proved by witnesses before Levin Woolford.

8 HD 195. March 31, 1795. John Smith to the State of Maryland: Bond as Inspector of Tobacco, with Jno. Eccleston and Thomas Smith as sureties. Witnesses: John Muir, James Roney. Proved by witnesses before Jno. Reed and David Smith, Justices.

8 HD 196. October 30, 1794. Isaac Nicols, Thomas Nicols and Jeremiah Nicols of Caroline County to Mark Noble of Dorchester County: part of "Addition to Rawley" on the road dividing Dorchester and Caroline Counties, containing 55 acres ½ more or less. Also part of "Addition to Rawley" between Thomas Nicols' sawmill and where Samuel McGee lives, containing 5 acres more or less. Witnesses: Joseph Douglass, Joseph Nicols. Acknowledged by Isaac, Thomas, and Jeremiah Nicols and by Sualy Nicols, wife of said Isaac, before Joseph Douglass and Joseph Nicols, Justices for Caroline County. Tho. Richardson, Clk.

8 ED 200. February 21, 1795. Mary Beard to Negro Charles: Manumission. Witnesses: Hooper Eucim, Henry Arnett. Acknowledged before Levin Woolford, Justice.

8 ED 201. February 2, 1795. James Steele and Mary his wife of Dorchester County to John Maguire of the same county: part of "Daniels Helicon," containing 48 acres more or less. Witnesses: Jno. Stevens, Levin Woolford. Acknowledged before Jno. Stevens and Levin Woolford, Justices.

8 HD 203. February 21, 1795. Rachel Phillips of Dorchester County to William Insley of the same county "Originall Outlett," "Raccoon Ridge" and "Partnership." Witnesses: Jno. Keene, Henry Lake. Acknowledged before Jno. Keene and Henry Lake Justices.

8 HD 204. February 23, 1795. Levin LeCompte to Negro slaves: Manumission. Witnesses: Thomas Lockerman Jr., Stephen LeCompte. Acknowledged before Levin Woolford, Justice.

8 ED 205. February 23, 1795. Walter Rawley of Dorchester County to Negro slaves: Manumission. Witnesses: Jno. Tootell, Geo. Ward. Acknowledged before Jno. Stevens, Justice.

8 HD 206. February 23, 1795. Stephen LeCompte of Dorchester County to Negro slaves: Manumission. Witnesses: Geo. Ward, Levin LeCompte. Acknowledged before Jno. Stevens, Justice.

8 HD 207. July 31, 1794. Agreement between Jonathan Patridge and Benjamin Keene re sale of part of "Buckfield" by said Patridge to said Keene, adj. part of the same tract sold by Patridge to John Scott. Witness: Saml. W. Pitt.

8 HD 208. February 2, 1795. Jonathan Patridge of Dorchester County to Benjamin Keene of the sarre county: part of "Buckfield" on the road from the upper bridge of Blackwater to Halls Branch, adj. "Ecclestons Regulation Rectified," adj. lands of Edward Brodess and John Brierwood, and containing 70 acres more or less. Witnesses: Jno. Stevens, Levin Woolford. Acknowledged before Jno. Stevens and Levin Woolford, Justices.

8 HD 212. November 6, 1794. James Shaw of Talbot County, trustee appointed by the Chancellor of Maryland to sell the real estate of Cuthbert Heron late of Dorchester County deceased, to Alexander Douglass of Dorchester County: lot in Vienna. Witnesses: David Smith, John Reed. Acknowledged before David Smith and John Reed, Justices.

8 HD 214. February 17, 1795. Benjamin Travers of Colberd County to Thomas Travers of Dorchester County: Negro slave named Jacob. Witnesses: Travers Tolley, Matthew Travers.

8 HD 215. February 26, 1795. William Bramble of Dorchester County to John Griffith of the same county: Negro girl slave about 12 years old, named Love. Witness: Henry Lake. Acknowledged before Henry Lake, Justice.

8 HD 216. February 17, 1795. Levin Fitzhugh of Dorchester County to Ezekiel Jones of the same county: part of two tracts called "Sheep Pasture" and "Addition to Sheep Pasture," containing 20 3/4 acres more or less. Witnesses: Tho. Jones, John Williams. Acknowledged by Levin Fitzhugh and Sarah his wife before Tho. Jones and Jno. Williams, Justices.

8 HD 218. January 21, 1795. Clement Vickars of Dorchester County to John Colston of the same county: part of "Preston" or "North and South Preston" on the east side of Little Choptank River and the North side of Vickars's Creek. Witnesses: Richd. PattisonJ Levin Woolford. Acknowledged before Levin Woolford and Richd. Pattison, Justices.

8 HD 221. September 11, 1794. Thomas McCrackin of Clark County, Kentucky to Peter Rich of Caroline County: part of a tract formerly called "Haywards Lott" but since resurveyed by Anthony Dawson and called "Dawsons Lott," on the road from the two bridges to the County School, containing 20 acres more or less. Also part of "Exchange" adj. the free school land and containing 65 ½ acres more or less. Witnesses: Wm. Whiteley, James Dixon. Acknowledged before William Whiteley and James Dixon, Justices for Caroline County. Tho. Richardson, Clk.

8 HD 224. February 7, 1795. Robert Stewart of Dorchester County to Vachel Keene of the same county: personal property. Witnesses: Levin Woolford, Francis Roberts. Acknowledged before Levin Woolford, Justice.

8 HD 225. March 3, 1767. Matthew Bright of Dorchester County, planter, to Robert Wilson of the same county: lands in Potters Neck on a branch of Blackwater River, called "Grove" (containing 40 ½ acres) and "White Oak Range" (containing 33 acres). Witnesses: Henry Hooper, Wm. Ennalls. Acknowledged before Henry Hooper, Justice of Provincial Court.

8 HD 229. March 12, 1795. John Muir of Dorchester County to William Winder of the same county: Negro slave named Draper, aged about 14 years. Witness: Alexr. Smith. Acknowledged before John Reed, Justice.

8 HD 230. March 6, 1795. Levi Insley of Dorchester County to Crissey Insley: personal property. Witness: Henry Lake. Acknowledged before Henry Lake, Justice.

8 HD 232. March 6, 1795. Levi Insley of Dorchester County to Althadora Insley: livestock, furniture and cider casks. Witness: Henry Lake. Acknowledged before Henry Lake, Justice.

8 HD 233. February 21, 1795. Levi Insley of Dorchester County to Letisha Insley: one heifer. Witness: Henry Lake. Acknowledged before Henry Lake, Justice.

8 HD 234. March 6, 1795. Levi Insley of Dorchester County to Leah Insley: livestock and other personal property. Witness: Henry Lake. Acknowledged before Henry Lake.

8 HD 235. February 21, 1795. Levi Insley and William Insley of Dorchester County to Althadora Insley of the same county: part of "Andrews Fortune"

between "Bettys Lot" and "Goose Creek Swamp." Witnesses: Jno. Keene, Henry Lake. Acknowledged before John Keene and Henry Lake, Justices.

8 HD 238. March 17, 1794 - September 5, 1794. Commission to Thomas Jones, Richard Pattison, Solomon Frazier and Arthur Whiteley of Dorchester County, Gent., to perpetuate bounds of Thomas LeCompte's land called "St. Anthonys," on Great Choptank River, and Return. Deposition of Joseph LeCompte, of full age, mentions his grandmother Mary LeCompte who showed him a bounder of St. Anthonys about 60 years ago. Also mentions his uncle Moses. Deposition of John Jones, of full age. Deposition of Ann Wingate, of full age. Deposition of Moses LeCompte, of full age who was present with the Commissioners on said land about 26 years ago.

8 HD 242. October 28, 1794. Levin Traverse and Mary his wife of Dorchester County to Charles Shenton of the same county: land on Hoopers Island called "Lower Island Regulated" (1/5 interest devised to said Levin Traverse by Last Will and Testament of Levin Traverse deceased). Witnesses: Tho. Jones, Jno. Keene. Acknowledged before Tho. Jones and Jno. Keene, Justices.

8 HD 245. March 6, 1795. John Riddle of Dorchester County to John Campbell of Dorchester County: Negro slaves. Witness: David Smith. Acknowledged before David Smith, Justice.

8 HD 246. March 17, 1795. Margaret Davis of Dorchester County, widow, to Nehemiah Whiteley of the same county, planter: "Fishers Chance" on Blackwater River, adj. "Tarcells Neck" and containing 250 acres more or less. Witnesses: Jno. Stevens, David Smith. Acknowledged before Jno. Stevens and David Smith, Justices.

8 HD 248. March 17, 1795. Charles Stewart of Dorchester County to Nehemiah Whiteley and William Whittington of Dorchester County: Negro slaves, livestock and other personal property. Witnesses: Jno. Stevens, Jno. Laing. Acknowledged before Jno. Stevens, Justice.

8 HD 249. March 17, 1795. Major John Hooper of Dorchester County to Matthew Traverse of the same county: part of a tract called "Hoopers Island" on Hungar River and Cedar Point, containing 203 ½ acres. Witnesses: Richd. Pattison, Levin Woolford. Acknowledged by John Hooper and Elizabeth his wife before Richd. Pattison and Levin Woolford, Justices.

8 HD 254. "Dorchester County Sst. 16th November 1793. I Nicey Lewis do

hereby agree and give my consent that Charles Shenton may marry whom he pleases and when he pleases As Witness my hand the day and year aforesaid.

her
Nicey W Lewis"
mark

Witness: Richd. Tubman. "I do hereby Testify to have joined in the bands of Matrimony Charles Shenton and Elizabeth Booze the Nineteenth day of November one Thousand seven hundred and ninety three, being present, Ann Tubman, Mary Tubman and Henry Phillips. Given under my hand this seventeenth day of January one Thousand seven hundred and Ninety five -

Charles Wheelan
Cath. Pst ."

8HD 254. February 5, 1795. Henry Hodson Senr. of Dorchester County, farmer, to Doctor Wm. Winder of the same county: lease of a lot in Vienna between the house of Susannah Jones and Alexander Douglass's Tavern, now occupied by John Reed, Esq. Witnesses: John Reed, David Smith. Acknowledged before John Reed and David Smith, Justices.

8 HD 256. February 21, 1795. Abraham Mister of Dorchester County to Joseph Wheeler of the same county: part of a tract called "Long Acre" on the east side of Hungar River and the west side of Charles Creek, containing 51 acres more or less. Witnesses: Jno. Keene, Henry Lake. Acknowledged before Jno. Keene and Henry Lake, Justices.

8 HD 258. March 19, 1795. William Vaughn of Dorchester County to Negro Esther: Manumission. Witnesses: Richd. Pattison, Marcellus Slacum. Acknowledged before Richd. Pattison, Justice.

8 HD 259. March 12, 1795. John Muir of Dorchester County to Alexander Douglass of the same county: Negro man named George, about 23 years of age. Witness: Jno. Reed. Acknowledged before Jno. Reed, Justice.

8 HD 260. March 12, 1795. John Muir of Dorchester County to John Henry of the same county: silver plate, slaves and furniture. Witnesses: David Smith, Jno. Reed. Acknowledged before Jno. Reed and David Smith, Justices.

8 HD 262. March 12, 1795. John Muir of Dorchester County to John Henry of the same county: "Partnership" containing 506 acres more or less; and "Support" containing 45 acres more or less. (Mortgage). Witnesses: Jno. Reed, David Smith. Acknowledged before John Reed and David Smith, Justices.

8 HD 264. March 14, 1795. Jacob Wright to Negro slaves: Manumission. Witnesses: Medford Andrews, Fras. Rowins. Acknowledged before Jno. Gooding, Justice.

8 HD 265. August 23, 1793. Jeremiah Pattison of Dorchester County to David Sare of the same county: part of "Pattisons Privilege" on Slaughter Creek, adj. "Davids Chance," adj. land of John Brohawn and containing 9 3/4 acres. Witnesses: Moses LeCompte, Richd. Pattison. Acknowledged before Moses LeCompte and Richd. Pattison, Justices.

8 HD 268. November 17, 1794. David Sares of Dorchester County to Standley Matkin of the same county: part of "Cupids Folly," part of "Pleasant Grove," part of "Davids Chance" and part of "Pattisons Privilege" except the part sold to John Brohawn; all lying on Slaughter Creek, where said David Sares now lives. Witnesses: Moses LeCompte, Richd. Pattison. Acknowledged before Richd. Pattison and Moses LeCompte.

8 HD 269. February 21, 1795. Mary Woodland, widow of Richard, of Dorchester County to John Starling Woodland of the same county: "Hansteed" on a branch of Fern Creek, near John Wingate's land called "Head of Firm," containing 50 acres more or less. Witnesses: Jno. Keene, Henry Lake. Acknowledged before Jno. Keene and Henry Lake, Justices.

8 HD 272. November 1, 179-. Articles of Agreement between W. V. Murray and Triffany Hammond, both of Dorchester County, re lease by said Murray to the said Triffany Hammond of a house and lot near Cambridge where said Triffany now lives. Witness: John Murray.

8 HD 273. March 23, 1795. David Dean of Caroline County to John Green of Dorchester County: 19 1/4 acres of "Deans Discovery." Witnesses: Richd. Pattison, Jno. Gooding. Acknowledged before Richd. Pattison and Jno. Gooding.

8 HD 276. March 13, 1795. Nehemiah Whiteley of Dorchester County, planter, to Woolford Stewart of the same county, Blacksmith: part of "Fishers Chance" on Blackwater River, adj. "Tarcells Neck" and containing 200 acres. Witnesses: Richd. Pattison, Levin Woolford. Acknowledged by Nehemiah Whiteley and Rosannah his wife before 1 Richd. Pattison and Levin Woolford, Justices.

8 ED 279. January 27, 1795 Levin Hodson, Hannah Hodson his wife and Charles Hodson of Dorchester County to Anthony Manning of the same county:

part of "Hodsons Seat," adj. "Addition to Rockahook" and containing 200 acres; also part of "Turkey Land," containing 19 ½ acres. Witnesses: Jno. Gooding, Jno. Stevens. Acknowledged before Jno. Gooding and Jno. Stevens, Justices.

8 HD 283. January 27, 1795. Jonathan Ward of Dorchester County to Anthony Manning of the same county part of "Addition to Haywards Farme," adj. Beaverdam Range" and "McDaniels Desire" and containing 3 3/4 acres. Witnesses: Jno. Stevens, Jno. Gooding. Acknowledged before Jno. Stevens and Jno. Gooding, Justices.

8 HD 287. April 14, 1795. Roger Woolford Junior of Dorchester County to Thomas Cook of the same county: "Brannocks Addition" on the north side of Little Choptank River, adj. "Winfields Trouble" and containing 104 acres more or less; also "Barren Ridge," adj. Edward Dawson's land, on Hodsons Creek and containing 87 acres more or less. Levin Woolford and Jno. Williams, Justices.

8 HD 289. March 23, 1795. Levin Jones to Negro slaves: Manumission. Witnesses: Charles K. Bryan, George Ward. Acknowledged before Richd. Pattison.

8 HD 290. March 30, 1795. Certificate of Howes Goldsborough, son of John Goldsborough, re Negro, slaves moved by him from Delaware into Maryland.

8 HD 291. February 11, 1795. John Dossey to Negro slaves: Manumission. Witnesses: Moses LeCompte, Richard Keene. Acknowledged before Moses LeCompte, Justice.

8 HD 291. April 14, 1795. Rebecca Murray to Negro slaves: Manumission. Witnesses: W. V. Murray, Levin Woolford. Acknowledged before Levin Woolford, Justice.

8 HD 292. March 18, 1795. Levin Kirkman, Administrator DBN of Levin Kirkman late of Dorchester County, to William Stoddart Bond of Talbot County: Assignment of Kirkman's interest in a suit now depending in the High Court of Chancery against Alex Smith of Dorchester County for moneys due "my late father." Witnesses: Salathiel Fitchett, Thomas Fitchett.

8 HD 293. Copy of Judgment, Levin Kirkman vs. Alexander Smith. Witnesses: Elizabeth Messick, Elizabeth Howeth. James Earle Junr., Clk. of General Court of the Eastern Shore.

8HD 295. May 16, 1795. Peter Ferguson of the town of Cambridge, Mcht., and John Finley of the town of Cambridge, Dealer and Chapman, to Thomas Lockerman of the same town, Gent.: Whereas the said John Finley has named Robert Henderson and the said Peter Ferguson as his Attorneys under Power of Attorney dated November 29, 1792; whereas the Justices of Dorchester County on June 14, 1788 did lease unto Patrick Ewing for the term of 99 years renewable, a part of the prison lands in Cambridge, and whereas Robert Ewing, Administrator of said Patrick Ewing, has conveyed the said Patrick's leasehold estate to the aforesaid Finley, Finley and his attorney hereby sell and convey the said leasehold to Thomas Lockerman. Witnesses: Levin Woolford, Richd. Pattison. Acknowledged before Richd. Pattison and Levin Woolford, Justices.

8 HD 298. May 18, 1795. Thomas E. Hooper of Dorchester County, planter, and Sarah his wife to Jacob Wright of the same county, planter: land in Northwest Fork Hundred, called "Bradford," containing 180 acres. Witnesses: Jno. Gooding, Charles Adams. Acknowledged before Jno. Gooding and Chas. Adams, Justices.

8 HD 301. May 14, 1795. Thomas Smith of Dorchester County to John Reed of the same county: part of a tract called "Smiths Industry" at the fork of the roads from Vienna to Newmarket and from Vienna to Crotchers Ferry, containing 4 acres more or less. Witnesses: Jno. Eccleston, David Smith. Acknowledged before Jno. Eccleston and David Smith, Justices.

8 HD 305. April 7, 1795. Agreement of Henry Ennalls concerning manumission of a Negro slave named Jacob, bought from Edward Cole. Witness: Henry Haskins.

8 HD 305. May 9, 1795. William Sotherin of Dorchester County to John Griffith of the same county: Negro slaves. Witnesses: Jacob Todd, Phillip Grayham. Acknowledged before Henry Lake, Justice.

8 HD 307. March 30, 1795. Thomas Green and Peggy his wife of Dorchester County to Francis Turpin of the same county: "Bartlett Meadows," patented to William Bartlett August 4, 1757, containing 60 acres more or less. Also "Addition to Bartletts Meadows" adj. thereto, patented to Ezekiel Goslin November 11, 1769 for 32 ½ acres, excepting 1 acre within the lines of an elder survey called "Wrights Third Purchase." Also part of "Adams's Dear Purchase" containing 24 acres according to deed of December 6, 1768 from Handy Tull and wife to Ezekiel Goslin, excepting ½ acre within an elder survey called "Addition to Luck." Witnesses: Jno. Crapper, Chas. Adams. Acknowledged

before Jno. Crapper and Chas. Adams, Justices.

8 HD 311. May 23, 1795. McKeel Connerly of Dorchester County to James Payne of the same place: part of "Norrage" on the west side of the Northwest Fork of Nanticoke, adj. 100 acres of the same tract heretofore conveyed by Thomas Connerly to George Waters, and containing 9 ½ acres more or less. Witnesses: Jno. Crapper, Chas. Adams. Acknowledged by McKeel Connerly and Rebecca his wife before Jno. Crapper and Chas. Adams, Justices.

8 HD 315. March 31, 1795. William Waters of Somerset County Gent., to James Payne of Dorchester County: part of "Norrage" formerly conveyed by Thomas Connerly and Nancy his wife to George Waters for 100 acres. Also 176 acres, part of "Security to Pains Point." Also three separate parts of "Nancys Purchase," containing 11 1/4 acres, 81 ½ acres and 145 3/4 acres. Witnesses: John Reed, David Smith. Acknowledged before John Reed and David Smith, Justices.

8 HD 322. March 31, 1795. James Payne of Dorchester County, Gent., to Joshua Noble of the same county, planter: part of "Nancys Purchase" containing 18 3/4 acres; and part of "Security to Pains Point" containing 106 acres more or less. Witnesses: John Reed, David Smith. Acknowledged by James Payne and Elizabeth his wife before John Reed and David Smith, Justices.

8 HD 327. May 15, 1795. Moses Geoghegan to Negro Jim: Manumission. Witnesses: Moses LeCompte, Rosanna Granger. Acknowledged before Moses LeCompte,

8 HD 329. May 23, 1795. Thomas Kallender of Dorchester County to John Dorsey, William Geoghegan, Capewell Keene, John Fooks, Ezekiel Vickars, Henry Ennalls, Levin Keene, Ezekiel Johnson and Thomas Brierwood, Trustees for the Methodist Church: part of "White Haven" at the head of Church Creek, containing ½ acre, for a Meeting House. Witnesses: Moses LeCompte, Jno. Williams. Acknowledged by Thomas Kallender and Katharine his wife before Jno. Williams and Moses LeCompte, Justices.

8 HD 332. May 27, 1795. James Arnett of Casuel County, North Carolina, to Moses Martin of Dorchester County: part of "Bell Field" on the road from Cambridge to the head of Fishing Creek, near the Presbyterian Meeting House, containing one acre more or less . Witnesses: Thomas Jones, Jno. Williams. Acknowledged before Thos. Jones and Jno. Williams, Justices.

8 HD 335. May 30, 1795. William Phillips of Dorchester County, planter, to John Kirwan Taylor of the same county: "Rich Ridge" in Meekins Neck, on the road to Gadds Ferry, containing 50 acres more or less. Witnesses: Henry Lake, John Keene. Acknowledged before Henry Lake and John Keene, Justices.

8 HD 337. May 28, 1795. John Kirwan, "Taylor," of Dorchester County, to Henry Travers Phillips of the same county: part of a tract called "Taylors Addition to Rich Ridge" in Meekins Neck, containing 3 acres and 15 perches more or less. Witnesses: John Keene, Jno. Crapper. Acknowledged by John Kirwan and Bartholough (Barthuly) his wife before Jno. Keene and Jno. Crapper, Justices.

8 HD 342. March 31, 1795. Daniel Nicolls of Dorchester County, Gent., to Samuel Wright of the same county: part of "Hampton," adj. "Brills Hope" and containing 87 1/4 acres more or less; and part of "Addition" adj. the said part of "Hampton" and containing 31 1/4 acres more or less. Witnesses: Jno. Stevens, Jno. Gooding. Acknowledged before Jno. Stevens and Jno. Gooding, Justices.

8 HD 346. February 6, 1795. Agreement between James LeCompte and William LeCompte concerning a road across James' land. Witness: Hy. Waggaman.

8 HD 347. April 1795. James McCollister of Dorchester County to Thomas Anderson of the same county: livestock, furniture and other personal property. Witnesses: Jno. Stevens. Jno. M. Stevens. Acknowledged before Jno. Stevens.. Justice.

8 HD 349. April 20, 1795 James Sulivane of Dorchester County. Gent. to William Bingham of Philadelphia, Pennsylvania. Mcht., and Robert Gilmor of Baltimore, Maryland, Mcht.: "Littletons Last Shift," containing 100 acres more or less granted to Edmond Littleton; "Addition to York" containing 20 acres more or less, granted to Daniel Sulivane; two parts of "New Market" containing 216 acres in the first part, the second part adj. "Melvills Meadows" and containing 13 ½ acres. (Mortgage). Witnesses: Jno. Stevens.. Richd. Pattison. Acknowledged before Jno. Stevens and Richd. Pattison, Justices.

8 HD 356. May 18, 1795. Dorsey Wyvill, Doctor, to Thomas Colsten, Carpenter, both of Dorchester County: part of "White Haven" on the north side of Church Creek, conveyed to said Wyvill by Thomas Thompson and Prissillah his wife, containing one acre more or less. Witnesses: Henry Lake, Jno. Williams. Acknowledged by Dorsey Wyvill and Sarah his wife before Henry Lake and Jno. Williams, Justices.

8 HD 359. May 28, 1795. John Laing of Dorchester County to Alexander Smith of the same county: Negro girl named Sall, about 9 years of age. Witness: Jno. Reed. Acknowledged before Jno. Reed, Justice.

8 HD 360. March 23, 1795. Anne Muse of the Town of Cambridge to Nathan Breerwood of the same county: "Stanfords Chance," on the west side of Jonathan Bestpitch's land and containing 154 acres more or less. Witnesses: Jno. Stevens, Richd. Pattison. Acknowledged before Jno. Stevens and Richd. Pattison, Justices.

8 HD 363. May 2, 1776. John Ross of Dorchester County to Beauchamp Harper of the same county: Bond to convey parts of "Cumberland," "Rosse' s Lott," "Increase" and "Harpers Folly." Witnesses: Spencer Waters, Ambros Goslen, Matthew Smith Junr.

8 HD 365. June 15, 1795. Thos. Colsten, Carpenter, to Thos. Kallender, shipwright: part of "Tootels Venture," containing 115 3/4 acres. Witnesses: Jno. Williams, John Keene. Acknowledged before Jno. Williams and John Keene, Justices.

8 HD 368. June 15, 1795. Thomas Kallender of Dorchester County, ship carpenter, to William Buchanan and William Bond of Talbot County: "Chance" on the North west Branch of Blackwater River, at Southeys Creek, adj. "Butens Desire" taken up by Joseph Meekins and conveyed by him to said Kallender, containing 149 acres more or less. Also part of "Tootels Venture," containing 115-3/4 acres more or le ss. (Mortgage). Witnesses: John Keene, Jno. Williams. Acknowledged before John Keene and Jno. Williams, Justices.

8 HD 373. June 15, 1795. Record of the marks on the livestock of Elizabeth Hayes.

8 HD 373. June 15, 1795. John Tootell to the State of Maryland: Bond with Charles Hodson and Thos. Hicks as Sureties. Witnesses: W. M. Robertson, J. E. Gist. Sworn to by witnesses before Thos. Jones.

8 HD 374. May 30, 1795. David Moore of Dorchester County from John Kirwan of the same A county: part of "Dispute" near the head of Edgars Creek, containing 26 1/4 acres and part of "Horsey Downs" and part of the resurvey on !4 "Horsey Downs," containing 24 acres more or less. Witnesses: John Keene, Henry Lake. Acknowledged by John Kirwan and Sarah his wife before John Keene and Henry Lake, Justices.

8 HD 377. June 6, 1795. Jacob Insley and Keziah his wife of Sussex County, Delaware, to Henry Lake of Dorchester County: part of a tract called "Andrews Desire" that Summer Adams devised to his daughter Nancy by Last Will and Testament, on the road from the lower Chapel to Hoopers Straits, adj. lands of Solomon Woodland and Henry Lake on Charles Creek and containing 100 acres more or less. It is provided that John Woodland is to have the free use of said land as life tenant during his natural life. Witnesses: Jno. Crapperl David Smith. Acknowledged before Jno. Crapper and David Smithl Justices.

8 HD 380. May 22, 1795. Bartholomew Byus of Dorchester County, Mariner, and Joseph Byus of Calvert County, Mcht. to James Byus of Charles County, Mcht.: part of "Black Water Range," containing 250 acres. Witnesses: Tho. Parran, Joseph Byus, Moses Rawlings. Acknowledged before Tho. Parran and Joseph Byus, Justices for Calvert County. J. Morsell, Clk.

8 HD 383. June 14, 1795. William M. Robinson of Cambridge to William B. Martin of the same town: lease of a lot in Cambridge with the houses thereon. Witness: Jno. Murray.

8 HD 385. January 1, 1795. Jonathan Patridge to John Breerwood: Bond to convey part of "Buckfield," containing 6 3/4 acres. Witnesses: Woolford Stewart, Celia Staplefort.

8 HD 387. June 22, 1795. Peter Rea of Cambridge and Sarah his wife to William Goldsborough of the same place: part of "Lockermans Regulation" near the town of Cambridge. Witnesses: Jno. Stevens, Levin Woolford. Acknowledged before Jno. Stevens and Levin Woolford, Justices.

8 HD 390. June 22, 1795. William Goldsborough of Dorchester County and Sarah his wife to Peter Rea of the same county: part of "Ennalls's Outrange" purchased by said William Goldsborough from William Vans Murray and Charlotte his wife by deed dated September 15, 1794, containing 6 acres more or less. Witnesses: Jno. Stevens, Levin Woolford. Acknowledged before Jno. Stevens and Levin Woolford, Justices.

8 HD 394. June 24, 1795. Archibald Moncrieff of Baltimore Town, survivor of Charles Crookshanks, to Charles K. Bryan of Dorchester County: lot in Cambridge, adj. lands of Thomas Stewart, Jame s Conden and Mrs. Muse, and on the main street, sold in accordance with the Last Will and Testament of Archibald Pattison deceased. Witnesses: Robert Dorsey, Mark M. Pringle. Acknowledged before Thoroughgood Smith and James Calhoun, Justices for

Baltimore County. Wm. Gibson, Clk.

8 HD 397. March 23, 1795. Zebulon Mitchell and Sarah his wife of Dorchester County, planters, to Peter Ferguson of the same county, Mcht.: land on the south side of the main road from Cambridge to Elizabeth Glover's dwelling plantation, containing 2 acres more or less. Witnesses: Jno. Stevens, Richd. Pattison. Acknowledged before Jno. Stevens and Richd. Pattison, Justices.

8 HD 399. June 22, 1795. Jane Blair of Cambridge, widow and Administratrix of John Blair deceased, to Peter Ferguson of the same town, Mcht.: Lot No.4 of the Prison lands, leased by the Justices of Dorchester County to Ann Smith, and sold by said Ann Smith to William Tucker and by Wm. Tucker to John Blair deceased. Witnesses: Jno. Stevens, Levin Woolford. Acknowledged before Levin Woolford and Jno. Stevens, Justices.

8 HD 403. June 6, 1795. Brigs Navey of Dorchester County to John Brohawn of the same county: part of "Laks Discovery" on a line formerly a division between Henry Navey and Thos. Phillips, containing 29 acres more or less. Witnesses: Moses LeCompte, Richd. Pattison. Acknowledged by Brigs Navey and Kesiah his wife before Moses LeCompte and Richd. Pattison, Justices.

8 HD 405. June 9, 1795. Mary Woodland of Dorchester County to William L. Dodge of the same county: Negro woman named Sarah. Witnesses: William Lake, Levin Lake.

8 HD 406. June 24, 1795. Archibald Moncrieff, surviving trustee of Archibald Pattison, to James Condon of Cambridge: lot in Cambridge on the main street, adj. lands of Charles Goldsborough, Charles K. Bryan and Ann Muse, also adj. the lot sold by Gustavus Scott to Patrick Kelly. Witnesses: Robert Dorsey, Mark M. Pringle. Acknowledged before Thoroughgood Smith and Jas. Calhoun, Justices for Baltimore County. Wm. Gibson, Clk.

8 HD 409. June 12, 1795. Lewis Griffith Junr. of Dorchester County and Mary his wife to Edward Griffith of the same county: part of "Hoopers Range" on the east side of Worlds End Creek, adj. "Worlds End," containing 150 acres more or less (all of said tract except a small part deeded to George Grayham). Witnesses: Henry Lake, Jno. Keene. Acknowledged before Henry Lake and John Keene, Justices.

8 HD 411. June 13, 1795. Littleton Willey and Hannah his wife of Dorchester County to Edward Griffith of the same county: part of "Venture" on the east

side of Worlds End Creek, adj. "Griffiths Adventure" and containing 16 1/4 acres more or less. Witnesses: Henry Lake, John Keene. Acknowledged before Henry Lake and John Keene, Justices.

8 HD 413. June 13, 1795. Philip Graham of Dorchester County to Edward Griffith of the same county: part of "Nuners Discovery" on the southeast side of Worlds End Creek, adj. "Griffith Adventure" and containing 8 acres and 20 Rod more or less. Witnesses: Henry Lake, John Keene. Acknowledged by Philip Graham and Mary his wife before Henry Lake and John Keene, Justices.

8 HD 415. June 13, 1795. Edward Griffith of Dorchester County to Lewis Griffith Junr. of the same county: part of "Venture," part of "Hoopers Range" and part of "Griffith Beginning," adj. "Worlds End" and containing 82 acres more or less. Witnesses: Henry Lake, John Keene. Acknowledged by Edward Griffith and Ales his wife before Henry Lake and John Keene, Justices.

8 HD 418. June 30, 1795. Philip Graham of Dorchester County, shipwright, to Edward Griffith of the same county, Gent.: Bond concerning a road. Witnesses: Henry Lake, John Keene.

8 HD 418. May 23, 1795. Henry McCotter of Dorchester County to Edward Woollen of the same county: part of "Lockermans Regulation," containing ten acres more or less. This deed is given to correct an error in an earlier deed between the same parties, for the same land. Witnesses: Tho. Jones, Jno. Williams. Acknowledged before Tho. Jones and Jno. Williams, Justices.

8 HD 421. January 8, 1795. James Steele to Moses W. Nisbett: lease of part of "Town Neck Composition," for 12 years (adj. the farm rented to Wm. Smith). Witne ss: Hannah Maynadier.

8 ED 423. July 1, 1795. Robert White of Somerset County to James Birckhead and Brother of the same county: personal property. Witness: John Reed. Acknowledged before Jno. Reed, Justice.

8 ED 424. July 7, 1795. Henry Steele Esq. of Dorchester County to Negro Jack Hollis: Manumission. Witnesses: Sarah Clark, Isaac Steele, John Reed. Acknowledged before Jno. Reed, Justice.

8 HD 425. May 16, 1795. James Sulivane of Dorchester County to Catharine Webster of the same county: parts of "Hickory Ridge Regulated," "Addition to Hickory Ridge," "Johns Outlett" and "Turkey Nest," all adj. each other and adj.

"Sarahs Delight Enlarged," in accordance with deed of July 16, 1785 from David Harper to James Sulivane, adj. "Long Survey" and containing 141 acres more or less. Witnesses: Jno. Eccleston, Jno. Stevens. Acknowledged by James Sulivane and Mary his wife before Jno. Eccleston and Jno. Stevens, Justices.

8 HD 428. July 8, 1795. Daniel Sulivane Senr. of Dorchester County to John Eccleston of the same county: "House Town" adj. the land where said Eccleston now lives, containing 85 ½ acres more or less. Witnesses: John Reed, Jno. Gooding. Acknowledged before Jno. Reed and Jno. Gooding, Justices.

8 ED 430. May 14, 1795. John McCollister and Lucy his wife of Dorchester County to John Eccleston of the same county: part of "Carpenters Square" not heretofore sold to Rebecca Richardson, containing 21 1/4 acres more or less. Witnesses: Jno. Reed, David Smith. Acknowledged before John Reed and David Smith, Justices.

8 HD 433. July 13, 1795. Henry Ennalls of Dorchester County to Joseph Ennalls of the same place: part of "Bartholomews Neck" (adj. part of said land which Henry Ennalls gave to his son Thomas Ennalls) on Tranequakin River, adj. "Timberyard" and containing 333 acres more or less. Witnesses: Richd. Pattison, Levin Woolford. Acknowledged before Richd. Pattison and Levin Woolford, Justices.

8 HD 434. July 13, 1795. Henry Ennalls of Dorchester County to Joseph Ennalls of the same place: "Addition," surveyed for Joseph Ennalls, within the lines of "Ennalls's Purchase" and to the southward of the new Indian line. Witnesses: Richd. Pattison, Levin Woolford. Acknowledged before Richd. Pattison and Levin Woolford, Justices.

8 HD 436. March 3, 1795. Deposition of William Sotherin, aged about 45 years, mentions George Slacum deceased and Joseph Brown in the year 1794, and a Negro boy named Draper. Witness: Jno. Keene.

8 HD 436. March 3, 1795. Deposition of David Tyler, aged about 48 years, mentions George Slacum deceased and Joseph Brown in the year 1794, a Negro boy named Draper, and Brown's wife named Dolley. Witness: Jno. Keene.

8 HD 436. July 20, 1795. John Rogers of Dorchester County to Negro Richard: Manumission. Witnesses: Richard Pattison, R. Woolford. Acknowledged before Richard Pattison, Justice.

151

8 HD 437. July 20, 1795. Mary Wells of Dorchester County to her two children Elizabeth Elecson and Robert Elecson: all her personal property. Witnesses: Richd. Pattison, John Rs. Acknowledged before Richd. Pattison, Justice.

8 HD 439. May 23, 1795. William Madkin of Dorchester County to Henry Macotter of the same county: parts of "Philips Discovery" and "Outlett," containing three acres. Witnesses: Tho. Jones, Jno. Williams. Acknowledged before Tho. Jones and Jno. Williams, Justices.

8 HD 441. July 27, 1795. William Pitt to the State of Maryland: Bond as Examiner of Tobacco at Ennalls Ferry Warehouse, with Charles Hodson and Thomas Hicks as sureties. Witnesses: Ezekiel Wall, Thos. Parrott. Sworn to by witnesses before Richd. Pattison, Justice.

8 HD 442. May 23, 1795. Henry Macotter of Dorchester County to John Tall of the same county: part of "Philips Discovery" containing 5 3/4 acres. Also part of "Outlett" containing by estimation 1/4 acre. Acknowledged by Henry Macotter and Sarah his wife before Tho. Jones and Jno. Williams, Justices.

8 HD 444. June 20, 1795. Stanley Matkins of Dorchester County to John Tall of the same county: "Outlet," containing 30 acres in Peters Neck, adj. "Talls Forrest"; and part of "Beaver Dam Addition" containing 12 3/4 acres, bought by said Matkins from Henry Macotter. Witnesses: Moses LeCompte, Richd. Pattison. Acknowledged by Stanley Matkins and Elizabeth his wife before Moses LeCompte and Richd. Pattison, Justices.

8 HD 446. June 20, 1795. Henry Macotter of Dorchester County to Stanley Matkin of the same county: part of "Beaver Dam Addition," containing 12 3/4 acres, "that the said Macoter bought of the aforesaid Matkins." Witnesses: Moses LeCompte, Richd. Pattison. Acknowledged before Moses LeCompte and Richd. Pattison, Justices.

8 HD 448. July 18, 1795. Daniel Bean of Dorchester County to Negro Minty: Manumission. Witnesses: Jeremiah Beckwith, Elias Gaither. Acknowledged before Thos. Barnett, Justice.

8 HD 449. August 7, 1794. Samuel Phillips of Dorchester County to Edward Riggin of the same county: Negro man named Dennis. Witnesses: Edward Phillips, Samuel P. Fargerson. Acknowledged before Jno. Reed, Justice.

8 HD 450. August 1, 1795. Thomas Woolford of Dorchester County to Richard

Linthicum of the same county: part of "Woolfords Foresight" on the road from Fishing Creek Church to Taylors Island Ferry, adj. another part of .the same tract conveyed by Woolford to Linthicum in 1794; and containing 8 acres more or less. Witnesses: Richd. Pattison, Jno. Williams. Acknowledged before Richd. Pattison and John Williams, Justices.

8 HD 452. June 1, 1795. Stanley Byus of Dorchester County and Sarah his wife to Col. William Whiteley of Caroline County: during the natural life of said Sarah, her right of dower in "Stevens Regulation" on Choptank River and Jenkins Creek, land of John Stevens deceased, the former husband of said Sarah Byus. Witnesses: Jno. Stevens, Levin Woolford. Acknowledged before Jno. Stevens and Levin Woolford, Justices.

8 HD 455. April 18, 1795. Dorrington Chance of Dorchester County and Esther his wife to Lemuel Davis of Caroline County, planter: part of "Addition to Noviscotia" between the Northwest and Northeast Forks of Nanticoke River, containing 18 acres more or less. Witnesses: Joseph Douglass, Thos. Nicols. Acknowledged before Joseph Douglass and Thomas Nicols, Justices for Caroline County. Tho. Richardson, Clk.

8 HD 459. August 4, 1795. Perry Spencer and Richard Spencer, Shipcarpenters of Talbot County, to John Jones of Dorchester County, Mariner: 2/3 of the Schooner "Liberty." Witnesses: Wm. N. Lambdin, John Harrington.

8 HD 460. July 20, 1795. Jean (Jane) Blair of Dorchester County to John Jones: Negro woman named Binah. Witnesses: John Jones, Thos. Jones Junr.

8 HD 461. March 5, 1795. Samuel Chew and John Chew of Kent County, Maryland, to James Murphy of Dorchester County, planter: lands formerly in Dorchester County but now mostly in Caroline County, called "Mount Pleasant," containing 45 acres more or less; "Smiths Forest," containing 50 acres more or less; "Thicket," containing 50 acres more or less; and "Moores Addition," containing 142 acres more or less. The said lands were formerly mortgaged by Risdon Moore and Mary his wife, on May 18, 1767, to Samuel Chew, John Clayton and John Chew, and are now the property of the said Samuel and John Chew by foreclosure proceedings in the High Court of Chancery, the said Moore and wife having defaulted on payment of the Mortgage and the said John Clayton having died, leaving the said Samuel and John as surviving Mortgagees. Joseph Douglass of Caroline County, Gent., is named as Attorney for grantors. Witnesses: And. Wiesenthal, John Bordley. Acknowledged before And. Wiesenthal and John Bordley, Justices for Kent

County. Ben Chambers, Clk. Receipt of Benjamin Chew for the consideration money of the above deed, paid to him as executor of the Last Will and Testament of Joseph Turner, surviving trustee of Messrs. Amos & Strettle and Joseph Turner, to whom the property of the company formerly known as Chew, Clayton & Chew was heretofore assigned. in trust for the purposes of the assignment. Witnesses: Henrietta Chew, Philip Nicklin. Joseph Douglass, as Attorney for grantors, entered and took possession of premises in the occupation, respectively, of Lemuel Davis, John Chipley and Heber Jones, and delivered the possession of same to James Murphy, in the presence of Charles Adams and Wm. Davis.

8 HD 469. April 15, 1795. Division of lands on Wrotens Island: a tract called "Stondwick" is divided between Thomas Wroten and Mathew Wroten (on the east side of Honger River); a second tract on said river is divided between the same parties, and Thomas acknowledges all his right of the said lands to be the property of his son Levin Wroten after his decease. Witnesses: Levin Booze, James Booze.

8 HD 470. August 10, 1795. Mary Airey of Dorchester County to Smith Goslin of the same county: lease of land on the Southwest side of the Northwest Fork of Nanticoke River, late the property of John Pitt Airey deceased and now the portion of said Mary Airey of his estate. Witnesses: Ezekiel Trego. Peter Stoaks.

8 HD 472. May 23, 1795. Jonathan Patridge of Dorchester County to William Reed of the same county: part of " Anchor of Hope" on the Southwest side of Blackwater River, on a branch called Green Branch near said Reed's present dwelling house containing 50 acres more or less. Witnesses: Moses LeCompte, Jno. Williams. Acknowledged before Moses Lecompte and Jno. Williams, Justices.

8 HD 474. March 26, 1795. Henry Meekins of Dorchester County, planter, to Levin Phillips of the same county: "Busicks Defiance," now called "Reliance," on a path from Henry Dean's to John Brohawn's plantation, beginning at the original boundary of "Busicks Venture" and containing 94 acres. Also "Busicks Venture," containing 29 acres. Witnesses: Tho. Jones, Jno. Williams. Acknowledged before Tho. Jones and Jno. Williams, Justices.

8 HD 476. April 11, 1795. James McCallister of Dorchester County to Garretson McCallister of the same county: "the Neglect" according to the original certificate dated August 28, 1792, containing 21 3/4 acres more or less. Witnesses: John Reed, David Smith. Acknowledged before John Reed and

David Smith, Justices.

8 HD 478. June 22, 1795 - July 13, 1795 Deposition taken by W. B. Martin" Attorney, in a dispute between Henry Ennalls and John Stevens. Wm. Frazier makes oath before Levin Woolford, Justice, that he delivered notice to Henry Ennalls. Deposition of Thomas Colsten, of lawful age, concerns Henry Ennalls, Thomas Colsten Junr. and Nathan Wright who were securities on the bond of John Stevens as Sheriff of Dorchester County; and a house and lot in Delaware transferred by said Stevens to the said Henry Ennalls to secure him and the other sureties.

8 HD 480. August 7, 1795. John Randall of Annapolis, Trustee appointed by the Chancellor of Maryland for completion of sale of the real estate of Levin Kirkman, to James Frazier of Dorchester County: part of "Lower Black Walnut Landing" and part of lot No.4 of the Nanticoke Indian Lands heretofore laid off and sold under acts of the General Assembly of Maryland; 200 acres in all hereby conveyed, having been sold to Frazier by James Shaw, late of Talbot County, deceased, former trustee for sale of the lands of said Levin Kirkman, the said Shaw having died before the complete execution of his trust. Witnesses: James Price, David Kerr. Acknowledged before David Kerr and James Price, Justices for Talbot County. Wm. S. Bond, Clk.

8 HD 485. June 6, 1795. Charles Stewart of Ann Arundel County to Jacob Todd of Dorchester County: two tracts on Hungar River called "New Markett," containing 22 acres, and "Bennetts Pasture," containing 6 acres, or 28 acres more or less in all, sold by said Charles Stewart, Administrator of John Bennett deceased, per decree of the Chancellor for the payment of said Bennett's debts. Witness: Richd. Tilghman 5th. Acknowledged before Jeremiah Townley Chase, one of the Judges of the General Court.

8 HD 486. August 10, 1795. Thomas Thompson of Dorchester County to Jacob Todd of the same county: livestock. Witnesses: Isaac Smith, Edward Griffith.

8 HD 487. August 17, 1795. John Henry of Dorchester County to Isaac Hurley of the same county: lease of 'Pasture Neck," now in the possession of David Smith. Witness: Martin Davis.

8 HD 490. August 18, 1795. James Tregoe and Levin Woolford (of Thos.), both of Dorchester County, to Henry Keene of the same county: part of "Robinsons Lot" containing 13 1/4 acres more or less, conveyed April 15, 1791 to said Henry Keene by said James Tregoe, whose title was doubtful. Witnesses: Moses

Lecompte, Richd. Pattison. Acknowledged before Moses LeCompte and Richd. Pattison, Justices.

8 HD 492. July 25, 1795. Thomas Kilman of Dorchester County to George Brannock of the same county: Negro girl named Lyne. Witness: John Jones. Acknowledged before Tho. Jones, Justice.

8 HD 493. July 29, 1795. James Sulivane Senr. of Dorchester County to Thomas Hodson Senr. of the same county: part of "Friends Discovery" surveyed by Christopher Short Badly on a branch of Chicamacomico River. Witnesses: Jno. Reed, David Smith. Acknowledged before Jno. Reed and David Smith, Justices.

8 HD 495. August 18, 1795. Levin Woolford and James Tregoe of Dorchester County to Thomas Tolley of the same county: part of "Robsons Lott" on Taylors Island, containing 79 acres more or less, adj. lands of Henry Keene and Thomas Traverse. Witnesses: Richd. Pattison, Moses LeCompte. Acknowledged by Levin Woolford and Mary his wife and James Tregoe before Richd. Pattison and Moses LeCompte.

8 HD 497. August 18, 1795. Levin Woolford and Mary his wife of Dorchester County to George Brannock of the same county: part of "Grace Reding" or "Grass Reading" at the head of St. Stephens Creek. Witnesses: Moses LeCompte, Richd. Pattison. Acknowledged before Moses LeCompte and Richd. Pattison, Justices.

8 HD 499. August 25, 1795. William Vans Murray Esq. of Dorchester County and Charlotte Murray his wife to John Green of the same county: 162 1/4 acres called "Andrews Venture," adj. "Deans Beginning." Witnesses: Levin Woolford, Richd. Pattison. Acknowledged before Richd. Pattison and Levin Woolford, Justices.

8 HD 502. August 25, 1795. Thomas Bowdle of Dorchester County to Negro slaves: Manumission. Witnesses: Edwd. White, Jr., Henry Bowdle. Acknowledged before Levin Woolford, Justice.

8 HD 503. May 18, 1795. Elizabeth Caile of Talbot County, widow, to Daniel Sulivane Junr. of Dorchester County, physician: all her claim to a lot in Cambridge adj. the Church land, leased by David Murray March 15, 1763 to John Caile for 50 years, devised by said John Caile to his nephew Hall Caile and by said Hall Caile to his mother Elizabeth Caile, party to this deed, for her lifetime with remainder, if she dies before the expiration of the term aforesaid,

to Hall Harrison. Witnesses: Jno. Stevens, Levin Woolford. Acknowledged before Levin Woolford and Jno. Stevens, Justices.

8 HD 505. August 10, 1795. Thomas Thompson of Dorchester County to Edward Griffith of the same county: personal property. Witnesses: Isaac Smith, Jacob Todd.

8 HD 506. March 7, 1795. Joseph Robson, Ayres Busick and Mary his wife, William Vass and Elizabeth his wife, all of Dorchester County, to Levin Woolford and James Tregoe of the same county: part of "Robsons Lott" on Taylors Island, on the bay side, containing 105 acres more or less. Witnesses: Richd. Pattison, John Keene. Acknowledged before Richd. Pattison and John Keene, Justices.

8 HD 508. October 27, 1794 - August 14, 1795. Commission to Richard Pattison, Jonathan Patridge, Edward Wright, John Braughan and William Pattison, all of Dorchester County, Gent., to perpetuate bounds of John Bromwell's land called "Bromwells Adventure" adj. land called "Woolfords Pasture" belonging to John Jones, and Return. Deposition of John Frazier, of full age, re line between John Bromwell, Thomas Jones and this deponent. Deposition of Roger Woolford, aged about 65 years. Land surveyed by Richard Pattison with John Tall and William Hubbert as chain carriers.

8 HD 512. April 22, 1795. Joshua Johnson and Levin Johnson, both of Dorchester County, to Mark Meekins of the same county: Bond concerning a road on the said Johnson's land, adj. Ichabud Shinton's line. Witnesses: John King, Dorothy King.

8 HD 513. August 26, 1795. Robert Ewing of Talbot County to Levin Hodson of Dorchester County: part of "Francis's Cottage" on the east side of Transquakin River, as in deed from Francis Hayward to John Nixon dated October 7, 1776, containing 3 acres more or less. Witnesses: Moses LeCompte, Jno. Eccleston. Acknowledged before Moses LeCompte and Jno. Eccleston, Justices.

8 HD 515. August 24, 1795. Thos. Walters and John Riddell, both of Dorchester County, to David Smith: one sorrel horse. Witness: Jno. Reed. Acknowledged before Jno. Reed, Justice.

8 HD 516. August 27, 1795. William Taylor of Dorchester County to Negro slaves: Manumission. Witnesses: Levin Woolford, Edwd. White, Jr.

Acknowledged before Levin Woolford, Justice.

8 HD 517. August 27, 1795. Joseph Daffin of Dorchester County to William Bonner of the same county: "Widows Purchase," containing 232 ½ acres. Witnesses: Richd. Pattison, Levin Woolford. Acknowledged before Richd. Pattison and Levin Woolford, Justices.

8 HD 518. August 27, 1795. Major John Hooper of Dorchester County to James Ruark of the same county: part of "Lower Island Regulated" on the lower end of Hoopers Island, containing 377 acres more or less. Witnesses: Moses LeCompte, Richd. Pattison. Acknowledged by John Hooper and Elizabeth his wife before Moses LeCompte and Richd. Pattison, Justices.

8 HD 520. August 24, 1795. Henry Wright of Dorchester County to Anthony Tall of the same county: Bond to convey "Linceys Range," "came and heired by Marrage of a certain Dorothy Webb, decd." Witnesses: William Medes, George Brannock.

8 HD 521. August 18, 1795. Henry Kilman of Dorchester County to William Martin of the same county: parts of "Lockermans Regulation" purchased by said Henry Kilman from John Jones (of Morgan) by deed dated February 25, 1792, containing 40 3/4 acres more or less in all. Also 1 ½ acres of said tract purchased from Nathan Stevens. Witnesses: Moses LeCompte, Richd. Pattison. Acknowledged by Henry Kilman and Delia his wife before Moses LeCompte and Richd. Pattison, Justices.

8 HD 523. August 18, 1795. Edward Woollen of Dorchester County to William Martin of the same county: part of "Morgans Venture" near the head of St. Stephens Creek, containing 27 acres more or less; and part of "Lockermans Regulation" purchased by said Woollen from Henry McCotter, containing 10 acres more or less. Witnesses: Moses LeCompte, Richd. Pattison. Acknowledged by Edward Woollen and Levina his wife before Moses LeCompte and Richd. Pattison, Justices.

8 HD 524. August 28, 1795. Robert Muir and John Muir of Dorchester County to Lemuel Beckwith of the same county: part of "Noels Closure" in Castle Haven Neck, adj. "Stewarts Place," "Contention" and "Beckwiths Addition" and containing 47 acres more or less. Witnesses: Richd. Pattison, Levin Woolford. Acknowledged by Robert Muir and Anne his wife and John Muir before Richd. Pattison and Levin Woolford, Justices.

8 HD 527. May 23, 1795. John Tall of Dorchester County to Levin Woollen of the same county: 3 acres of "Phillips Discovery." Witnesses: Tho. Jo.nes, Jno. Williams. Acknowledged before Tho. Jones and Jno. Williams, Justices.

8 HD 529. May 30, 1795. John Kirwan and Sarah Kirwan his wife of Dorchester County to Gabriel Slacum of Dorchester County: "Todd Point" on the east side of Farham Creek, containing 65 acres more or less. Witnesses: Henry Lake, John Keene. Acknowledged before Henry Lake and John Keene, Justices.

8 HD 531. September 7, 1795. John Mitchell Stevens and Pamela Stevens, legal representatives of Robertson Stevens Esq., late of Dorchester County, deceased, to Tubman Cannon, son of Curtis Cannon late of Dorchester County, deceased: part of "Waters's Last Choice" between the forks of Nanticoke River, containing 148 3/4 acres more or less. Witnesses: Jno. Stevens, Levin Woolford. Acknowledged before Jno. Stevens and Levin Woolford, Justices.

8 HD 533. September 7, 1795. John Mitchell Stevens and Pamela Stevens, legal representatives of Robertson Stevens late of Dorchester County, deceased, to James Wilson of the same county: part of "Waters's Last Choice," containing 120 ½ acres more or less. Witnesses: Jno. Stevens, Levin Woolford. Acknowledged before Jno. Stevens and Levin Woolford, Justices.

8 HD 534. August 22, 1795. John Maguire and Sarah his wife of Dorchester County to Thomas Hicks, Mcht., of Cambridge: part of a water lot and storehouse in Vienna (lot No. 14), where Capt. Thomas Wall now lives. Witnesses: Jno. Reed, David Smith. Acknowledged before David Smith, Justice.

8 HD 537. August 15, 1795. Thomas Walters and Anne his wife of Dorchester County to Thomas Hicks of the same county: part of a lot in Vienna where Ezekiel Mason now lives, being the remainder of the lot sold to John Maguire by Wm. Angell and the said Anne Walters, who was then the wife of said Wm. Angell deceased. Also the dower interest in "Maidens Forrest," "Traverses Honeysucker" and three other tracts, names unknown, all lying near Vienna in Dorchester County, formerly the property of John Hicks Traverse late of Dorchester County deceased, former husband of the said Anne, and now in the tenure and occupation of Matthew Travers, son of said John Hicks Traverse. Witnesses: Levin Woolford, Jno. Stevens. Acknowledged before Levin Woolford and Jno. Stevens, Justices.

8 HD 540. September 8, 1795. Thomas Woolford of Dorchester County, Gent., to Roger Woolford, (son of James) of the same county, Mcht.: "Winfells

Trouble" containing 200 acres more or less; "Hydes Chance" adj. thereto, containing 34 acres more or less; and "Baron Ridge" and "Addition to Baron Ridge," adj. said tracts. Witnesses: Levin Woolford, Stanley Byus. Acknowledged by Thomas Woolford and Priscilla his wife before Levin Woolford and Stanley Byus, Justices.

8 HD 542. September 8, 1795. James Sulivane of Dorchester County, Gent., and Mary his wife to Charles LeCompte Junior of the same county, Gent.: land in New Market where John McClaran now lives, adj. a lot sold by said James Sulivane to William Riley about seven years since. Witnesses: Jno. Stevens, Jno. Reed. Acknowledged by James Sulivane and Mary his wife before Jno. Stevens and Jno. Reed, Justices.

8 HD 544. April 18, 1795. Zorababel Marine of Dorchester County to Marget Framptom of Caroline County: part of "Marines Addition," "Goslins Join" and containing 36 ½ acres more or less. Witnesses: Joseph Douglass, Thos. Nicols. Acknowledged before Joseph Douglass and Thos. Nicols, Justices for Caroline County. Tho. Richardson, Clk.

8 HD 547. August 24, 1795. John Turpin to Joseph Wheatley: Negro slaves. Witness: George Gale.

8 ED 547. September 16, 1795. William M. Robertson of Dorchester County to Negro slaves: Manumission. Witnesses: Edwd. White Jr., Levin Woolford. Acknowledged before Levin Woolford, Justice.

8 HD 548. June 13, 1795. Capt. Edward Griffith of Dorchester County to Phillip Graham of the same county: part of four tracts on the Southeast side of Worlds End Creek called "Worlds End," "Griffiths Adventure," "Griffiths Beginning" and "Hoopers Range." George Graham is mentioned as son of said Phillip. Witnesses: Henry Lake, John Keene. Acknowledged by Capt. Edward Griffith and Ales his wife before Henry Lake and John Keene, Justices.

8HD 552. September 28, 1795. Hugh Maguire of Dorchester County, Cordwinder, to Thomas Kallender of the same county, shipwright: Lot No. 7 of "White Haven" containing 2 acres more or less; and Lot No. 6 of "White Haven," except the part sold to Charles Beacham, containing one acre more or less. Witnesses: Tho. Jones, Jno. Williams. Acknowledged before Tho. Jones and Jno. Williams, Justices.

8HD 554. September 24, 1795. Thomas Hodson Senr. of Dorchester County to his grandson Samuel Smoot, son of the late Edward Smoot of Dorchester County: Negro boy named Tom, about 11 years of age. Witnesses: John Laing, Jas. Hodson.

8 HD 555. July 18, 1795. William Littleton of Dorchester County to Charles Dean of the same county: part of two tracts adj. each other, called "Maiden Forrest" and "Hickory Ridge Enlarged," containing 25 3/4 acres more or less. Witnesses: Jno. Reed, David Smith. Acknowledged by William Littleton and Gracy his wife before Jno. Reed and David Smith, Justices.

8 HD 557. September 8, 1795. Abner Shanks to Robert Dennis and Thos. Hingson of Dorchester County: Negro girl called Priscilla, aged about 16 years. Witnesses: Littleton Lankford, Wm. Draera, Chas. Adams. Acknowledged before Chas. Adams, Justice.

8 HD 559. May 30, 1795. Levi Insley of Dorchester County to William Insley of the same county: part of "Insleys Priviledge" adj. "Andrews Fortune" and containing 43 acres, devised to Jacob Insley by Last Will and Testament of James Insley deceased. Witnesses: Henry Lake, Jno. Keene. Acknowledged by Levi Insley and Joyce his wife before Henry Lake and Jno. Keene, Justices.

8 HD 561. September 28, 1795. Deposition of James Harper, aged 27 years, or thereabouts, states that his brother John Harper, now apprenticed to Joseph Davidson, Cooper, in Baltimore town, was born in May 1774.

8 HD 562. September 8, 1795. Roger Woolford Junr. of Dorchester County to Thomas Cook of the same county: "Brannocks Addition" on the north side of Little Choptank River, adj. "Winfields Trouble" and containing 104 acres more or less. Also "Barren Ridge" adj. Edward Dawson's land, on Hudsons Creek, containing 87 acres more or less. Witnesses: Levin Woolford, Stanley Byus. Acknowledged before Levin Woolford and Stanley Byus, Justices.

8 HD 565. October 1, 1795. Joseph Andrews and Elizabeth his wife of Dorchester County to John Bramble of the same county: part of "Gootees Lott" adj. "Batchchellors Folly" and containing 4 acres and 23 Rod. Witnesses: Henry Lake, John Keene. Acknowledged before Henry Lake and John Keene, Justices.

8 HD 567. September 3, 1795. William Price of Dorchester County from William Craswell of Somerset County: "Middle Island" on the north end of Cotneys Island, containing 53 1/4 acres more or less. Witnesses: John Keene, Henry Lake. Acknowledged by Wm. Craswell and Patience his wife before John

Keene and Henry Lake, Justices.

8 HD 569. October 8, 1795. Nancy Hooper of Dorchester County, spinster, to Jacob Wright of the same county, Yeoman: land in Northwest Fork Hundred called "Bradford," containing 180 acres more or less. Witnesses: Jno. Crapper, Chas. Adams. Acknowledged before Jno. Crapper and Chas. Adams, Justices.

8 HD 571. October 8, 1795. Jacob Wright and Isaac Wright, both of Dorchester County, and Jesse Wright of Caroline County, Executors of Edward Wright Senior, to Noah Cannon of the same county, planter: part of "Wrights Regulation," containing 44 ½ acres more or less. Witnesses: Jno. Crapper, Chas. Adams. Acknowledged before Jno. Crapper and Chas. Adams, Justices.

8 HD 574. October 8, 1795. Tubman Cannon of Dorchester County, Yeoman, and Betsy his wife, to Jacob Wright of the same county, planter: part of "Portroyal" and part of "Waterses Last Choice," containing 166 acres more or less. Witnesses: Chas. Adams, Jno. Crapper. Acknowledged before Chas. Adams and Jno. Crapper, Justices.

8 HD 576. August 1, 1794. Daniel Nicols from Isaac Canter: Receipt for purchase money for "Staintons Purches," formerly bought by Canter from Magary Stainton, now the wife of Bartho. Fletcher. Witnesses: Arthur Pritchard, Jacob Jacobs.

8 HD 577. July 29, 1795. Thomas Hodson of Dorchester County to James Sulivane of the same county: "Hodsons Venture," containing 76 acres more or less. Witnesses: Jno. Reed, David Smith. Acknowledged before John Reed and David Smith, Justices.

8 HD 579. May 16, 1795. James Sulivane of Dorchester County to Daniel Sulivane Junr. of the same county: "Adventure" on a branch of Chicamacomico River, adj. "Bradleys Lott" and containing 94 acres more or less. Witnesses: Jno. Eccleston, Jno. Stevens. Acknowledged before Jno. Eccleston and Jno. Stevens, Justices.

8 HD 582. July 30, 1795. Certificate of John Hooper and Theophilus Marshall re manumission of Negro Dick in the Last Will and Testament of William Ennalls Hooper deceased, dated July 14, 1795, the testator having died the 15th of the same month.

8 HD 583. May 16, 1795. Daniel Sulivane Junr. of Dorchester County to James

Sulivane of the same county: "Hickory Ridge Regulated," containing 151 ½ acres; and part of "Sarahs Delight Enlarged," containing 142 1/4 acres. Witnesses: Jno. Eccleston, Jno. Stevens. Acknowledged before Jno. Eccleston and Jno. Stevens, Justices.

8 HD 586. August 15, 1795. Thomas Hicks and Sarah his wife of Dorchester County to Peter Rea of the same county: all their lands in Dorchester County or elsewhere. (Mortgage). Witnesses: Jno. Stevens, Levin Woolford. Acknowledged before Jno. Stevens and Levin Woolford, Justices.

8 HD 589. October 20, 1795. Nehemiah Whiteley of Dorchester County, planter, to Woolford Stewart of the same place, blacksmith: livestock, etc. Witnesses: Isaac Patridge, Mary Stewart.

8 HD 590. April 18, 1795. Lemuel Davis of Caroline County to Esther Chance of Dorchester County: part of "Marains Addition," containing 3 acres more or less. Witnesses: Joseph Douglass, Thos. Nicols. Acknowledged before Joseph Douglass and Thos. Nicols, Justices for Caroline County. Tho. Richardson, Clk.

8 HD 593. October 18, 1795. Joseph Kerby of Dorchester County to John Crapper of the same county: livestock and furniture. Witnesses: Thomas Kerby, Sally Kerby.

8 HD 594. August 8, 1795. Sophia Roberts of Dorchester County to Robson Cator of Baltimore town: part of a tract near where Capt. John Bennett formerly lived, called "All Three of Us," containing 11 3/4 acres more or less. Witnesses: Henry Lake, John Keene. Acknowledged before Henry Lake and John Keene, Justices.

8 HD 596. May 30, 1795. John McNamara Pritchett and Elizabeth his wife of Dorchester County, planter, to Edward Hart of the same county, planter: part of "Hazzard" on the road from the Chapel to Marcus Andrews and on the east side of Mary Woodland's land, adj. "Head of Farham" and containing 6 acres more or less. Witnesses: Henry Lake, John Keene. Acknowledged before Henry Lake and John Keene, Justices.

8 ED 599. September 15, 1795. Levin Woollen of Dorchester County to Jabin Todd of the same county: part of "Matkins Forrest," containing 110 acres more or less. Also part of "Philips Discovery," containing 3 acres. Witnesses: Tho. Jones, John Williams. Acknowledged by Levin Woollen and Priscilla his wife before Tho. Jones and John William, Justices.

8 HD 602. May 27, 1795. Andrew McDonald of Dorchester County, Carpenter, to Rhoads Riggen of the same county: part of "St. Bartholomew" and part of "Weston." Witnesses: John Reed, David Smith. Acknowledged by Andrew McDonald and Catharine his wife before John Reed and David Smith, Justices.

8 HD 605. October 27, 1795. Bartholomew Ennalls of Dorchester County to John Craig of the same county: lands willed by his father Bartholomew Ennalls deceased to his granddaughter Elizabeth Ennalls. Witnesses: Jno. Stevens, Thos. Barnett. Acknowledged before Jno. Stevens and Thos. Barnett, Justices.

8 HD 607. October 28, 1795. John Griffith of Dorchester County to Negro Robert, formerly the property of Archibald Patison: Manumission. Witnesses: Chas. Goldsborough, Thos. McKeel. Acknowledged before John Keene, Justice.

8 HD 607. October 27, 1795. Henry Lord of Dorchester County to Robert Dennis and Thomas Hingson of the same county: livestock, etc. Witnesses: Charles Stainton, Littleton Langford. Acknowledged before Jno. Stevens, Justice.

8 HD 609. November 1793. Certificate of survey of division line between lands of Abraham Neild, James Dail and James Busick. Witness: Wm. Barrow.

8 HD 610. January 20, 1795. Phillip, Thomas, Daniel and Isaiah LeCompte of Dorchester County to Nicholas LeCompte of the same county: Bond re award of Moses LeCompte, Solomon Fraizer and Levin Woolford Esquires, Arbitrators in a dispute concerning division of "Saint Anthonys." Witnesses: Richard Pattison, John McKeel.

8 HD 612. July 15, 1795. Award by Moses LeCompte, Solomon Frazier and Levin Woolford in a dispute concerning "Saint Anthonys." William LeCompte deceased is mentioned as father of Phillip, Thomas, Daniel and Isaiah LeCompte; Joseph LeCompte deceased is mentioned as father of Nicholas LeCompte; 1/3 of the land in question was held by Samuel LeCompte and by him devised to the said parties after the death of Joseph LeCompte (of Peter) and his wife Elizabeth; and the entire tract appears to be divided into thirds in accordance with a devise by Moses LeCompte deceased, "to his sons who had had the misfortune of losing their sight." It is mentioned that a certain John LeCompte set up a right to said tractJ Which right was purchased by the said Phillip, Thomas, Daniel, Isaiah and Nicholas LeCompte.

8 HD 618. October 13, 1795. Certificate of Survey of "St. Anthonys" by

Theophilus Marshall by direction of Capt. Solomon Frazier and Levin Woolford, Arbitrators.

8 HD 622. February 13, 1795. John Span Conway and Chaplin Conway of Somerset County to Henry Lake of Dorchester County: Bond concerning "Walnut Point" and "Taylors Point" devised by Last Will and Testament of Solomon Chaplin to his daughter Susanna Conway and Ann Chaplin, and now the property of John Span Conway, Chaplin Conway, John Conway, Thomas Conway, Henry Conway and Robert Conway. Witness: George Robertson. Assigned by Henry Lake to Moses Barns, September 21, 1795. Witness: John Foxwell.

8 HD 625. October 28, 1795. John Tootell of Dorchester County, Physician, to Lydia Pennington: Negro man named Solomon Cornish. Witnesses: Nathaniel Manning Junr., Samuel Rust. Acknowledged before Jno. Stevens, Justice.

8 HD 626. November 3, 1795. Lydia Pennington to Solomon Cornish: Manumission. Witnesses: Stanley B. Lockerman, Wm. Piercy. Acknowledged before Jno. Stevens, Justice.

8 HD 627 December 16, 1794. Mitchell Russum of Dorchester County to John Eccleston of Dorchester County: Negro slaves. Witnesses: Nanney Polk, John Gooding. Acknowledged before John Gooding, Justice. "Received 1st Feby. 1795 of John Molock the sum of Seventy Pounds Currt. Money of Maryland in full consideration of the within mentioned Negroes, and I certify that I have no claim, Title or Demand of either of the Negroes aforesaid -Witness my Hand - Jno. Eccleston."

INDEX

(References are to Liber and Folio in the original records, as shown at upper left of each abstract.)

Aaron, John 4 HD 69, 542; 6 HD 412
Aaron, Sarah 6 HD 328
Abbet, Thomas 4 HD 587
Abbett, Thomas 3 HD 593, 601; 8 HD 87
Abbot, Sarah 3 HD 78
Abbott, Samuel 4 HD 174
Ackworth, James 6 HD 10, 432, 633
Acworth, James 4 HD 624
Acworth, Priscilla 4 HD 624
Adams, Amy 4 HD 172
Adams, Charles 6 HD 445, 446, 447; 8 HD 461, 557
Adams, Charles, Justice 8 HD 298, 307, 311, 557, 569, 571, etc.
Adams Dear Purchase [tract] 3 HD 487; 8 HD 307
Adams, Edward 3 HD 74; 6 HD 356
Adams, Henry 6 HD 445, 447
Adams, Nancy 8 HD 377
Adams, Summer 8 HD 377
Adams Venture" 3 HD 485
Addition to Anything [tract] 4 HD 631
Addition to Baron Ridge [tract] 8 HD 540
Addition to Bartletts Meadows [tract] 8 HD 307
Addition to Bramble Hope [tract] 3 HD 424
Addition to Britts Hope [tract] 6 HD 283
Addition to Buttons Intent [tract] 8 HD 124
Addition to Fair Dealing [tract] 3 HD 202
Addition to Fishers Landing [tract] 4 HD 115; 6 HD 405
Addition to Fitchews Range [tract] 4 HD 103
Addition to Francis Cottage [tract] 3 HD 148
Addition to Galloway [tract] 6 HD 241
Addition to Green Bank [tract] 3 HD 371
Addition to Greens Adventure [tract] 8 HD, 134
Addition to Harwick [tract] 4 HD 151
Addition to Haywards Farme [tract] 8 HD 283
Addition to Hickory Ridge [tract] 8 HD 425
Addition to Hog Quarter [tract] 3 HD 477
Addition to Hoopers Pasture [tract] 4 HD 612
Addition to Joneses Chance [tract] 3 HD 624
Addition to Keenes Delight [tract] 3 HD 183
Addition to KeenesTimber Yard [tract] 6 HD 499
Addition to Kilmons Folly [tract] 3 HD 410, 444; 6 HD 266
Addition to LeComptes Chance [tract] 3 HD 363
Addition to Leinster [tract] 6 HD 332
Addition to Liberty [tract] 4 HD 463

Addition to Luck [tract] 8 HD 307
Addition to Moores Meadows [tract] 3 HD 447
Addition to New Town [tract] 3 HD 264
Addition to Noviscotia [tract] 8 HD 455
Addition to Outlett [tract] 4 HD 229; 6 HD 630; 8 HD 114
Addition to Rawley [tract] 8 HD 191, 196
Addition to Reeds Chance [tract] 3 HD 315, 318, 494
Addition to Rockahook [tract] 8 HD 279
Addition to Rosses Chance [tract] 3 HD 355; 6 HD 475
Addition to Second Chance [tract] 3 HD 355
Addition to Sharps Point [tract] 6 HD 37
Addition to Sheep Pasture [tract] 8 HD 216
Addition to Shentons Advantage [tract] 8 HD 77
Addition to Skinners Choice [tract] 3 HD 329; 6 HD 213
Addition to Small Profit [tract] 3 HD 136
Addition to Stave Landing [tract] 6 HD 195
Addition to Stewarts Marsh [tract] 6 HD 415, 418
Addition to Teverton [tract] 8 HD 134
Addition to the End of Strife [tract] 6 HD 356
Addition to Timber Swamp [tract] 3 HD 202
Addition to Turkey Neck [tract] 4 HD 229; 6 HD 630
Addition to White Fryers [tract] 3 HD 410
Addition to White Haven [tract] 6 HD 329, 381, 478, 612, 615
Addition to Whiteleys Choice [tract] 3 HD 183
Addition to York [tract] 8 HD 349
Addition to White Haven [tract] 4 HD 275
Addition [tract] 3 HD 253, 275, 404; 4 HD 582; 6 HD 283, 420; 8 HD 342, 434
Adly, William 4 HD 65
Adventure [tract] 8 HD 579
Affins Increase [tract] 4 HD 13
Airey, John Pitt 4 HD 399; 8 HD 470
Airey, Mary 8 HD 470
Airey, Thomas 3 HD 604
Airey, Thomas Hill 3 HD 45, 282, 324, 411, 584; 4 HD 402, 605; 6 HD 167
Aireys Chapel 8 HD 65
Aireys Regulation [tract] 3 HD 324
Akers, Daniel 3 HD 47; 6 HD 454
Alford, Richard 3 HD 309, 377; 8 HD 22
All Three of Us [tract] 6 HD 529, 532, 534, 536; 8 HD 594
Allegany County 3 HD 224
Allen, Shadrack 6 HD 604
Anchor or Hope [tract] 8 HD 472
Anderson, Edward 3 HD 257
Anderson, Henry 3 HD 309; 4 HD 574
Anderson, John M. 4 HD 580
Anderson, Joseph 3 HD 257
Anderson, Thomas 3 HD 309; 4 HD 582; 8 HD 347

Andertons Desire [tract] 3 HD 195
Andrew, Thomas 4 HD 574
Andrews Desire [tract] 8 HD 377
Andrews, Elizabeth 3 HD 20, 76; 6 HD 305; 8 HD 565
Andrews Fortune [tract] 4 HD 165, 167, 353, 601; 6 HD 141, 147, 261, 523; 8 HD 235, 559
Andrews, Isaac 3 HD 111; 4 HD 334; 6 HD 141, 147, 164; 8 HD 65, 108
Andrews, John 4 HD 535
Andrews, Joseph 3 HD 20, 21, 39, 76, 111, 423, 424; 4 HD 208; 6 HD 303, 305; 8 HD 142, 565
Andrews, Judah 4 HD 208
Andrews, Marcus 8 HD 596
Andrews, Medford 3 HD 42; 8 HD 65, 264
Andrews, Reubin 3 HD 572; 4 HD 208; 6 HD 307, 361
Andrews, Sarah 8 HD 65
Andrews Venture [tract] 8 HD 499
Angell, Anne 8 HD 537
Angell, Nancy 3 HD 416
Angell, William 8 HD 537
Angell, William C. 3 HD 416; 4 HD 559, 589
Ann Arundel County 3 HD 589; 4 HD 90, 330; 6 HD 387, 415, 418, 537; 8 HD 109, 485
Annapolis 3 HD 394, 487, 589; 4 HD 90; 6 HD 495; 8 HD 480
Anthonys Priviledge [tract] 6 HD 379
Appin Forrest [tract] 3 HD 259
Appleby [tract] 3 HD 10, 127
Applegarth, George 6 HD 475
Armstrongs Bay 3 HD 348
Armstrongs Folly [tract] 4 HD 425, 444

Armstrongs Hog Pen Regulated [tract] 6 HD 387
Armstrongs Quarter [tract] 6 HD 1
Armstrongs Venter [tract] 4 HD 459
Arnal, John 3 HD 502
Arnett, Henry 8 HD 91, 200
Arnett, James 4 HD 513; 6 HD 70, 78; 8 HD 332
Arnett, Mary 6 HD 70
Arnett, Mary Ann 6 HD 78
Arthur & Betty [tract] 8 HD 109
Arthurs Discovery [tract] 6 HD 37
Ayres, James 4 HD 293
Bachelors Forrest [tract] 8 HD 80
Back Creek 6 HD 317, 326
Bacon Quarter [tract] 4 HD 65, 94
Badley, Christopher Short 3 HD 491; 8 HD 493
Badley, Jane 3 HD 491
Badley, Richard 3 HD 491
Badley, William 3 HD 115
Baker, John Martin 4 HD 516
Bakers Chance [tract] 4 HD 516, 520
Bakers Marsh [tract] 4 HD 516, 520
Ball, John 3 HD 47, 419; 4 HD 249; 6 HD 112
Ball, Levin 4 HD 561; 8 HD 114
Baltimore County 3 HD 1, 361; 6 HD 37, 89, 96, 348, 374; 8 HD 394, 406
Baltimore Town 3 HD 1, 571; 4 HD 238; 6 HD 37, 89, 167, 348, 515; 8 HD 349, 394, 561, 594
Bansbury [tract] 4 HD 470
Baptist Church 8 HD 64
Baptists 6 HD 582
Bare Gardain Creek 6 HD 144
Barkly, James 6 HD 601
Barnes, Daniel 4 HD 371
Barnes, Elizabeth 6 HD 459, 462

Barnes, John 4 HD 129, 374, 463
Barnes, Mace 6 HD 459, 462
Barnes, Mary 6 HD 511
Barnes, Moses 4 HD 318; 6 HD 511
Barnes, Robson 6 HD 459, 462, 509, 511
Barnes, Thomas 4 HD 318, 371, 374, 463
Barnes, William 6 HD 425, 459
Barnett, Thomas 4 HD 127
Barnett, Thomas, Justice 6 HD 126, 132, 266, 310, 312, 475, 615; 8 HD 94, 96, 99, 137, 448, 605
Barns, Aney 3 HD 623
Barns, John 3 HD 326, 327; 4 HD 74
Barns, Moses 8 HD 82, 622
Barns, Robson 3 HD 164
Barns, Thomas 3 HD 327, 573
Barren Ridge [tract] 8 HD 287, 540, 562
Barron, Joseph 6 HD 172
Barron, Sarah 6 HD 172
Barrow, William 3 HD 27, 236, 279, 555; 6 HD 254, 515; 8 HD 56, 609
Bartholomew Ennalls Chapel 8 HD 65
Bartholomews Neck [tract] 6 HD 107; 8 HD 433
Bartlett Meadows [tract] 8 HD 307
Bartlett, William 8 HD 307
Batchelders Hope [tract] 3 HD 333
Batchellors Folly [tract] 8 HD 565
Batchelors Forrest [tract] 4 HD 307
Batsey, Margaret 6 HD 20
Batsey, Richard 6 HD 20
Bayly, Benjamin 4 HD 65
Bayly, Josiah 4 HD 566, 568; 6 HD 274, 285, 344, 346

Beacham, Charles 6 HD 552, 557; 8 HD 552
Beall, Brooke 4 HD 466
Bean, Daniel 8 HD 448
Beard, Mary 8 HD 200
Beard, Thomas 4 HD 601
Beaston, Peregrine 3 HD 467, 593, 601; 6 HD 219, 271, 287; 8 HD 87
Beaverdam Addition [tract] 6 HD 296, 298; 8 HD 444, 446
Beaverdam Range [tract] 8 HD 283
Beckwith Chapel 8 HD 65
Beckwith, Jeremiah 4 HD 623; 8 HD 12, 448
Beckwith, Lemuel 3 HD 363; 4 HD 623; 8 HD 524
Beckwith, Nehemiah 3 HD 172
Beckwiths Addition [tract] 8 HD 524
Bellefield (Belfield, Bell Field) [tract] 3 HD 210, 236, 279, 345, 442, 549; 4 HD 259, 513; 6 HD 70, 78; 8 HD 332
Bell, Arthur 3 HD 402; 4 HD 125
Bell, Isaac 3 HD 159, 397, 573
Bell, John 4 HD 441
Bennett, Frederick 6 HD 466; 8 HD 143
Bennett, John 3 HD 489; 8 HD 485, 594
Bennetts Pasture [tract] 8 HD 485
Benson, Joseph 6 HD 557
Berrys Chance [tract] 6 HD 277
Bestpitch, Jonathan 4 HD 480, 573; 8 HD 114, 360
Bestpitch, Levin 4 HD 65
Betties Lott [tract] 4 HD 165, 167
Bettys Desier [tract] 3 HD 111
Bettys Inlargement [tract] 3 HD 414

Bettys Lot [tract] 6 HD 523; 8 HD 235;
Billingsleys Chance [tract] 6 HD 274
Bingham, William 3 HD 1; 8 HD 349
Birckhead, James & Bro. 8 HD 423
Birckhead, James 4 HD 19, 21, 494, 625, 626
Birckhead, Jane 6 HD 41
Birckhead, Solomon 3 HD 35, 608; 6 HD 41
Birckhead, Solomon, Justice 3 HD 6, 10, 27, 43, 45, 47, 48, etc.
Bird, Jonathan 3 HD 428
Black Swamp [tract] 3 HD 202, 226
Black Walnut Island [tract] 4 HD 491
Black Water Range [tract] 8 HD 380
Blackwater Bridge 3 HD 40
Blackwater Range [tract] 3 HD 304, 386
Blackwater River 3 HD 48, 76, 122, 124, 155, 173, 175, 226, 302, 423, 510, 573, 589; 4 HD 74, 147, 246, 314, 334, 371, 466, 503, 545, 573, 585; 6 HD 175, 307, 359, 361, 464, 493, 503, 511, 525; 8 HD 65, 77, 124, 142, 152, 155, 208, 225, 246, 276, 368, 472
Blackwell, Ann 4 HD 297, 300
Blair, Jane (Jean) 8 HD 399, 460
Blair, John 3 HD 50, 236, 345, 549; 4 HD 454, 497, 513, 594; 70, 78, 184, 344, 346; 8 HD 399
Blinkhorns Creek 3 HD 579; 6 HD 132; 8 HD 22
Boar Brook [tract] 3 HD 572
Bond, William & Co. 3 HD 480
Bond, William 8 HD 176, 368
Bond, William L. 3 HD 350

Bond, William S. 4 HD 19, 545; 6 HD 439; 8 HD 92, 292, 480
Bonner, William 6 HD 574; 8 HD 517
Bonnewell, George 4 HD 65
Bonwill, Elizabeth (Betty) 4 HD 98; 6 HD 396
Bonwill, George 3 HD 617; 4 HD 77, 94, 157, 628
Bonwill, Mary 3 HD 53, 56; 4 HD 57, 98, 175, 189, 309
Bonwill, Michael Hall 3 HD 53, 56; 4 HD 57, 78, 94, 97, 98, 157, 175, 189, 194, 309, 431, 628; 6 HD 396
Bonwills Expitible Lott [tract] 3 HD 53, 56, 62
Bonwills Lott [tract] 3 HD 53
Bonwills Regulation on Halls Seat [tract] 4 HD 98, 157; 6 HD 396
Booth, Hartly 3 HD 564
Booth, John 3 HD 572
Booze, Dennis 8 HD 143
Booze, Elizabeth 8 HD 254
Booze, James 3 HD 155, 573; 8 HD 469
Booze, Levin 8 HD 469
Booze, Teresa 8 HD 143
Bordley, John 8 HD 461
Boston, Massachusetts 3 HD 617
Boston [tract] 6 HD 37, 277
Bourbourk [tract] 4 HD 208
Bourburk [tract] 6 HD 361
Bowdle, Henry 8 HD 502
Bowdle, Thomas 8 HD 502
Boxalls Lott [tract] 6 HD 52
Boyle, Anthony 4 HD 227, 587
Boyus, William 8 HD 16
Bozman, Betsey 8 HD 142
Bozman, Risdon 8 HD 142

Bozmans Beginning [tract] 8 HD 142
Bradford [tract] 3 HD 282; 8 HD 298, 569
Bradley, Kelbey 3 HD 105
Bradley, Mrs. 3 HD 98
Bradley, Nathan 3 HD 195
Bradley, Purnall 3 HD 105
Bradley, William 6 HD 391
Bradleys Intention [tract] 3 HD 115
Bradleys Lott [tract] 8 HD 579
Bradshaw, John 4 HD 497; 6 HD 162, 271
Bramble, David 4 HD 611
Bramble, Edmondson 3 HD 355; 6 HD 123, 144, 303
Bramble, Gabriel 6 HD 20
Bramble, Job 6 HD 151
Bramble, John 6 HD 144; 8 HD 565
Bramble, Peter 4 HD 81
Bramble, Priscilla 3 HD 157
Bramble, William 3 HD 157; 6 HD 448, 450, 451, 453; 8 HD 69, 104, 106, 173, 215
Brambles Delight [tract] 4 HD 321
Brambles Hope [tract] 3 HD 547
Brannock, Ann 8 HD 100
Brannock, Edmond 3 HD 168; 6 HD 455, 617, 620
Brannock, George 6 HD 624; 8 HD 121, 492, 497, 520
Brannock, Mary 3 HD 613
Brannock, Philemon 3 HD 613; 8 HD 100, 121
Brannock, Sidney 8 HD 121
Brannock, Thomas 3 HD 10, 608
Brannocks Addition [tract] 8 HD 287, 562
Brannocks Regulation [tract] 8 HD 121
Brannoclrs Chance [tract] 3 HD 10

Brannon, John 8 HD 16
Brannooks Point [tract] 8 HD 121
Braughan, John 3 HD 431; 4 HD 612; 6 HD 412; 8 HD 508
Braughan, Patrick 3 HD 81, 158, 159, 289, 290
Breeden, John 3 HD 544
Breeden, Mary 3 HD 544
Breerwood, John 6 HD 12, 20, 22; 8 HD 385
Breerwood, Nathan 8 HD 360
Breerwood, Thomas 6 HD 12
Brewington, Caty 4 HD 107
Briley, Thomas 3 HD 178
Brice, John 3 HD 589
Brickell, Isaiah 4 HD 339
Brickell, Macall 4 HD 339
Bridge Neck [tract] 4 HD 118, 628; 6 HD 489, 549
Brierwood, John 8 HD 208
Brierwood, Thomas 8 HD 329
Bright, Benjamin 3 HD 91; 4 HD 618
Bright, Matthew 6 HD 175; 8 HD 225
Bright, Rhoda 4 HD 618
Bright, Richard 3 HD 117, 119, 122
Bright, Solomon 4 HD 618
Bright; Elizabeth 3 HD 91
Brights Addition to the Grove [tract] 3 HD 117, 119, 122
Brills Hope [tract] 8 HD 342
Brinchfield, James 3 HD 309
Broad Cove 4 HD 477
Brodess, Edward 4 HD 201, 573; 8 HD 208
Brodess, Jonathan 3 HD 25; 8 HD 114
Brodess, Joseph 8 HD 114
Brodess, Richard 8 HD 114
Brodess, Tabitha 3 HD 25

Brohawn, John 3 HD 83, 243; 4 HD 140, 473; 8 HD 265, 268, 403, 474
Brohawn, Mary 4 HD 140
Brohawn, Patrick 4 HD 140
Bromwell, Edward 8 HD 22
Bromwell, John 6 HD 431, 546; 8 HD 508
Bromwells Adventure [tract] 6 HD 546; 8 HD 508
Brook, Stephen 6 HD 604
Brooks Outhold [tract] 3 HD 472
Brooks, Robert 6 HD 420
Brooks, William 6 HD 420
Brown, Anderton 4 HD 179
Brown, Betsey 4 HD 395
Brown, Betty 4 HD 179
Brown, Charles 3 HD 402, 457; 4 HD 179
Brown, Dolley 8 HD 436
Brown, Eccleston 3 HD 447; 4 HD 618; 6 HD 57
Brown, Edward 4 HD 395
Brown, George 3 HD 419; 6 HD 405, 407
Brown, Humphriss 3 HD 422
Brown, James 4 HD 65, 77, 94, 97, 395
Brown, Joseph 8 HD 436
Brown Neglect [tract] 4 HD 393, 420
Brown, Rebeccah 3 HD 402, 457
Brown, Samuel 4 HD 552, 582; 6 HD 162, 279, 294, 295, 437, 438
Brown, White 3 HD 422
Browns Meadow [tract] 4 HD 94, 98, 395
Browns Mistake [tract] 6 HD 112
Bruce, A. B. 8 HD 124
Bruce, Abner B. 6 HD 617
Bruce, John 6 HD 481

Bruckses Creek 8 HD 52
Bruffit, Gardner 6 HD 254
Bruffit, Garner 3 HD 159
Bruffitt, Daniel 4 HD 435
Bruffitt, Garner 4 HD 435, 607
Bryan, Charles K. 6 HD 436; 8 HD 65, 289, 394, 406
Bryan, Elizabeth 6 HD 436
Bryans Branch 4 HD 446
Bryerwood, John 6 HD 224
Buchanan, James A. 3 HD 361
Buchanan, William 4 HD 545; 6 HD 439; 8 HD 368
Buck Range [tract] 3 HD 408
Buck Valley [tract] 4 HD 318; 6 HD 511
Buckfield [tract] 3 HD 173, 434; 4 HD 483; 6 HD 224; 8 HD 207, 208, 385
Budd, Rebecca 4 HD 196
Burn, Thomas 4 HD 244
Burne, John 3 HD 15
Busby [tract] 3 HD 213, 338
Busick, Abey 6 HD 286
Busick, Anne 3 HD 137
Busick, Ayres 3 HD 308; 6 HD 464, 493, 503; 8 HD 506
Busick, James 3 HD 137; 8 HD 145, 609
Busick, Mary 6 HD 464, 493, 503; 8 HD 506
Busick, Thomas 4 HD 574
Busicks Defiance [tract] 4 HD 473; 8 HD 474 ,
Busicks Lott [tract] 4 HD 103
Busicks Range [tract] 4 HD 41
Busicks Tryal [tract] 3 HD 302
Busicks Venture [tract] 4 HD 140, 473; 8 HD 474
Butens Desire [tract] 8 HD 368

Butten, Elizabeth 6 HD 65, 75
Butten, William 6 HD 65, 75
Buttons Intent [tract] 8 HD 124, 126
Byus, Bartholomew 8 HD 380
Byus, James 3 HD 304; 8 HD 380
Byus, Joseph 3 HD 495; 8 HD 380
Byus, Sarah 8 HD 452
Byus, Stanley 3 HD 287; 4 HD 109; 6 HD 569; 8 HD 128, 452
Byus, Stanley, Justice 3 HD 529, 532, 535, 547, 584; 4 HD 151, 163, 339, 350, 388, 473, etc.; 6 HD 8, 18, 266, 277, 279, 280, etc.; 8 HD 134, 540, 562
Cabin Creek 3 HD 425, 428, 460, 579; 4 HD 412, 428, 574, 582; 6 HD 52
Cabin Creek Mills 8 HD 71
Cabin Creek Neck 8 HD 22
Caile, Elizabeth 6 HD 607, 609; 8 HD 503
Caile, Hall 6 HD 607; 8 HD 503
Caile, John 6 HD 607; 8 HD 503
Caile, John Hall 6 HD 607
Caile, Margaret 6 HD 607
Caile, Rebecca 6 HD 607
Calhoun, James 6 HD 37, 89; 8 HD 394, 406
Callahan, John, Register 3 HD 234
Callander, Capriel 4 HD 65
Callis [tract] 3 HD 20, 76, 423, 526; 4 HD 314; 6 HD 123, 303, 305
Calvert County 8 HD 380
Cambridge 3 HD 35, 43, 50, 65, 145, 150, 160, 218, 221, 236, 244, 279, 335, 345, 437, 517, 520, 529, 535, 552, 601, 604, 611; 4 HD 113, 240, 259, 275, 350, 388, 454, 548, 590, 597; 6 HD 41, 162, 207, 210, 219, 238, 271, 329, 483, 486, 495, 515, 552, 557, 576, 582, 607, 609; 8 HD 71, 147, 272, 295, 332, 383, 387, 394, 397, 399, 406, 503
Cambridge [tract] 3 HD 23
Campbell, Henry 4 HD 170
Campbell, John 8 HD 245
Campbell, Levin H. 6 HD 391
Campbell, William 6 HD 537
Cannon, Betsy 8 HD 574
Cannon, Curtis 8 HD 531
Cannon, James 6 HD 151
Cannon, Jesse 4 HD 25
Cannon, Noah 8 HD 571
Cannon, Richard 6 HD 541
Cannon, Tubman 8 HD 531, 574
Cannon, William 6 HD 151
Canter, Isaac 3 HD 86; 4 HD 386; 8 HD 576
Cantwell, Joseph 6 HD 555
Caroline County 3 HD 133, 289, 290, 361, 397, 447, 477, 578, 579; 4 HD 157, 179, 232, 357, 535, 618; 6 HD 52, 181, 475; 8 HD 22, 191, 196, 221, 273, 452, 455, 461, 544, 571, 590
Carpenter, Sarah 4 HD 118
Carpenters Square [tract] 8 HD 430
Carrol, Rachel 4 HD 541
Carroll, Daniel 6 HD 403
Carroll, Denton 3 HD 218
Carroll, Nich. 4 HD 90
Carroll, Patrick 3 HD 234, 361
Carroll, William 3 HD 434
Carter, Ann 8 HD 22
Carter, Ann Ennalls 3 HD 579
Carter, James 3 HD 578, 579
Carthagenia [tract] 4 HD 379, 566, 568
Cassons Neck 4 HD 603

Castle Haven Creek 3 HD 306, 619; 4 HD 1
Castle Haven Neck 8 HD 524
Casuel County, North Carolina 8 HD 332
Cathagenia [tract] 3 HD 297, 299; 4 HD 377
Cator, Joseph 6 HD 55
Cator, Levin 6 HD 55, 399
Cator, Robson 8 HD 594
Causey, John 3 HD 565
Cedar Creek 4 HD 609; 6 HD 164
Cedar Point 8 HD 249
Cedar Point [tract] 3 HD 555
Chairs, John 8 HD 137
Chalmers, James 4 HD 466
Chalmors Chance [tract] 4 HD 466
Chambers, Ben 8 HD 461
Chance, Bethulia 6 HD 52
Chance, Dorrington 8 HD 455
Chance, Esther 8 HD 455, 590
Chance, Rich 6 HD 52
Chance [tract] 3 HD 231, 275, 302; 4 HD 503; 6 HD 132; 8 HD 368
Chapel 4 HD 388, 470; 8 HD 596
Chapel Creek 3 HD 267, 406
Chapel, the 6 HD 93
Chaplin, Ann 8 HD 622
Chaplin, Solomon 8 HD 622
Chapman, Catherine 6 HD 1, 374
Chapman, Nancy 4 HD 630; 6 HD 1
Chappell, Edwd. 4 HD 553
Chappell, Erasmus 4 HD 601
Chappell, Sarah 4 HD 553
Charles Branch 3 HD 122
Charles County 6 HD 481, 482; 8 HD 380
Charles Creek 3 HD 226; 4 HD 16, 211, 263, 283, 631; 6 HD 68; 8 HD 256, 377

Charles, Isaac 6 HD 241
Charles, John 3 HD 457
Chase, J. Toy., Judge of the General Court 3 HD 224, 487; 6 HD 415, 418
Chase, Jeremiah Townley, Justice of the General Court 8 HD 485
Chase, Samuel, Chief Justice of Maryland 6 HD 96, 515
Chesmans Gore [tract] 6 HD 132
Chesums Gore [tract] 3 HD 8
Chew, Benjamin 8 HD 461
Chew, Henrietta 8 HD 461
Chew, John 8 HD 461
Chew, Samuel 8 HD 461
Chezum, Elizabeth 3 HD 168
Chicamacomico Meeting House 8 BD 64
Chicamacomico River 3 HD 16, 575, 617; 4 HD 5, 78, 118, 175, 309, 524, 526 ; 6 HD 489, 549; 8 HD 493, 579
Chickawan Creek 4 HD 9; 6 HD 249
Chilcut, Thomas 4 HD 391
Chiltenham [tract] 8 HD 263
Chipley, John 8 HD 461
Chipman, Parris 3 HD 101, 178
Chisum (Chizum), James 6 HD 329, 612
Choptank River 4 HD 240; 8 HD 452
Church Creek 3 HD 377; 4 HD 275; 6 HD 381; 8 HD 100, 121, 329, 356
Church Creek Chapel 8 HD 65
Clark County, Kentucky 8 HD 221
Clark, John 3 HD 178
Clark, Sarah 8 HD 424
Clarriage, John 8 HD 52
Clayton, John 8 HD 461
Clerk, James 4 HD 568

Clift [tract] 8 HD 56
Clifton [tract] 3 HD 213, 338, 341, 455; 4 HD 350
Clow, Andrew & Co. 4 HD 185
Cochran, Alexander 4 HD 185
Cochran, William 4 HD 185
Cole, Edward 6 HD 135, 280, 437, 438; 8 HD 305
Cole, George 3 HD 544, 545; 8 HD 142
Cole, John 8 HD 142
Coleman, James 4 HD 574
Coles Creek 3 HD 544, 573, 595; 4 HD 13; 6 HD 361, 511; 8 HD 142
Coles Gift [tract] 6 HD 540
Coles Regulation [tract] 3 HD 544, 545, 547; 6 HD 540
Coles Venture [tract] 3 HD 544, 545, 547
Coleson, John 4 HD 557
Coleson, Thomas 3 HD 366; 6 HD 63
Collinson, Benjamin 3 HD 578, 579; 4 HD 428
Collinson, Edward 3 HD 428
Collinson, Mary 3 HD 579
Collison, Benjamin 3 HD 284, 377, 425, 428; 8 HD 22
Colsten, Betsey 4 HD 154
Colsten, Elizabeth 6 HD 455
Colsten, John 8 HD 218
Colsten - see Colston.
Colsten, Thomas 4 HD 41, 154, 160, 238, 246, 371; 6 HD 118, 139, 178, 329, 455, 478; 8 HD 8, 145, 356, 365, 478
Colsten, Thomas Junr. 4 HD 246
Colstens Industry [tract] 4 HD 154
Colston, Betsy 3 HD 40

Colston, Thomas 3 HD 40, 124, 127, 130, 136, 369, 371
Colstons Dispute [tract] 3 HD 124, 136
Colstons Industry [tract] 3 HD 40
Conclusion [tract] 4 HD 405
Conden, James 8 HD 394, 406; 4 HD 587
Condon, James 6 HD 55
Connelly - see also, Connerly.
Connelly, Thomas 3 HD 397
Connerly, McKeel 3 HD 246, 295, 475; 8 HD 311
Connerly, Nancy 8 HD 315
Connerly, Rebecca 3 HD 246, 295, 475; 8 HD 311
Connerly, Thomas 4 HD 22; 6 HD 332; 8 HD 311, 315
Connerly, William 3 HD 457
Connerlys Branch 3 HD 402
Connolly, Christopher 8 HD 22
Connolly, Dennis 8 HD 22
Connolly, Mary Ann 6 HD 281
Contention [tract] 3 HD 267, 363, 619; 4 HD 35; 8 HD 524
Conway, Chaplin 8 HD 622
Conway, Henry 8 HD 622
Conway, John 8 HD 622
Conway, John Span 8 HD 622
Conway, Robert 8 HD 622
Conway, Susanna 8 HD 622
Conway, Thomas 8 HD 622
Cook, Elizabeth 3 HD 406, 444; 6 HD 266
Cook, Hodson (Hudson) 3 HD 406, 408, 444; 6 HD 266
Cook, John 3 HD 472, 474, 507
Cook, Thomas 8 HD 287, 562
Cooks Point 3 HD 495, 555
Cooleys Branch 8 HD 158, 161

Cooper, James 8 HD 100
Corkran, James 4 HD 541
Corkran, Owen 4 HD 541
Corkran, Peter 8 HD 22
Corkran, Rachel 4 HD 541
Corkran, Timothy 3 HD 428
Corkrin, Henry 4 HD 357
Corner, Solomon Junr. 3 HD 289
Cornish, Solomon 8 HD 625, 626
Cornwell [tract] 3 HD 40, 374; 4 HD 90
Corse, Thomas 6 HD 3; 8 HD 138, 181
Cotmans Swamp [tract] 3 HD 213, 338
Cotneys Island 8 HD 567
Cottrell, Burford 6 HD 481, 482
Cottrell, Thomas 4 HD 297, 300
Couden, Robert 3 HD 589
Coulter, James 4 HD 146
Councell, Henry 8 HD 77
Councell, Sally 8 HD 77
Court House Land 3 HD 221
Covey, Richard 3 HD 30
Cow Garden [tract] 3 HD 72
Cow Pasture [tract] 4 HD 129; 8 HD 126
Cow Quarter [tract] 6 HD 274
Cow Range [tract] 4 HD 215
Cox, Peggy 4 HD 126; 8 HD 176
Coxes Addition to Bridge Neck [tract] 6 HD 489, 549
Craig, John 8 HD 605
Crapper, John 8 HD 593
Crapper, John, Justice 3 HD 246, 295, 299, 315, 397, 402, etc.; 4 HD 22, 26, 29, 125, 179, 386, 405, etc.; 6 HD 10, 27, 52, 57, 59, 86, 112, etc.; 8 HD 145, 181, 307, 311, 337, 377, 569, etc.

Craswell, Patience 8 HD 567
Craswell, William 8 HD 567
Cratchers Ferry 6 HD 86, 292
Craven County, N. C. 8 HD 82
Creaton, John 6 HD 326
Creaton, Nancy 6 HD 326
Creaton, Peggy 3 HD 466
Creighton, Isaac 6 HD 468, 470, 471
Creighton, Lilly 6 HD 471
Creighton - sse also, Creaton.
Creighton, Thomas 3 HD 264
Creighton, Vernon 6 HD 233, 470
Cripples Lott [tract] 3 HD 178
Crocket, Thomas 4 HD 106
Crockett, John 8 HD 168
Crockett, Mary 8 HD 168
Crooked Billet [tract] 4 HD 548
Crooked Ridge [tract] 4 HD 179
Crookshanks, Charles 3 HD 517, 520, 523; 4 HD 113, 238; 6 HD 37, 89, 348; 8 HD 394
Crotchers Ferry 3 HD 33, 81, 537; 6 HD 560; 8 HD 301
Cryer, John Jr. 3 HD 230
Cullenses Interest [tract] 6 HD 415, 418
Cumberland [tract] 3 HD 487; 8 HD 363
Cummins, Joseph 3 HD 354
Cupids Folly [tract] 8 HD 268
Daffin, Charles 3 HD 8, 25, 289, 290, 312; 6 HD 31
Daffin, Joseph 4 HD 607; 6 HD 574; 8 HD 517
Daffin, Mable 3 HD 289
Dail, James 4 HD 90; 6 HD 139; 8 HD 609
Dail, Nancy 6 HD 203
Dail, William 3 HD 329, 395; 4 HD 41, 151, 259; 6 HD 78, 203, 213

Dale, Thomas Junr. 4 HD 330
Dales Addition [tract] 4 HD 603
Dales Right [tract] 4 HD 603
Daley [tract] 6 HD 521
Danielly, Archy 4 HD 412
Daniels Choice [tract] 3 HD 565; 6 HD 227, 368; 8 HD 56
Daniels Choice Resurveyed [tract] 8 HD 56
Daniels Helicon [tract] 4 HD 65, 94, 98; 8 HD 169, 201
Dannelly, John 3 HD 377; 8 HD 22
Darby [tract] 4 HD 26, 29, 303; 6 HD 254
Darbys Addition Enlarged [tract] 4 HD 26, 303
Dare, Ann 4 HD 330
Dare, Henry 3 HD 165
Darley [tract] 3 HD 173, 175, 434; 4 HD 483, 529, 584; 6 HD 13, 519, 525
Davids Chance [tract] 3 HD 83; 8 HD 265, 268
Davidson, Joseph. 8 HD 561
Davies, Jehu 4 HD 118
Davies, Sarah 4 HD 118
Davis, Jehu 4 HD 157
Davis, Lemuel 8 HD 455, 461, 590
Davis, Margaret 8 HD 256
Davis, Martin 8 HD 487
Davis Point 6 HD 387
Davis, Sarah 4 HD 157
Davis, William 8 HD 461
Davis, William W. 8 HD 56
Davis, William Worthington 6 HD 609
Dawson - see also Dowson
Dawson, Anthony 8 HD 221
Dawson, Edward 8 HD 287, 562
Dawson, Elizabeth 3 HD 18; 8 HD 139
Dawson, John 3 HD 18; 8 HD 139
Dawson, Mary 4 HD 71
Dawsons Lott [tract] 3 HD 18; 8 HD 139, 221
Dawsons Security [tract] 8 HD 139
Dean, Allefare 4 HD 78
Dean, Charles 3 HD 617; 4 HD 78, 175; 8 HD 555
Dean, David 4 HD 535; 6 HD 181, 223; 8 HD 273
Dean, Edward 4 HD 357; 6 HD 352
Dean, George 3 HD 226; 6 HD 361
Dean, Henry 3 HD 308; 4 HD 473; 8 HD 474
Dean, James 6 HD 523
Dean, John 4 HD 446
Dean, Mary 4 HD 535; 6 HD 181
Dean, Noble 4 HD 239
Dean, Richard 8 HD 69, 171, 172
Deans Beginning [tract] 4 HD 535; 8 HD 499
Deans Chance [tract] 8 HD 177
Deans Discovery [tract] 6 HD 181; 8 HD 273
Deavors Choice [tract] 8 HD 94, 96
DeDrusina, James 4 HD 508
Deep Water Point [tract] 6 HD 475
Defiance [tract] 4 HD 140
Delahay, Moses 3 HD 254
Delaware 3 HD 81, 113, 164, 187, 189, 192, 302, 354, 397, 431, 455, 494, 573; 4 HD 118, 126, 157, 179, 431, 540, 560, 628; 6 HD 132, 300, 407, 468, 495; 8 HD 168, 290, 377, 478
Dennis, Rob, Justice 3 HD 53, 56, 67, 69, 78, 86, 89, etc.

Dennis, Robert 3 HD 165; 4 HD 65, 249; 6 HD 405, 630; 8 HD 145, 557, 607
Denwoods Resurvey [tract] 3 HD 96
Derby [tract] 4 HD 409
Dick, John 4 HD 65
Dickinson, H. 4 HD 225
Dickinson, H., Clk. 3 HD 428
Dickinson, Henry 3 HD 150, 195, 299, 559; 4 HD 566, 568, 592; 6 HD 495
Dickinson, James 4 HD 592
Dickinson, John. 3 HD 299
Discovery [tract] 3 HD 81, 229, 397; 4 HD 446, 456; 6 HD 59, 86, 420, 560
Dispute [tract] 8 HD 374
Dixon, James 8 HD 221
Dixons Discovery [tract] 3 HD 189; 4 HD 459
Dobson, Thomas 4 HD 185
Dodge, William L. 8 HD 405
Dodson, Joseph 3 HD 577; 4 HD 146
Done, John, Chief Justice 8 HD 64, 65
Done, John, Justice 3 HD 145, 517, 520, 523; 4 HD 240
Done, William 4 HD 494
Donnack- see Dunnock.
Dorchester County Court House 8 HD 8
Dorris, Angell 8 HD 124, 126
Dorris, John 8 HD 124, 126
Dorsey, Edward 3 HD 168
Dorsey, John 3 HD 168; 8 HD 329
Dorsey, Levin 3 HD 168
Dorsey, Robert 8 HD 394, 406
Dossey, John 8 HD 291

Douglass, Alexander 3 HD 480, 499, 594; 4 HD 367, 538; 6 HD 24; 8 HD 212, 254, 259
Douglass, James 3 HD 583; 4 HD 118, 157
Douglass, Joseph 4 HD 459; 6 HD 446; 8 HD 191, 196, 455, 461, 544, 590
Douglass, Mary N. 4 HD 386
Douglass, William 4 HD 118, 157
Dover (Delaware) 3 HD 354, 455; 6 HD 495
Dover [tract] 6 HD 1, 374
Downes, Henry 3 HD 290
Dowson, Joseph 3 HD 221, 239; 4 HD 508
Draera, William 8 HD 557
Draw Bridge 8 HD 64
Dunnock, Thomas 6 HD 420
Dunnock, William 6 HD 420, 590
Duvall, Gabriel 6 HD 537
Dyer, John 6 HD 332
Earle, James Junr. 8 HD 293
Easons Venture [tract] 3 HD 142
Easton, Town of 8 HD 92
Easum, Bartholomew 3 HD 142
Eccleston, Charles 3 HD 474, 555; 4 HD 623; 8 HD 12
Eccleston, Elizabeth 4 HD 201
Eccleston, Hugh 4 HD 201
Eccleston, John 3 HD 25, 167, 202, 209, 216, 239, 286, 333, 559, 571, 584; 4 HD 94, 97, 172, 219, 240, 402, 508, 552, 573; 6 HD 3, 70, 72, 74, 126, 281, 291, 502; 8 HD 22, 176, 195, 428, 430, 627
Eccleston, John, Justice 3 HD 416, 491, 499, 537, 579; 4 HD 5, 25, 57, 78, 98, 118, 157, 175, etc.; 8 HD 301 425, 513, 579, 583

Eccleston, Joseph 4 HD 623; 8 HD 12
Eccleston, Sarah 6 HD 563
Eccleston, William W. 6 HD 563
Ecclestons Regulation Rectified [tract] 4 HD 201, 573; 8 HD 208
Edgar, Arnold 6 HD 195
Edgar, Henry 3 HD 526; 4 HD 314; 6 HD 123, 303, 305
Edgar, Keziah 4 HD 314; 6 HD 123, 303
Edgar, Thomas 6 HD 195
Edgars Beginning [tract] 6 HD 195
Edgars Creek 8 HD 374
Edloes Purchase [tract] 6 HD 233, 470, 471
Edmondson, Elisabeth 4 HD 399
Edmondson, James 3 HD 302; 4 HD 140, 451
Edmondson, John 3 HD 85, 249; 4 HD 451
Edmondson, Moses 4 HD 451
Edmondson, Peter 3 HD 133; 8 HD 56
Edmondson, Pollard 4 HD 83, 399; 6 HD 412, 425
Edmondson, Samuel 4 HD 451
Edmondsons Regulation [tract] 4 HD 83, 399
Edwards, John 3 HD 589
Elecson, Elizabeth 8 HD 437
Elecson, Robert 8 HD 437
Ellett, John 4 HD 459
Elliot, Elizabeth 3 HD 133
Elliot, Francis 3 HD 133
Elliot, John 3 HD 103; 6 HD 129
Elliot, Nathaniel 3 HD 14, 183, 351
Elliot, Thomas 3 HD 1
Elliott, Hooper 3 HD 377; 6 HD 433
Elliott, John 4 HD 367; 8 HD 119
Elliott, Nathaniel 4 HD 89; 6 HD 195, 495
Eloner McGraw Desire [tract] 6 HD 584
End of Controversy [tract] 3 HD 168
End of Strife [tract] 3 HD 74, 109; 6 HD 371
Ending [tract] 3 HD 500
Ennalls, Andrew Skinner 6 HD 107
Ennalls, Ann 3 HD 167, 386, 589; 8 HD 152, 155
Ennalls, Anne 6 HD 46, 48
Ennalls, Bartholomew (Bartho.) 3 HD 72, 218, 254, 493, 560, 561, 562, 564; 4 HD 598; 6 HD 67, 224, 228 291; 8 HD 605
Ennalls, Elizabeth 3 HD 167; 4 HD 201, 607; 8 HD 605
Ennalls, Elizabeth G. 3 HD 353
Ennalls Ferry 3 HD 43
Ennalls Ferry Warehouse 3 HD 45; 6 HD 288; 8 HD 441
Ennalls, Henry 3 HD 6, 10, 43, 74, 109, 213, 221, 282, 338, 354, 394, 437, 442, 493, 560, 561, 562, 564, 577, 583, 604, 608, 611, 613; 4 HD 22, 47, 106, 107, 170, 324, 548, 600; 6 HD 63, 72, 74, 82, 107, 224, 261, 371, 495; 8 HD 65, 91, 305, 329, 433, 434, 478
Ennalls, John 3 HD 167; 4 HD 201; 6 HD 432
Ennalls, Joseph 3 HD 43, 45, 167, 202, 540; 4 HD 201, 224, 574; 6 HD 84, 107, 126; 8 HD 91, 433, 434
Ennalls Luck [tract] 3 HD 213, 338
Ennalls, Mary 3 HD 552; 6 HD 67, 401

Ennalls Outrange [tract] 3 HD 35, 386, 437, 442, 589; 6 HD 82
Ennalls Regulation [tract] 4 HD 201
Ennalls, Sarah 3 HD 6, 10, 43, 72, 74, 109, 221, 338, 354, 437, 604, 608, 611, 613; 4 HD 22; 6 HD 63, 495
Ennalls, Thomas 3 HD 167, 213, 571; 4 HD 201; 6 HD 46, 48, 377; 8 HD 433
Ennalls Town [tract] 3 HD 216
Ennalls Warehouse 3 HD 411; 4 HD 227
Ennalls, William 3 HD 167, 209; 4 HD 201, 480, 552; 6 HD 84 126; 8 HD 225
Ennalls's Friendshlp [tract] 6 HD 46
Ennalls's Outrange [tract] 6 HD 576; 8 HD 152, 155, 390
Ennallsls Purchase [tract] 8 HD 434
Episcopal Church 8 HD 71
Eppin Forrest [tract] 4 HD 57, 309
Errexson, Matthew (Matthew Errexsons Bridge) 4 HD 563
Eucim, Hooper 8 HD 200
Evans, Robert 6 HD 606
Evans, Samuel 6 HD 224
Ewing, Patrick.3 HD 218, 244, 254; 8 HD 295
Ewing, Robert 3 HD 145, 218, 244, 520; 4 HD 113; 8 HD 295, 513
Exchange [tract] 3 HD 251, 414; 4 HD 309, 357, 548; 6 HD 352, 457; 8 HD 158, 163, 169, 221
Fair Dealing [tract] 3 HD 202
Fallen, Daniel 6 HD 261
Fargerson, Samuel P. 8 HD 449
Fargusson, George 4 HD 359
Farham Creek 3 HD 199; 4 HD 601; 8 HD 529

Faunce, John 4 HD 572
Feirm Creek 3 HD 111
Feirm [tract] 3 HD 111
Ferguson, Peter 4 HD 183, 185, 238; 8 HD 295, 397, 399
Fern Creek 6 HD 450; 8 HD 106, 269
Ferry Point [tract] 6 HD 468
Finley, John 3 HD 244; 4 HD 183, 185, 238; 8 HD 295
Firm Creek 4 HD 165, 167, 609
Firm Creek Bridge 6 HD 141
Fisher, Henry 3 HD 352
Fishers Chance [tract] 8 HD 246, 276
Fishers Landing [tract] 4 HD 115; 6 HD 405
Fishers Title [tract] 4 HD 77, 97, 98
Fishing Bay 3 HD 202
Fishing Creek 3 HD 6, 10, 40, 127, 139, 210, 236, 279, 345, 549, 604, 611, 613; 4 HD 90, 151, 238, 259, 477, 506, 513; 6 HD 63, 89, 203, 213, 329, 379, 439, 455, 478, 569, 612, 615; 8 HD 1, 64, 100, 134, 332
Fishing Creek Church 6 HD 552, 557; 8 HD 450
Fishing Creek Point Regulated [tract] 3 HD 514
Fishing Creek Point [tract] 3 HD 514
Fishing Lot [tract] 6 HD 300
Fishlng Bay 6 HD 389
Fishwick, Jean 4 HD 90
Fishwick, William 4 HD 90
Fishwicks Adventure [tract] 4 HD 98; 8 HD 169
Fitchett, Salathiel 8 HD 292
Fitchett, Thomas 8 HD 292
Fitchew, Ezekiel 3 HD 377; 4 HD 103
Fitchews Industry [tract] 4 HD 103

Fitchu, Sarah 8 HD 145
Fitchu, Thomas 8 HD 145
Fitzgerald, Nancy 3 HD 561
Fitzhugh, Levin 8 HD 216
Fitzhugh, Sarah 8 HD 216
Fletcher, Bartholo. 8 HD 149, 576
Fletcher, Bartholomew 3 HD 86, 293; 4 HD 596
Fletcher, Benthal 4 HD 125
Fletcher, Magary 8 HD 576
Fletcher, Margery 3 HD 86
Fletcher, William 3 HD 96, 98
Fookes, John K. 6 HD 612, 615
Fookes's Regulation [tract] 3 HD 389, 391
Fooks, John 8 HD 329
Fooks, Levin 3 HD 168
Foresight [tract] 3 HD 117, 122
Fork Chapel 6 HD 292
Fork Neck 3 HD 251
Fort Cumberland 3 HD 224, 234
Foulue, John 4 HD 160
Fountain, John 6 HD 428
Four Sisters [tract] 6 HD 1, 374
Fourth Callis [tract] 3 HD 76
Fox Creek 4 HD 165, 167
Fox, Edward 4 HD 183
Foxwell, Abram 4 HD 287, 291
Foxwell, Elizabeth 4 HD 211
Foxwell, John 4 HD 279, 283; 8 HD 622
Foxwell, Levi 3 HD 434; 4 HD 609
Foxwell, Rhoda 4 HD 16
Foxwell, Roger 3 HD 107; 4 HD 16, 211, 287, 291, 609
Foxwell, Sarah 4 HD 279, 283
Foxwell, Shadrach 3 HD 107
Foxwells Endeavour [tract] 4 HD 609
Foxwells Lot [tract] 4 HD 16, 211, 279, 283; 6 HD 68

Foxwells Venture [tract] 3 HD 107
Fraizer, James 6 HD 155
Framptom, Marget 8 HD 544
Frampton, Hubird 6 HD 371
Francis's Cottage [tract] 3 HD 23, 148; 8 HD 513
Frazier, James 8 HD 480
Frazier, John 3 HD 495; 8 HD 508
Frazier, Solomon 3 HD 400; 4 HD 324; 8 HD 12, 56, 238, 610, 612, 618
Frazier, William 4 HD 545; 8 HD 478
Friends Assistance [tract] 4 HD 343, 431, 544
Friends Discovery [tract] 3 HD 491; 8 HD 493
Gadd, Richard. 4 HD 359
Gadds Ferry 8 HD 335
Gaither, Elias 8 HD 448
Gale, George 3 HD 94, 96, 98, 101, 103, 105; 4 HD 420; 6 HD 446; 8 HD 547
Gambrell, Abraham 6 HD 429
Gambrell, Richardson 6 HD 230, 429
Gay Street 3 HD 27
Geators Creek 3 HD 608
Geoghegan, John 4 HD 144, 425, 444
Geoghegan, Moses 4 HD 425, 438; 6 HD 412; 8 HD 327
Geoghegan, Rebecca 4 HD 438, 441, 444
Geoghegan, William 4 HD 438, 441, 444, 542; 6 HD 51, 441, 442; 8 HD 329
Geoghegen, John 8 HD 131
Georges Priviledge [tract] 6 HD 361
Gibson, William 3 HD 1; 6 HD 37, 89, 348, 374; 8 HD 394, 406
Giffin, John 8 HD 179, 181

Gift to My Daughter [tract] 4 HD 318, 371, 374
Gift [tract] 8 HD 139
Gilmor, Robert 3 HD 1; 8 HD 349
Gilmore, Robert 6 HD 167
Gist, J. E. 8 HD 64, 151, 373
Gist, John Elder 4 HD 508; 6 HD 135, 184, 439, 483
Gladsons Branch 3 HD 189
Glasgow [tract] 3 HD 218, 517, 532
Glover, Elizabeth 8 HD 397
Glover, Richard 3 HD 213, 338, 517; 4 HD 350, 597; 6 HD 184
Glover, Widow 6 HD 238
Godwin, Daniel 3 HD 8, 25, 195; 6 HD 31, 132
Godwin, Sarah 6 HD 31, 132
Golden Grove 3 HD 178
Goldsborough, Charles 3 HD 6, 139, 202, 213, 335, 338, 341, 354, 395, 520, 552; 6 HD 203, 210, 213, 495, 609; 8 HD 16, 56, 134, 406, 607
Goldsborough, Elizabeth 3 HD 455; 4 HD 43; 8 HD 134
Goldsborough, Howes 3 HD 168, 213, 354; 4 HD 43; 6 HD 495, 627; 8 HD 290
Goldsborough, John 3 HD 6, 139, 354; 6 HD 495, 515; 8 HD 147, 290
Goldsborough, R. 3 HD 329
Goldsborough, R., Judge of the General Court 3 HD 213, 394, 455; 4 HD 43; 6 HD 495, 627
Goldsborough, Rachel 3 HD 139, 335, 341, 354, 394
Goldsborough, Rebecca 3 HD 213, 354; 6 HD 495, 627

Goldsborough, Richard 3 HD 210, 213, 236, 279, 282, 335, 338, 341, 345, 354, 394, 442, 455, 549
Goldsborough, Richard 4 HD 259, 350, 388, 513; 6 HD 495, 609
Goldsborough, Robert 3 HD 6, 139, 159, 168, 213, 335, 338, 341, 394, 395, 455, 514, 613; 4 HD 43, 388; 6 HD 203, 213, 495, 627
Goldsborough, Sarah 3 HD 354; 8 HD 390
Goldsborough, William 3 HD 139, 213, 335, 341, 354, 414; 4 HD 43; 6 HD 495, 576, 609, 627; 8 HD 387, 390
Goldsboroughs Outlet [tract] 3 HD 210, 213, 338, 341
Good Intent [tract] 3 HD 287; 6 HD 348
Good Luck by Friendship [tract] 4 HD 412
Good Luck to Wallace [tract] 3 HD 15
Good Luck [tract] 6 HD 126; 8 HD 158, 161, 163
Gooding, John, Justice 4 HD 535; 6 HD 24, 31, 181, 241, 281, 341, etc.; 8 HD 74, 84, 119, 179, 264, 273, 279, etc.
Goodridges Choice [tract] 3 HD 8, 284, 425, 428, 460, 578, 579; 4 HD 428; 6 HD 132; 8 HD 22
Googe, John 8 HD 16
Goose Creek 3 HD 202
Goose Creek Swamp 6 HD 147
Goose Creek Swamp [tract] 8 HD 235
Goostree, Absolom 8 HD 143

Gootee, Andrew 3 HD 423
Gootee, Bedcar 6 HD 189
Gootee, Capewell 6 HD 189
Gootee, Edward 6 HD 189
Gootee, Elizabeth 6 HD 189
Gootee, Frederick 3 HD 355
Gootee, Jabus 4 HD 573
Gootee, John 6 HD 189
Gootee, Mary 6 HD 189
Gootee, Priscilla 3 HD 355, 423, 526
Gootee, Shadrach 6 HD 189
Gootee, Zebulon 6 HD 189
Gootees Choice [tract] 3 HD 526
Gootees Defiance [tract] 6 HD 305, 307
Gootees Lott [tract] 8 HD 565
Gootees Neck 3 HD 355
Gordon, Peter 3 HD 158, 218; 4 HD 22; 6 HD 162, 279, 280, 371, 401
Goslen, Ambros 8 HD 363
Goslen, John 4 HD 22
Goslen, Smith 8 HD 145, 470
Goslin, Ezekiel 8 HD 307
Goslins Join [tract] 8 HD 544
Goutee, Jacob 6 HD 495
Goutee - see Gootee.
Grace Reding (Grass Reading) [tract] 8 HD 497
Grace, Richard 6 HD 67
Grace, Thomas 6 HD 454
Graham, Philip 4 HD 13
Grainger, Edward 8 HD 22
Granger, Rosanna 8 HD 327
Grass Reading [tract] 6 HD 617, 620, 624
Gray, Archibald 4 HD 491
Gray, Thomas 4 HD 491
Gray, William 3 HD 545
Grayham, George 8 HD 409, 548

Grayham, Mary 8 HD 413
Grayham, Phillip 8 HD 305, 413, 418, 548
Great Britain 3 HD 354
Great Choptank Parish 6 HD 607, 609
Great Choptank River 3 HD 267, 287; 6 HD 162, 219, 271; 8 HD 16, 96, 238
Green Bank [tract] 3 HD 40
Green Branch 8 HD 472
Green, Esther 3 HD 584
Green, James 3 HD 309
Green, John 6 HD 313; 8 HD 273, 499
Green, Mary 3 HD 259
Green, Peggy 8 HD 307
Green, Thomas 3 HD 202, 259; 8 HD 307
Green, William 3 HD 309
Greens Adventure [tract] 8 HD 134
Greenwood, John 6 HD 230
Griffin, Fanny 3 HD 363, 410
Griffin, Nathan 3 HD 4, 383, 412
Griffith, Ales 8 HD 415, 548
Griffith, Amos 3 HD 234
Griffith Beginning [tract] 8 HD 415
Griffith, Edward 6 HD 151; 8 HD 171, 172, 409, 411, 413, 415, 418, 486, 505, 548
Griffith, John 3 HD 183; 4 HD 466; 6 HD 195, 534; 8 HD 63, 171, 172, 173, 215, 305, 607
Griffith, Lewis 3 HD 352; 8 HD 409, 415
Griffith, Mary 8 HD 409
Griffith, Robert 3 HD 297, 299, 326, 327, 464; 4 HD 377, 379; 6 HD 195

Griffiths Adventure [tract] 8 HD 411, 413, 548
Griffiths Beginning [tract] 8 HD 548
Grove [tract] 3 HD 412; 4 HD 438, 441, 444; 6 HD 175; 8 HD 225
Guilford County, N. C. 3 HD 545
Gum Swamp [tract] 3 HD 322; 4 HD 451
Hackaran [tract], 6 HD 582
Hackrin [tract] 4 HD 477
Hackron [tract] 3 HD 206
Hailes's Choice [tract] 3 HD 329, 395; 6 HD 203, 213
Hall, Joseph 4 HD 466
Halls Branch 4 HD 201, 4808 HD 208
Hambrooks Point 4 HD 240; 6 HD 515
Hamilton, John 3 HD 545
Hammilton, Elizabeth 4 HD 146
Hammond, Nicholas 3 HD 145, 150, 428; 8 HD 147
Hammond, Ns. 4 HD 560; 6 HD 439
Hammond, Tiffany 8 HD 272
Hammond, William 4 HD 371
Hampton [tract] 3 HD 253; 4 HD 574, 582; 6 HD 283; 8 HD 342
Hamsteed [tract] 8 HD 269
Handley, Handy 4 HD 431
Handleys Regulation [tract] 4 HD 431
Handsell 4 HD 9
Handsell [tract] 6 HD 249
Hanson, Alexander Contee 4 HD 489
Hanson, Alexander Contee, Chancellor 6 HD 24
Harcum, Thomas 4 HD 297, 300
Harcum, William 4 HD 297, 300
Hard Fortune [tract] 6 HD 560
Hardcastle, John 3 HD 290

Hardican, Robert 6 HD 283; 8 HD 22
Hardikin, Robert 4 HD 574
Harford County 4 HD 412
Harper, Beachamp 4 HD 393
Harper, Beauchamp 8 HD 363
Harper, Daniel 8 HD 149
Harper, David 3 HD 89; 6 HD 300; 8 HD 425
Harper, Hetty 3 HD 397, 573
Harper, James 8 HD 561
Harper, John 8 HD 561
Harper, Joseph 3 HD 397, 573
Harper, Thomas 3 HD 29
Harpers Folly [tract] 3 HD 487; 8 HD 363
Harpers Meadows [tract] 3 HD 397
Harpers Seat [tract] 3 HD 487
Harpers Third Purchase [tract] 3 HD 189
Harrington, Elizabeth 3 HD 579
Harrington, John 6 HD 546; 8 HD 459
Harrington, Nathan 3 HD 257, 284, 377, 460, 578, 579; 8 HD 22
Harrington, Peter 3 HD 117, 119, 121; 4 HD 359; 6 HD 420
Harris, Edward 4 HD 402
Harrison, Hall 6 HD 607; 8 HD 503
Harrison, Robert 3 HD 145, 150, 202; 6 HD 82, 238; 8 HD 147, 152, 155
Harrison, Robert, Justice 3 HD 150, 210, 216, 244, 254, 286, etc.; 4 HD 1, 115, 146, 147, 240, 435, etc.; 6 HD 63, 78, 118, 167, 203, 213, 439
Harrison, Sam 4 HD 330
Harrison, Samuel 8 HD 109
Harriss, Risdon 4 HD 129
Hart, Edward 8 HD 596

Hart, Naboath 3 HD 111
Hart, Naboth 6 HD 151, 261; 8 HD 69, 173
Hart, Richard , 4 HD 609
Harwood, Nicholas (Nich.) 3 HD 589; 4 HD 90, 330; 8 HD 109
Harwoods Choice [tract] 3 HD 10, 127, 608, 613; 6 HD 63, 455; 8 HD 100, 121
Haskins, Henry 8 HD 91, 305
Haskins, Joseph 6 HD 107
Haskins, Sarah 6 HD 107
Haskins, William 6 HD 405
Hawhill Security [tract] 6 HD 420
Hay-Land [tract] 3 HD 329, 395
Hayes, Elizabeth 8 HD 373
Hayland [tract] 6 HD 203, 213
Hayward, Alin 6 HD 536
Hayward, David 6 HD 529
Hayward, Francis 3 HD 148; 8 HD 119, 513
Hayward, Harriot 8 HD 92
Hayward, John 3 HD 148
Hayward, Mary 6 HD 584, 587, 595, 598
Hayward, Rebeckah 6 HD 266
Hayward, Richard 4 HD 145
Hayward, William 3 HD 148, 158, 267, 411, 619; 4 HD 1, 127; 6 HD 266, 312, 313, 584, 587, 595, 598; 8 HD 179
Haywards Lott [tract] 8 HD 221
Haywards Regulation [tract] 3 HD 148
Hazzard (Hazzard) [tract] 3 HD 355; 4 HD 229, 391; 6 HD 630; 8 HD 596
Head of Farham [tract] 8 HD 596
Head of Firm [tract] 8 HD 269

Head Range [tract] 3 HD 40; 4 HD 90, 334; 6 HD 89, 552; 8 HD 65
Henderson, Robert 4 HD 183, 185; 8 HD 295
Hengson, Thomas 4 HD 572
Henly, Hooper 4 HD 65
Henry, Ezekiel 4 HD 357
Henry, John 4 HD 85; 6 HD 391; 8 HD 260, 262, 487
Henry, Sary 4 HD 357
Henrys Delight [tract] 3 HD 89
Hereford [tract] 8 HD 82
Heron, Cuthbert 8 HD 212
Heron, Elizabeth 4 HD 555
Heron, Robert 4 HD 555
Heron, Susanna 4 HD 555
Herring Run Branch 6 HD 352
Hickory Point [tract] 6 HD 292
Hickory Ridge Enlarged [tract] 4 HD 78, 175, 189; 8 HD 555
Hickory Ridge Regulated [tract] 8 HD 425, 583
Hicks, Denwood 6 HD 430
Hicks Field [tract] 6 HD 112
Hicks, Henry 3 HD 537; 4 HD 574; 8 HD 22
Hicks, Henry H. 6 HD 433
Hicks, John 6 HD 525
Hicks, Mary 3 HD 213, 338
Hicks, Sarah 3 HD 173, 175; 4 HD 483; 6 HD 13, 135, 184, 344, 346, 525; 8 HD 586
Hicks, Thomas 3 HD 47, 173, 175, 434, 537; 4 HD 483, 529, 545, 548, 584; 6 HD 13, 135, 184, 288, 344, 346, 430, 519, 521, 525; 8 HD 373, 441, 534, 537, 586
Hicks, William Ennalls 3 HD 173, 175; 4 HD 201; 6 HD 525

Hill, Eben 3 HD 1
Hill, Elizabeth 8 HD 8
Hill, James 8 HD 8
Hill, John 3 HD 514, 594
Hill, Mary 8 HD 8
Hills Point 4 HD 388
Hingson, Thomas 3 HD 165; 4 HD 459, 581, 596; 6 HD 86, 129; 8 HD 145, 557, 607
Hocady Creek 4 HD 607
Hockadays Branch. 4 HD 483
Hodson, Anne 6 HD 274, 285
Hodson Branch 8 HD 82
Hodson, Catharine 4 HD 293; 6 HD 46
Hodson, Charles 3 HD 242, 286, 559; 4 HD 225, 383, 402, 524, 526, 552; 6 HD 224, 274, 285, 435, 502, 537; 8 HD 279, 373, 441
Hodson, Elizabeth 3 HD 59; 4 HD 5
Hodson, Hannah 8 HD 179, 279
Hodson, Henry 3 HD 59, 175; 4 HD 5, 307; 6 HD 567; 8 HD 254
Hodson, James 3 HD 16, 167, 213; 4 HD 293; 6 HD 46; 8 HD 554
Hodson, John 3 HD 213; John 4 HD 5
Hodson, John Senr. 3 HD 167
Hodson, Levin 4 HD 225; 6 HD 72; 8 HD 179, 279, 513
Hodson, Thomas 3 HD 419, 491, 617; 4 HD 249; 6 HD 96; 8 HD 493, 554, 577
Hodson, Thomas Ennalls 3 HD 213
Hodsons Creek 3 HD 483, 502, 505, 507; 8 HD 287
Hodsons Seat [tract] 8 HD 279
Hodsons Venture [tract] 8 HD 577
Hog Quarter [tract] 3 HD 111, 326
Hog Range [tract] 3 HD 189

Hogg Marsh 4 HD 129
Hogg Quarter [tract] 4 HD 74
Hogg Range [tract] 6 HD 214, 407
Hogg Ridge [tract] 3 HD 326
Hogg Yard [tract] 3 HD 94, 96, 98, 101, 103, 105, 224
Holland, Isaac 3 HD 589
Holland, Jane 3 HD 589
Holliday, Clement 6 HD 537
Holliday, Richard 6 HD 440
Hollidays, Mr. 4 HD 611
Hollock, James 4 HD 560
Hollock, John 4 HD 560
Hollock, Thomas 4 HD 82
Hollock, William 4 HD 82
Holt, Jonathan 8 HD 56
Hongar River 8 HD 469
Honourable Division [tract] 4 HD 334; 8 BD 65
Hooper, Ann 3 HD 33, 72
Hooper, Betty 8 HD 114
Hooper, Elizabeth 6 HD 468; 8 HD 249, 518
Hooper, Ennalls 3 HD 579
Hooper, Henry 3 HD 33, 72, 173, 177, 202, 377; 6 HD 317
Hooper, Henry, Col. 8 HD 22
Hooper, Henry, Gen. 8 HD 22
Hooper, Henry, Justice of Provincial Court 8 HD 225
Hooper, Henry of Ennalls 8 HD 22
Hooper, Henry Qs. 4 HD 65; 8 HD 114, 158, 163, 176
Hooper, James 3 HD 284, 623; 4 HD 612; 8 HD 22
Hooper, John (or Henry) 6 HD 41
Hooper, John 3 HD 46, 562, 564; 4 HD 548, 598, 600; 6 HD 3, 228, 291, 425, 468; 8 HD 582
Hooper, John, Major 8 HD 249, 518

Hooper, John or James 6 HD 394, 399
Hooper, Joshua 4 HD 359
Hooper, Mary 3 HD 33; 4 HD 612
Hooper, Nancy 4 HD 612; 8 HD 569
Hooper, Nathaniel 3 HD 45
Hooper, Roger A. 4 HD 548; 6 HD 245, 502
Hooper, Samuel 3 HD 38, 168, 286, 400, 512, 559; 4 HD 563
Hooper, Sarah 3 HD 33, 72; 8 HD 298
Hooper Straits 6 HD 93
Hooper, Thomas 4 HD 612; 8 HD 22
Hooper, Thomas E. 8 HD 298
Hooper, Thomas Junr. 3 HD 282
Hooper, William Ennalls 3 HD 33, 72, 289, 290; 8 HD 582
Hoopers Beginning [tract] 3 HD 512
Hoopers Conclusion [tract] 4 HD 612
Hoopers Delight [tract] 4 HD 246
Hoopers Fortune [tract] 6 HD 274
Hoopers Island 6 HD 314, 317, 322, 326, 338; 8 HD 242, 518
Hoopers Island [tract] 8 HD 249
Hoopers Labour [tract] 4 HD 601
Hoopers Outlett [tract] 8 HD 158
Hoopers Range [tract] 3 HD 229; 8 HD 409, 415, 548
Hoopers Strait 8 HD 109, 377
Hope [tract] 6 HD 564
Hopewell [tract] 4 HD 179
Hopkins's Island [tract] 6 HD 495
Hoplite Creek 6 HD 151
Horn [tract] 8 HD 56
Horsey Downs [tract] 8 HD 374
House Town [tract] 8 HD 428
Howard, Samuel H. 8 HD 88
Howard, William 4 HD 89
Howards Lott [tract] 3 HD 18

Howells Regulation [tract] 6 HD 82
Howeth, Elizabeth 8 HD 293
Hubbard, James 4 HD 145
Hubbard, John 8 HD 137
Hubbard, Joseph 3 HD 474, 483, 505
Hubbard, Thomas 6 HD 266, 270, 544
Hubbert, Levin 3 HD 502
Hubbert, Samuel 8 HD 12
Hubbert, Thomas 3 HD 444
Hubbert, William 8 HD 508
Huburtts Hazard [tract] 6 HD 52
Hudnall, Richard 4 HD 297, 300
Hudson, James. 3 HD 254
Hudsons Branch 3 HD 137
Hudsons Creek 3 HD 472; 6 HD 475; 8 HD 562
Huffington, John 4 HD 163
Huggins, Hannah 4 HD 47
Hungar River 3 HD 198, 199, 489; 4 HD 35, 220, 266, 269, 279, 283, 287, 291, 631; 6 HD 317, 373, 495, 587, 595, 598; 8 HD 249, 256, 485
Hunting Creek 3 HD 8; 4 HD 412, 574, 582; 6 HD 132, 283, 352
Hunting Creek Church 3 HD 402, 457
Hurdle, Hardy 6 HD 617; 8 HD 124
Hurley, Isaac 4 HD 81; 8 HD 487
Hurley, William 4 HD 81
Hurlock, William 6 HD 563
Hust, Levi 4 HD 170
Hust, Samuel 8 HD 167, 625
Hutchinson, John 3 HD 420
Hydes Chance [tract] 8 HD 540
Increase [tract] 3 HD 487; 8 HD 363
Indian Lands 3 HD 213, 404; 4 HD 219; 8 HD 480

Indian Quarter [tract] 3 HD 472, 474, 483, 505
Indian Ridge [tract] 3 HD 406, 410, 444; 6 HD 266
Ingrum, Paul 8 HD 16
Inlett [tract] 4 HD 129
Insley, Althadora 8 HD 232, 235
Insley, Andrew 3 HD 166; 6 HD 261
Insley, Crissey 8 HD 230
Insley, Esau 4 HD 601
Insley, Gabriel 6 HD 261, 389, 523
Insley, Jacob 4 HD 165; 6 HD 261; 8 HD 377, 559
Insley, James 4 HD 165, 167; 6 HD 261; 8 HD 559
Insley, John 3 HD 166; 6 HD 261
Insley, Joice 4 HD 167, 353
Insley, Joseph 6 HD 261
Insley, Joyce 8 HD 559
Insley, Keziah 8 HD 377
Insley, Leah 8 HD 234
Insley, Letisha 8 HD 233
Insley, Levi 4 HD 165, 167, 353; 6 HD 147, 261; 8 HD 230, 232, 233, 234, 235, 559
Insley, Thomas 3 HD 187, 189; 4 HD 581; 6 HD 407
Insley, Valentine 4 HD 601; 6 HD 261
Insley, William 4 HD 167; 6 HD 147, 164, 261, 389, 523; 8 HD 203, 235, 559
Insleys Folly [tract] 6 HD 164
Insleys Prevention [tract] 3 HD 111;
Insleys Priviledge [tract] 8 HD 559
Insleys Purchase [tract] 6 HD 389
Isaac Venture [tract] 3 HD 189, 469
Jacobs, Elizabeth 3 HD 315, 318
Jacobs, Jacob 3 HD 315, 318; 8 HD 145, 576

Jacobs, Jonathan 3 HD 315, 318
James Island 4 HD 425, 438, 441, 444; 6 HD 387
James, Mary 3 HD 254
Jarrell Neck [tract] 4 HD 147
Jarrett, Jemima 4 HD 16
Jarrett, Matthew 4 HD 16
Jeams, Joseph 3 HD 575
Jenkins Creek 3 HD 213, 338, 341; 8 HD 452
Jesseys Lott [tract] 6 HD 96
Jib, the [tract] 3 HD 489
Jinkins, Henry 6 HD 437, 438
Jinkins, Thomas 6 HD 437
Jockeys Cabbin Branch 4 HD 601
Johns Adventure [tract] 4 HD 580
Johns Beginning [tract] 6 HD 462, 509
Johns Creek 8 HD 16
Johns Delight [tract] 3 HD 53, 56; 6 HD 65, 75
Johns Desire [tract] 3 HD 236, 279, 345
Johns Industry [tract] 4 HD 94, 118; 6 HD 489, 549, 579; 8 HD 169
Johns Labour [tract] 8 HD 161
Johns Outlett [tract] 8 HD 425
Johns Venture [tract] 4 HD 438, 441
Johnson, Ann 6 HD 170
Johnson, Annaritta 4 HD 81
Johnson, Charles 4 HD 416; 6 HD 27
Johnson, Ezekiel 3 HD 15; 8 HD 329
Johnson, John 3 HD 575; 4 HD 561
Johnson, Joseph 4 HD 81
Johnson, Joshua 3 HD 264; 8 HD 512
Johnson, Levin 8 HD 512
Johnson, Mary 3 HD 264
Johnson, Nathan 4 HD 65
Johnson, Randolph 3 HD 575; 4 HD 174, 561; 6 HD 121, 170

Johnson, Thomas 3 HD 572
Johnson, Whitington 6 HD 261, 523
Johnson, William 4 HD 585
Johnsons Chapel 8 HD 65
Johnsons Contrivance [tract] 3 HD 185
Johnsons Last Purchase [tract] 6 HD 507
Johnsons Misfortune [tract] 6 HD 75
Johnsons Plane [tract] 6 HD 507
Jones, Ann 3 HD 56
Jones, Catherine 4 HD 554
Jones, Cloudsbury 3 HD 254
Jones, Delitha 3 HD 425
Jones, Eleanor 4 HD 544
Jones, Ezekiel 8 HD 216
Jones, Heber 8 HD 461
Jones, James 4 HD 343
Jones, James B. 3 HD 347
Jones, James Junr. 4 HD 343
Jones, John 3 HD 206, 450, 452, 514, 571, 624; 4 HD 49, 135, 138, 343; 6 HD 235; 8 HD 8, 238, 459, 460
Jones, John, Justice 8 HD 492
Jones, John of Morgan 8 HD 521
Jones, John of Thos. 8 HD 52
Jones, Keziah 4 HD 263
Jones, Laben 6 HD 292
Jones, Leonard 4 HD 343
Jones, Levin 8 HD 289
Jones, Lunaria (Lurania) 3 HD 450, 452
Jones, Lurana 4 HD 49, 138
Jones, Luranah 6 HD 235
Jones, Mary 4 HD 343
Jones, Morgan 3 HD 53, 450, 452, 487; 4 HD 49, 135, 138; 6 HD 100, 116, 235, 592
Jones, Nancy 3 HD 53
Jones, Obadiah 6 HD 288
Jones, Roger 3 HD 377, 624; 4 HD 103
Jones, Solomon 4 HD 83; 6 HD 409
Jones, Susannah 8 HD 254
Jones, Thomas 3 HD 495, 570; 4 HD 359; 6 HD 155, 175, 286, 287, 385, 407, 409, 410, 412, 425; 8 HD 8, 52, 238, 460, 508
Jones, Thomas Junr. 3 HD 137, 168, 571; 4 HD 193
Jones, Thomas, Justice 3 HD 10, 16, 18, 35, 38, 40, 43, etc.; 4 HD 41, 49, 54, 61, 83, 103, 132, etc.; 6 HD 8, 18, 35, 100, 116, 139, etc.; 8 HD 65, 100, 121, 126, 130, 216, etc.
Jones, Washington 4 HD 224
Jones, William 3 HD 425, 428, 460, 571; 4 HD 65, 224, 249, 559; 6 HD 121, 289, 489, 549, 579; 8 HD 22, 64, 508
Jones, Zepheniah 4 HD 65
Jumps Point [tract] 4 HD 232
Kadjers Straits 4 HD 297, 300
Kallendar, Thomas 3 HD 366
Kallender, Catherine 6 HD 329, 478
Kallender, Katharine 8 HD 329
Kallender, Thomas 4 HD 41, 371, 501, 503; 6 HD 118, 139, 178, 329, 381, 439, 478; 8 HD 82, 329, 365, 368, 552
Keene, Benjamin 3 HD 251, 308, 489, 584; 4 HD 359; 6 HD 373, 457, 534, 536; 8 HD 158, 163, 207, 208
Keene, Benjamin Junr. 4 HD 359
Keene, Benjamin, Justice 3 HD 14, 20, 21, 76, 107, 111, etc.

Keene, Capewell 4 HD 266, 269, 542; 6 HD 328, 442; 8 HD 329
Keene, Ezekiel 3 HD 168; 6 HD 296; 8 HD 63
Keene, Hartly (Booth) 3 HD 564
Keene, Henry 3 HD 181; 6 HD 412, 420; 8 HD 490, 495
Keene, John 3 HD 198; 6 HD 189, 420; 8 HD 4, 69
Keene, John, Justice 3 HD 595, 624; 4 HD 13, 16, 74, 140, 165, 167, etc.; 6 HD 1, 5, 65, 68, 75, 93, 104, 110, etc.; 8 HD 77, 89, 126, 203, 235, 242, 256, etc.
Keene, Kitturah 3 HD 14
Keene, Kitty (Catherine) 3 HD 183
Keene, Levin 3 HD 326, 489, 584; 4 HD 605; 6 HD 151, 195, 373; 8 HD 185, 188, 329
Keene, Levin of Ben 6 HD 189
Keene, Lucrecy 6 HD 1
Keene, Mary 4 HD 334
Keene, Matthew 3 HD 21, 183, 185, 351; 6 HD 104, 189, 420
Keene, Nancy 3 HD 251, 489
Keene, Richard 3 HD 38, 130, 168, 198, 206, 230, 308; 6 HD 1, 104, 329, 478, 499; 8 HD 291
Keene, Sally 3 HD 21
Keene, Samuel 3 HD 308
Keene, Sarah 6 HD 499
Keene, Susanna 4 HD 554
Keene, Thomas 6 HD 224
Keene, Vachel 3 HD 464; 4 HD 279, 283; 6 HD 68; 8 HD 63, 224
Keene, William 3 HD 39, 424, 573; 4 HD 321; 6 HD 412; 8 HD 88, 89
Keene, Zebulon Senior 3 HD 464
Keene, Zechariah 3 HD 14, 183
Keenes Discovery [tract] 3 HD 21

Keenes Inclosure [tract] 3 HD 464
Keenes Landing [tract] 6 HD 104
Keenes Neglect [tract] 3 HD 198
Keenes Outlet [tract] 3 HD 130
Keenes Regulation [tract] 3 HD 489; 8 HD 188
Keenes Rest [tract] 3 HD 185
Keenes Security [tract] 3 HD 464
Keenes Timber Yard [tract] 3 HD 489; 6 HD 499
Kelly, Patrick 4 HD 113; 8 HD 406
Kemp, Benjamin 3 HD 593
Kemp, Geo. 4 HD 185
Kemp, James 8 HD 151
Kendals Chance [tract] 6 HD 93
Kennard, Ebenezer 6 HD 67
Kennedy, Catharine 4 HD 386
Kennedy, Henry Co 4 HD 592
Kennedy, John 6 HD 332
Kennedy, Priscilla 6 HD 332
Kennerd, Ebenezer 4 HD 571
Kenny, John 3 HD 535
Kent County 8 HD 461
Kent County, Delaware 3 HD 397, 431; 4 HD 118, 157, 431, 628; 6 HD 132, 300
Kentucky 8 HD 221
Kerby, Joseph 8 HD 593
Kerby, Sally 8 HD 593
Kerby, Thomas 8 HD 593
Kerr, David 6 HD 537; 8 HD 480
Key, Ann 6 HD 418
Key, John Ross 6 HD 418
Key, Philip Barton 6 HD. 415, 418
Keys, Levin 3 HD 411
Killman, Delilah 3 HD 322
Killman, Edward 6 HD 592
Killman, Henry 3 HD 322, 450, 452; 8 HD 52, 521
Killrnan, John 8 HD 52

Kilman, Delia 8 HD 521
Kilman, Edward 4 HD 49
Kilman, Henry 4 HD 54; 6 HD 35
Kilman, Reanace 4 HD 61, 135
Kilman, Thomas 3 HD 450, 452; 4 HD 61, 135, 232, 616; 8 HD 492
Kilmans Cove 4 HD 438, 441
Kilmans Neck 4 HD 425
Kilmons Folly [tract] 3 HD 444; 6 HD 266
King, Dorothy 8 HD 512
King, Edward 6 HD 12
King, Elizabeth 6 HD 443
King, John 3 HD 577; 6 HD 65, 443; 8 HD 126, 512
King, Thomas Senr. 4 HD 393
Kings Chance [tract] 3 HD 113; 4 HD 416; 6 HD 27
Kings Misfortune [tract] 3 HD 309; 6 HD 283
Kirkman, Levin 4 HD 77; 8 HD 292, 293, 480
Kirkman, Levin, Justice 6 HD 332
Kirkman, Thomas 3 HD 293
Kirwan, Sarah 8 HD 374, 529
Kirwan, Andrew 3 HD 562
Kirwan, Barthologh (Barthuley) 8 HD 337
Kirwan, Betsy 4 HD 291
Kirwan, John 6 HD 450; 8 HD 106, 335, 337, 374, 529
Kirwan, John Tyler 4 HD 291
Kirwan, Mary 6 HD 195
Kirwan, Peter 4 HD 287, 291; 6 HD 195
Kirwan, Thomas 8 HD 88, 89
Labrook Regulated [tract] 8 HD 158
LaBrook [tract] 8 HD 158
Laing, Alexander 3 HD 480
Laing, Charles 3 HD 81
Laing, Eleanor 3 HD 480
Laing, John 3 HD 81, 480; 4 HD 446; 6 HD 59; 8 BD 248, 359, 554
Laing, Rosanna (Rosanah) 3 HD 81, 480; 4 HD 446; 6 HD 59
Lake, George 8 HD 112
Lake, Henry 6 HD 195, 261; 8 HD 173, 194, 377, 622
Lake, Henry, Justice 3 HD 4, 14, 20, 21, 39, 76, 107, etc.; 4 HD 9, 13, 16, 74, 165, 167, 199, etc.; 6 HD 93, 110, 123, 141, 144, 147, etc.; 8 HD 69, 77, 89, 104, 106, 108, 112, etc.
Lake, Levin 8 HD 405
Lake, William 4 HD 470; 8 HD 69, 405
Lakes Discovery [tract] 8 HD 8, 403
Lambdin, William N. 8 HD 459
Lancaster Lot [tract] 4 HD 516, 520
Land of Promise [tract] 4 HD 115
Langfitt, John 4 HD 94, 628; 6 HD 489, 549
Lankfit, James 3 HD 564
Lankford, Littleton 8 HD 557, 607
Last Vacancy [tract] 4 HD 318; 6 HD 511
Laybrook Regulated [tract] 6 HD 457
Laybrook [tract] 6 HD 457
Layton, Charles 3 HD 180
Layton, Daniel 3 HD 189, 192,
Layton, James 4 HD 589
Layton, Levin 6 HD 429
Layton, Mary 3 HD 180
Laytons Chance [tract] 4 HD 179
Leatherbury, John 4 HD 115
Leatherbury, Jolley 4 HD 115, 383
Leatherbury, Robert 4 HD 383
LeCompte, Anthony 3 HD 408, 444; 6 HD 266

LeCompte, Becky 3 HD 410
LeCompte, Charles 3 HD 18, 414; 4 HD 324, 548, 563; 8 HD 16, 139, 542
LeCompte, Daniel 8 HD 130, 610, 612
LeCompte, Elizabeth 3 HD, 386; 4 HD 557; 8 HD 12, 612
LeCompte, Isaiah 8 HD 130, 610, 612
LeCompte, James 3 HD 328, 386; 4 HD 111; 8 HD 346
LeCompte, John 3 HD 180, 328; 4 HD 5; 8 HD 16, 94, 99, 612
LeCompte, Joseph (of Peter) 8 HD 612
LeCompte, Joseph 6 HD 603; 8 HD 238, 612
LeCompte, Levin 4 HD 5; 8 HD 204, 206
LeCompte, Levin Junr. 4 HD 309
LeCompte, Mary 8 HD 238
LeCompte, Moses 3 HD 206, 271, 326, 327, 464, 555; 4 HD 359, 423, 516, 520; 6 HD 155, 254, 425; 8 HD 4, 8, 238, 610, 612
LeCompte, Moses, Justice 3 HD 4, 27, 35, 38, 40, 83, 85, etc.; 4 HD 1, 9, 32, 35, 49, 54, 61, 69, 72, etc.; 6 HD 5, 12, 20, 22, 51, 55, 67, 68, etc.; 8 HD 100, 131, 132, 147, 157, 176, etc.
LeCompte, Nancy 3 HD 271; 4 HD 69; 6 HD 51; 8 HD 131
LeCompte, Nicholas 8 HD 610, 612
LeCompte, Philemon 3 HD 18; 8 HD 139
LeCompte, Phillip 8 HD 130, 610, 612
LeCompte, Rebecca 3 HD 363

LeCompte, Samuel 8 HD 612
LeCompte, Sarah 4 HD 324
LeCompte, Stephen 8 HD 204, 206
LeCompte, Thomas 8 HD 130, 238, 610, 612
LeCompte, William 3 HD 287, 312, 328, 408, 410; 8 HD 16, 194, 346, 612
LeCompte, William G. 6 HD 266
LeCompte, William Harrison 3 HD 363, 406, 444; 4 HD 127; 6 HD 544, 555; 8 HD 12
LeCompte, Windsmore 8 HD 16
LeComptes Addition [tract] 4 HD 438
Lee, Abraham 3 HD 242, 348, 495, 555; 6 HD 310; 8 HD 137
Lee, Edward 3 HD 348
Lee Grand [tract] 4 HD 259
Lee, John 3 HD 555; 6 HD 155
Lee, Philip Ludle 6 HD 481, 482
Lee, Thomas 3 HD 348; 6 HD 310
Lee, William 3 HD 495, 555; 6 HD 155
Leinster [tract] 6 HD 332
Levering, Nathan 8 HD 69, 173
Levertons Chance [tract] 3 HD 31, 469, 485; 8 HD 74
Lewis, Aaron 3 HD 544, 545
Lewis, Abraham 3 HD 544, 545, 547; 4 HD 236; 6 HD 281
Lewis, Dezilla 8 HD 143
Lewis, George 8 HD 143
Lewis, Joseph 8 HD 143
Lewis, Mary 8 HD 143
Lewis, Nicey 8 HD 143, 254
Lewis, Raymond 8 HD 143
Lewis, Thomas 3 HD 547
Liberty (Schooner) 8 HD 459
Liberty [tract] 6 HD 144

Lightwood Knott Chapel 8 HD 64
Linceys Range [tract] 8 HD 520
Linchacome, Richard 8 HD 1
Lingan, James Maccubbin 4 HD 466
Lingrell, Nehemiah 8 HD 166
Linthicum, Ann 6 HD 18
Linthicum, Edward 6 HD 8
Linthicum, Richard 8 HD 450
Linthicum, Thomas 6 HD 8, 18
Lisbor, 3 HD 410
Little Brittain [tract] 4 HD 140, 473
Little Choptank River 3 HD 218, 287; 4 HD 232, 324, 557; 6 HD 277, 348, 569, 620; 8 HD 52, 218, 287, 562
Little Creek Point [tract] 4 HD 74
Little House Cove 3 HD 472
Littleton, Edmond 8 HD 349
Littleton, Gracy 8 HD 555
Littleton, Mark 3 HD 377; 8 HD 22
Littleton, William 4 HD 189; 8 HD 555
Littletons Last Shift [tract] 8 HD 349
Littleworth [tract] 3 HD 306
Lockerman, Hill 4 HD 49
Lockerman, Jacob 6 HD 286
Lockerman, Lovey 4 HD 49
Lockerman, Stanley B. 8 HD 626
Lockerman, Thomas 3 HD 160, 502; 4 HD 118, 172, 590; 6 HD 235, 549, 579; 8 HD 204, 295
Lockerman, William 8 HD 128
Lockermans Mills 6 HD 489; 8 HD 64
Lockermans Regulation [tract] 3 HD 450, 452, 517, 523, 529, 601; 4 HD 54, 61, 132, 135, 138, 240, 454, 497, 531, 590, 594, 597, 616; 6 HD 35, 100, 219, 235, 238; 8 HD 387, 418, 521, 523

Logan, Thomas 3 HD 78
London 3 HD 354
Long Acre [tract] 8 HD 256
Long, John 6 HD 230; 8 HD 80
Long Ridge [tract] 3 HD 89
Long Survey [tract] 8 HD 425
Long, William 6 HD 230
Loockerman, Thomas 3 HD 282
Lord, Henry 3 HD 431; 8 HD 607
Lott [tract] 6 HD 584
Lowe, Isaac 3 HD 309
Lower Black Walnut Landing [tract] 8 HD 480
Lower Island Regulated [tract] 8 HD 242, 518
Luck by Chance [tract] 4 HD 118
Lynthecum, Thomas 3 HD 555
McBryde, Sarah 4 HD 494
McBryde, William & Co. 3 HD 439
McBryde, William 4 HD 494
McCall - See McColl.
McCall, Hugh 3 HD 502
McCall, James 6 HD 603
McCauley, William 8 HD 124
McCkredey, John 4 HD 81
McClaran, John 8 HD 542
McColl (McCall), Hugh 4 HD 169, 244, 557, 558, 562; 6 HD 432, 603
McCollister, Daniel 3 HD 420
McCollister, Garretson 8 HD 476
McCollister, James 6 HD 283; 8 HD 347, 476
McCollister, John 8 HD 430
McCollister, Lucy 8 HD 430
McCollister, Nathan 4 HD 581
McCollister, William 3 HD 254
McCotter, Henry 4 HD 54, 61, 132; 8 HD 418, 523
McCotter, James 6 HD 291

McCotter, John 3 HD 253, 309; 4 HD 574, 582; 6 HD 283
McCotter, Philip 6 HD 291
McCrackin, Thomas 8 HD 221
McCray, Elizabeth 6 HD 72
McDaniel, John 6 HD 170
McDaniels Desire [tract] 6 HD 48; 8 HD 283
McDonald, Andrew 3 HD 440; 4 HD 115; 6 HD 405; 8 HD 8, 602
McDonald, Catharine 8 HD 602
McDonnell, Daniel 4 HD 160
McDonnell, Daniel (Danl.) 3 HD 42; 6 HD 13, 55, 67, 519, 537
McFarlin, John 6 HD 241
McGee, Samuel 4 HD 556; 6 HD 281; 8 HD 196
McGraw, Elloner 6 HD 534, 536
McGraw, Rosanna 4 HD 89; 6 HD 584, 587, 595, 598
McGraws Outlett [tract] 6 HD 587, 595, 598
McGuire, Hugh 6 HD 89, 552
McGuire, John 3 HD 254, 416; 4 HD 94; 6 HD 287
McKeel, John 4 HD 324, 339, 435; 6 HD 37, 227, 277, 368, 569; 8 HD 610
McKeel, Mary 4 HD 324; 6 HD 569
McKeel, Thomas 4 HD 47, 106, 107, 170, 172, 324, 598, 600
McKeel, Thomas (Thos.) 3 HD 560, 561, 562, 564, 577, 583; 8 HD 607
McKeel, Thomas, Clk. 6 HD 3, 72, 74
McKenney, Kenneth 3 HD 257, 571
McKinny, Kenneth 8 HD 22
McMahan, Charles 3 HD 145
McNamara, Levin 6 HD 411

McNamara, Thomas 8 HD 142
McNemara, John 3 HD 206
McNemara, John Stewart 3 HD 155
McNemara, Levin 3 HD 202, 206
McNemara, Lovey 3 HD 155
McNemara, Thomas 3 HD 547, 573; 4 HD 208
McWilliams, John 4 HD 459
McWilliams, Rebecca 4 HD 459
Maccubbin, James 4 HD 466
Mace, Angell 6 HD 617, 620
Mace, Dinah 3 HD 38
Mace, Edmond 3 HD 369, 374
Mace, Ezekiel 6 HD 617, 620; 8 HD 124, 126
Mace, John 4 HD 90; 6 HD 178
Mace, Josias 3 HD 137; 6 HD 617, 620; 8 HD 124
Mace, Mary 4 HD 90
Mace, Thomas 3 HD 374
Mace, William 3 HD 371, 374
Maces Back Range [tract] 3 HD 369, 371
Maces Purchase [tract] 3 HD 137
Machthacutawakin [tract] 4 HD 57
Mackeel, John 3 HD 4
Mackey, Thomas 4 HD 572
Macnemara, John 8 HD 142
Macoter, Henry 3 HD 510
Macotter, Henry 4 HD 616; 6 HD 35, 296; 8 HD 439, 442, 444, 446
Macotter, Sarah 4 HD 616; 8 HD 442
Madkin, William 8 HD 439
Madkins Forrest [tract] 4 HD 251
Madkins Venture [tract] 4 HD 251
Maguire (Macguire), John 4 HD 65, 97, 98
Maguire, Hugh 8 HD 552
Maguire, John 3 HD 47; 6 HD 396; John 8 HD 169, 201, 534, 537

Maguire, Sarah 8 HD 169, 534
Maiden(s) Forrest [tract] 3 HD 617; 4 HD 78, 157, 175, 189, 307; 8 HD 537, 555
Maidens Lot [tract] 3 HD 206; 6 HD 411
Maids Choice [tract] 3 HD 414
Mann, William 6 HD 224
Manning, Anthony 3 HD 53, 56, 59, 62, 195, 540; 4 HD 5; 8 HD 279, 283
Manning, John 4 HD 597
Manning, Nathaniel 3 HD 555; 4 HD 563; 8 HD 12, 94, 96, 625
Manning, Nathaniel Junr. 4 HD 174, 238
Mannings Marsh [tract] 6 HD 415, 418
Mannlng, John 6 HD 135
Manumissions 3 HD 35, 38, 159, 167, 177, 180, 230, 243, 271, 282, 294, 347, 354, 422, 466, 467, 493, 570, 607, 623; 4 HD 25, 69, 71, 72, 73, 111, 126, 144, 146, 194, 367, 542, 554, 560, 630; 6 HD 22, 51, 67, 279, 293, 294, 295, 328, 401, 428, 430, 435, 436, 440, 441, 442, 454, 630; 8 HD 112, 113, 130, 131, 137, 138, 151, 157, 176, 200, 204, 205, 206, 258, 264, 289, 291, 305, 327, 424, 436, 448, 502, 516, 547, 582, 607, 626
Marains Addition [tract] 8 HD 590
Marine, Zorobabel 8 HD 544
Marines Addition [tract] 8 HD 544
Marlborough County, South Carolina 3 HD 544
Marsh Pasture [tract] 4 HD 489

Marshahope Regulated [tract] 4 HD 129
Marshall, Andrew 3 HD 495; 6 HD 310
Marshall, Daniel. 8 HD 56
Marshall, Elijah 3 HD 555; 6 HD 310
Marshall, Elizabeth 4 HD 379
Marshall, John 4 HD 379
Marshall, Levin 3 HD 30, 159, 377; 4 HD 428, 581; 6 HD 86; 8 HD 22
Marshall, Mary 4 HD 428; 6 HD 86
Marshall, Theo. (Theophilus) 3 HD 195, 213, 253, 299, 309; 4 HD 97, 239, 377, 379, 548, 574, 592; 6 HD 283, 420; 8 HD 22, 84, 582, 618
Marshall, Thomas 6 HD 437, 438; 8 HD 166
Marshall, Thomas John 3 HD 299
Marshall, William 4 HD 592; 6 HD 440
Marshalls Chance [tract] 3 HD 297; 4 HD 377, 379; 8 HD 84
Martain, William 3 HD 510, 512; 4 HD 616
Martin, Elijah 6 HD 1, 374
Martin, Elizah 4 HD 630
Martin, Joseph 4 HD 26, 29, 303; 6 HD 254
Martin, Moses 4 HD 244; 8 HD 332
Martin, Nancy 4 HD 303
Martin, Richard 4 HD 26, 303, 409; 6 HD 254
Martin, Sally 4 HD 26, 29
Martin, Sarah 6 HD 374
Martin, Solomon 6 HD 437
Martin, Thomas 4 HD 26, 29, 227, 560; 6 HD 228
Martin, Tristram 4 HD 26, 29

Martin, William 6 HD 100, 116; 8 HD 521, 523
Martin, William B. 8 HD 128, 383, 478
Martins Beginning [tract] 6 HD 116
Maryland, State of 3 HD 38, 45, 47, 202, 209, 224, 286, 400, 411, 419, 559; 4 HD 224, 225, 227, 249, 489, 552; 6 HD 287, 288, 289, 502; 8 HD 194, 195, 290, 373, 441
Mason, Ezekiel 8 HD 537
Masons Vineyard [tract] 4 HD 359; 6 HD 420
Massachusetts Bay, Province of 3 HD 617
Matkin, Elizabeth 8 HD 132, 444
Matkin, Standley 8 HD 132, 268, 444, 446
Matkins, Elizabeth 6 HD 296, 298
Matkins Forrest [tract] 8 HD 132, 599
Matkins, Stanley 6 HD 296, 298
Matkins, William 6 HD 296
Matney, Henry 6 HD 314
Maybury, John 3 HD 617
Maynadier, Daniel 6 HD 415, 418
Maynadier, Elizabeth 6 HD 415
Maynadier, Hannah 8 HD 421
Maynadier, Henry 6 HD 415, 418
Meadow [tract] 4 HD 489
Meddis, William 3 HD 377; 4 HD 65, 501
Medes, William 8 HD 520
Medford, William 3 HD 42
Medkin, William 4 HD 251
Medland [tract] 6 HD 37
Meekins, Abram 4 HD 359
Meekins, Catherine 4 HD 359; 6 HD 420
Meekins, Ezekiel 3 HD 573

Meekins, Henry 4 HD 473, 570; 8 HD 474
Meekins, Henry Junr. 4 HD 359
Meekins Hope [tract] 3 HD 121; 4 HD 359
Meekins, John 4 HD 359; 6 HD 420
Meekins, John Denwood 8 HD 4
Meekins, Joseph 4 HD 503; 6 HD 317, 409; 8 HD 368
Meekins, Joshua 3 HD 185; 4 HD 359, 585; 6 HD 420
Meekins, Mark 6 HD 5, 75; 8 HD 512
Meekins, Mary 4 HD 359
Meekins, Matthew 6 HD 420
Meekins Neck 3 HD 121; 4 HD 35, 506, 516, 520, 580; 6 HD 590; 8 HD 335, 337
Meekins, Richard 4 HD 359; 8 HD 4
Meekins, Thomas 6 HD 420
Meekins, Thomas M. 6 HD 420
Meekins, Thomas Mace 4 HD 359
Meekins's Hope [tract] HD 4
Meekinses Creek 3 HD 14; 4 HD 74, 321
Meekinsl Mark 4 HD 359, 585
Meeting House 6 HD 78
Meeting House Survey 3 HD 549
Meeting Houses 8 HD 64, 65
Megraw, John 3 HD 572
Melloy, Sarah 4 HD 236
Melloy, Thomas 4 HD 236
Melvill, Lydia 6 HD 363, 366
Melvill Meeting House 8 HD 64
Melvills Meadows [tract] 8 HD 349
Meredith, John 6 HD 110, 307
Meredith, Thomas 6 HD 110, 601
Meredith, William 6 HD 110, 601
Merediths Inclosure [tract] 6 HD 601
Merideth, Jeene 3 HD 573

Messick, Eliza 3 HD 485
Messick, Elizabeth 8 HD 293
Messick, George 3 HD 485
Methodist Church 8 HD 329
Methodist Episcopal Church 8 HD 65
Methodist Meeting House 3 HD 584; 4 HD 605; 6 HD 167, 329, 612
Middle Island [tract] 8 HD 567
Middle Land [tract] 3 HD 275
Middle Range [tract] 3 HD 276
Middleton, George 4 HD 118
Miller & Abercrombe 4 HD 185
Mills, Betsey (Elizabeth) 4 HD 74
Mills, David 4 HD 109; 6 HD 293
Mills, Jacob 3 HD 168
Mills, John 3 HD 573; 4 HD 74, 109
Mills, Levin 3 HD 168
Mills's Choice [tract] 4 HD 109
Mills's Course [tract] 4 HD 109
Mills's Security [tract] 4 HD 109
Minitree, Andrew 6 HD 481
Mister, Abraham 3 HD 199; 8 HD 256
Mitchel, Rubin 3 HD 347
Mitchell, Cyrus 3 HD 447; 4 HD 236; 6 HD 31; 8 HD 22
Mitchell, Sally 3 HD 294
Mitchell, Sarah 3 HD 447; 4 HD 236; 8 HD 397
Mitchell, Zebulon 8 HD 397
Mobray, Henry 3 HD 460
Molock, John 3 HD 493; 8 HD 627
Moncrieff, Archibald 3 HD 517, 520, 523; 4 HD 113, 238; 6 HD 37, 89, 348; 8 HD 394, 406
Montgomery County 4 HD 466
Moore, David 8 HD 374
Moore, Eba 4 HD 416
Moore, James 3 HD 297; 4 HD 85; 6 HD 287, 431; 8 HD 82
Moore, Mary 3 HD 297; 8 HD 461
Moore, Pheby 6 HD 431
Moore, Risdon 8 HD 461
Moores Addition 8 HD 461
Moore, William 4 HD 416
More, Sarah 3 HD 81
More, Thomas 3 HD 81
More, William 3 HD 113
Morefields Addition [tract] 4 HD 287, 291
Morgan, David 3 HD 583
Morgans (Morgins) Venture [tract] 4 HD 49; 6 HD 592; 8 HD 523
Morris, John 8 HD 56
Morsell, J. 8 HD 380
Morton, Jacob 8 HD 124
Moseleys Addition [tract] 3 HD 185
Moses Liberty [tract] 4 HD 318; 6 HD 511
Mount Pleasant [tract] 6 HD 373; 8 HD 461
Mowbray, Henry 3 HD 257
Mowbray, James 3 HD 257; 8 HD 22
Muir, Adam 3 HD 27; 4 HD 113
Muir, Ann 8 HD 524
Muir, Charity 6 HD 564
Muir, Charles 4 HD 377, 383
Muir, James 4 HD 456; 6 HD 560, 564
Muir, John 3 HD 158, 487, 568; 4 HD 477; 8 HD 195, 229, 259, 260, 262, 524
Muir, Robert 3 HD 158; 4 HD 238; 8 HD 524
Muir, Samuel 3 HD 4, 383, 412, 439, 499; 4 HD 383
Muirs Good Luck [tract] 3 HD 10
Muirs Inspection [tract] 3 HD 4, 383; 4 HD 339
Mulbery Island [tract] 6 HD 389

Mullican, Sarah 3 HD 386
Mullican, Samuel 3 HD 386
Mureign, Stephen 8 HD 124
Murphy- see also Murphey.
Murphey, James 3 HD 560, 598
Murphey, William 3 HD 598
Murphey, William B. 3 HD 561
Murphy, James 8 HD 461
Murphy, William B. 4 HD 598
Murray, Anthony 3 HD 309
Murray, Charlotte 3 HD 35, 329; 4 HD 151; 6 HD 207, 210, 213, 576; 8 HD 390, 499
Murray, David 8 HD 503
Murray, H., Dr. 6 HD 210
Murray, Henry 3 HD 221
Murray, James 4 HD 90; 6 HD 515
Murray, John 3 HD 47, 159, 535; 4 HD 145; 6 HD 162, 207, 210, 219, 271; 8 HD 272, 383
Murray, Rebecca 8 HD 291
Murray, Sarah 4 HD 90
Murray, W. V. 8 HD 272, 291, 390, 499
Murray, William 3 HD 309
Murray, William Vans 3 HD 35, 279, 329; 4 HD 151; 6 HD 162, 203, 207, 210, 213, 576
Murrays Chance [tract] 6 HD 213
Murrays Friendship [tract] 3 HD 386, 589; 6 HD 415, 418; 8 HD 152, 155
Murrays Settlement [tract] 3 HD 279; 4 HD 151, 259
Muse, Ann (Anne) 3 HD 27, 150; 6 HD 223; 8 HD 147, 360, 406
Muse, Mrs. 3 HD 571
Nancys Purchase [tract] 8 HD 315, 322

Nanticoke Indian Lands 4 HD 219; 8 HD 480
Nanticoke Manor 6 HD 96, 112
Nanticoke River 3 HD 31, 91, 94, 96, 98, 101, 103, 105, 113, 142, 295, 315, 318, 494; 4 HD 9, 163, 236, 330, 383, 395, 405, 446, 611; 6 HD 249, 300, 332, 356, 371; 8 HD 311, 455, 470, 531
Nash, John 4 HD 541; 8 HD 22
Navey, Briggs 8 HD 8, 403
Navey, Henry 8 HD 8, 403
Navey, John 6 HD 155
Navey, Kesiah 8 HD 403
Navey, Richard 8 HD 8
Navey, Sarah 8 HD 8
Navey, Thomas 6 HD 155; 8 HD 8
Neglect [tract] 8 HD 476
Negro slaves (see also, Manumissions) 8 HD 87, 92, 114, 214, 215, 229, 245, etc.
Neild, Abraham 6 HD 118
Neighbourly Kindness [tract] 2 HD 89; 6 HD 341
Neild, Abraham 8 HD 609
Nevitts Double Purchase [tract] 3 HD 27
New Market (Newmarket) 3 HD 8, 25, 133, 312, 437; 6 HD 31, 86, 560; 8 HD 301, 542
New Market Episcopal Church 8 HD 71
New Market [tract] 3 HD 25, 133, 312; 4 HD 377; 8 HD 71, 349, 485
New Town [tract] 3 HD 264
Newton, Ebenezer 3 HD 404; 4 HD 115, 239
Newton, William 6 HD 245
Newton, Willis 4 HD 548

Newtons Interest [tract] 3 HD 404
Newtons Regulatlon [tract] 3 HD 404
Nichols, Dolly 3 HD 545
Nichols, Isaac 3 HD 545
Nichols, Nehemiah 3 HD 165
Nicklin, Philip 8 HD 461
Nicolls, Daniel 3 HD 86, 89, 159, 253, 257, 293, 431, 571
Nicolls, Elizabeth 4 HD 574
Nicolls, Isaac 4 HD 574
Nicolls, John 4 HD 574
Nicolls, Levin 4 HD 574
Nicolls, Mark 4 HD 574
Nicolls, Nehemiah 4 HD 574
Nicolls, Thomas 4 HD 535
Nicols, Daniel 4 HD 369, 574; 6 HD 283, 403; 8 HD 149, 342, 576
Nicols, Isaac 8 HD 196
Nicols, Jeremiah 8 HD 196
Nicols, Joseph 8 HD 191, 196
Nicols, Thomas 8 HD 191, 196, 455, 544, 590
Nimcock [tract] 3 HD 348, 495, 555
Nisbett, Moses W. 4 HD 85; 6 HD 170; 8 HD 421
Nixon, John 8 HD 513
Noble, John 6 HD 313, 429
Noble, Joshua 8 HD 322
Noble, Mark 8 HD 191, 196
Noel, Edward , 4 HD 563, 623
Noel, Edward, Justice 3 HD 6, 35, 48, 50, 231
Noels Closure [tract] 8 HD 524
Noels Regulation [tract] 4 HD 623
Norage [tract] 4 HD 236
Norman, William 4 HD 21
Norrage [tract] 8 HD 311, 315
Norris, Robert 3 HD 593
North and South Preston [tract] 8 HD 218
North Carolina 3 HD 202, 428, 545; 6 HD 604, 606, 617, 620, 624; 8 HD 82, 124, 126, 332
North Division [tract] 3 HD 239
North, George 3 HD 48
North, John 3 HD 30
North, Rebecca 4 HD 145
North, Thomas 3 HD 85, 322
Norths Range [tract] 3 HD 48
Northumberland County, Virginia 3 HD 249; 4 HD 297, 300
Northwest Fork 3 HD 74, 109, 475, 477; 6 HD 59, 129, 181, 481
Northwest Fork Bridge 6 HD 57
Northwest Fork Hundred 8 HD 298, 569
Nuners Discovery [tract] 4 HD 13; 8 HD 413
Nuners Pasture Enlarged [tract] 6 HD, 189
Nutterwell, John 6 HD 286
Obscurity [tract] 3 HD 302
Orange County, N. C. 6 HD 617, 620, 624; N. C. 8 HD 124, 126
Orem, Hugh 4 HD 557
Original Outlett [tract] 8 HD 203
Outlet(t) [tract] 3 HD 40, 137; 4 HD 41, 154, 409; 6 HD 341; 8 HD 158, 439, 442, 444
Owens, Isaac 6 HD 238
Owens, John 3 HD 568
Ox Pasture [tract] 6 HD 274
Paddison, William 3 HD 159, 295; 6 HD 540
Pagan, Henry H. 6 HD 425
Pagan, John 6 HD 425
Palmer, William 4 HD 563
Paris [tract] 3 HD 155
Parker, Daniel Junr. 4 HD 587
Parker, Edward 4 HD 444

Parker, Levin 4 HD 330
Parker, Thomas 6 HD 338
Parker, William 4 HD 574
Parks, Joseph 8 HD 56
Parran, Thomas 8 HD 380
Parrott, Thomas 8 HD 157, 441
Parsons Creek 4 HD 616; 6 HD 35
Partnership [tract] 3 HD 67, 404, 537; 4 HD 480; 6 HD 245, 569; 8 HD 203, 262
Passapae, Moses 6 HD 540
Pasture Neck [tract] 8 HD 487
Pasture [tract] 4 HD 612
Pasture Point [tract] 6 HD 420
Patison, Archibald 3 HD 48, 158, 218, 517, 520, 523; 4 HD 113, 160, 238, 590, 597; 6 HD 37, 89, 135, 162, 329, 348, 515
Patison, James 6 HD 203
Patison, John 3 HD 560
Patison, Thomas James 6 HD 213
Patricks Wells [tract] 6 HD 155
Patridge, Isaac 8 HD 589
Patridge, Jonathan 3 HD 168, 206, 495; 4 HD 409, 488; 6 HD 224, 254, 261, 405; 8 HD 56, 207, 208, 385, 472, 508
Patridges Regulation [tract] 4 HD 488
Pattison, Archibald 8 HD 394, 406, 607
Pattison, Jacob 3 HD 164; 4 HD 425
Pattison, James 4 HD 425; 6 HD 387
Pattison, Jeremiah 3 HD 83, 85; 4 HD 83, 272, 399, 451, 612; 6 HD 412, 425; 8 HD 8, 52, 2b5
Pattison, John 4 HD 558
Pattison, Margaret 4 HD 129
Pattison, Mary 4 HD 129
Pattison, Nancy 3 HD 83, 85

Pattison, Richard 3 HD 164, 168, 173, 175, 243, 271, 555, 565; 4 HD 129, 144, 359, 563, 612; 6 HD 1, 135, 155, 189, 254, 412, 425, 442; 8 HD 4, 8, 52, 63, 157, 238, 508, 610
Pattison, Richard, Justice 3 HD 466, 467, 502, 510, 512, 623; 4 HD 26, 29, 32, 35, 83, 126, 154, etc.; 6 HD 35, 41, 65, 70, 75, 139, 175, etc.; 8 HD 82, 121, 132, 158, 161, 163, etc.
Pattison, Sarah 4 HD 425
Pattison, T. 3 HD 38
Pattison, Thomas 4 HD 444
Pattison, Thomas James 3 HD 329; 4 HD 129
Pattison, William 4 HD 129, 488; 8 HD 8, 508
Pattison, William Junr. 4 HD 266, 269, 425
Pattisons Addition to Ennalls's Gift [tract] 6 HD 37
Pattisons Beginning' 4 HD 129
Pattisons Priviledge [tract] 3 HD 83; 4 HD 272, 451; 8 HD 265, 268
Paul, Daniel 8 HD 166
Paul, Lewis Griffith 6 HD 495
Paul, Ralph 4 HD 107; 6 HD 402
Pauls [tract] 8 HD 163
Payne, Daniel 3 HD 89; 4 HD 369; 6 HD 129, 540
Payne, Elizabeth 8 HD 322
Payne, James 3 HD 402; 6 HD 181, 241; 8 HD 311, 322
Payne, Mary 3 HD 253; 4 HD 369
Paynes Mill [tract] 3 HD 457
Pearson, Edward 4 HD 631
Pearson Laban 4 HD 631
Pearson, Lidia 4 HD 470

Pearson, Stephen 4 HD 470
Peers, Valentine 3 HD 594
Pennington, Lydia 8 HD 625, 626
Pennington, William 8 HD 16
Pennsylvania 3 HD 1; 8 HD 349
Perry, Thomas 4 HD 169
Perth [tract] 3 HD 589; 8 HD 152, 155
Peterkin, David 8 HD 94
Peters Neck 3 HD 510; 4 HD 466; 6 HD 175; 8 HD 444
Philadelphia, City of 3 HD 1; 4 HD 183, 185; 8 HD 349
Philadelphia Range [tract] 4 HD 516, 520
Phillips Discovery [tract] 6 HD 135, 184, 296; 8 HD 439, 442, 527, 599
Phillips, Edward 8 HD 449
Phillips, Ellet 4 HD 359
Phillips, Henry 8 HD 254;
Phillips, Henry Travers 6 HD 5; 8 HD 337
Phillips, John 3 HD 555; 4 HD 196
Phillips, Levin 4 HD 140, 473, 570; 8 HD 474
Phillips Liberty [tract] 8 HD 77
Phillips Lot [tract] 3 HD 477
Phillips, Major 6 HD 503
Phillips, Nancy 6 HD 5
Phillips, Rachel 8 HD 203
Phillips, Samuel 8 HD 52, 449
Phillips, Thomas 6 HD 155; 8 HD 403
Phillips, William 3 HD 568; 8 HD 335
Phillips's Creek 6 HD 555
Phillips's Discovery [tract] 3 HD 65
Phillips's Liberty [tract] 6 HD 65
Pickron, John, 4 HD 359

Piercy, William 4 HD 607; 8 HD 626
Pike, John 4 HD 65
Pilgrimage [tract] 3 HD 584; 4 HD 402, 605; 6 HD 167
Pilgrims Rest [tract] 6 HD 394, 399, 425
Pine Point [tract] 4 HD 35
Piney Grove [tract] 3 HD 322
Piney Neck 4 HD 83
Piney (Piny) Point [tract] 4 HD 266, 269; 6 HD 555; 8 HD 12
Pinkney, Jona. 3 HD 257
Pinkney, Jonathan 8 HD 22
Pinkneys Chance 3 HD 351, 489
Pitt County, N. C. 3 HD 202; 6 HD 604, 606
Pitt, John 3 HD 45, 324, 411, 584; 4 HD 73, 227, 255, 605; 6 HD 167, 288, 295
Pitt, Mary 4 HD 72, 73, 255
Pitt, Samuel (Saml.) W. 6 HD 430, 525; 8 HD 207
Pitt, William 3 HD 45, 177, 324, 411, 467; 4 HD 72, 73, 227; 6 HD 288, 294; 8 HD 441
Pitts Desire 4 HD 255
Pleasant Grove Regulated [tract] 4 HD 451
Pleasant Grove [tract] 3 HD 85; 8 HD 268
Plymouth [tract] 6 HD 320
Point Good Hope [tract] 6 HD 274
Pokety [tract] 4 HD 563
Polk, Nanney 8 HD 627
Pollard, William 6 HD 155
Pollards Choice [tract] 6 HD 155
Polly (Schooner) 4 HD 193
Poor House 3 HD 604
Poplar Neck [tract] 3 HD 251
Poppelar Point [tract] 4 HD 196

Porpeigham [tract] 8 HD 114
Porter, Levin 6 HD 615
Portroyal [tract] 8 HD 574
Possump Ridge [tract] 6 HD 96
Potters Neck 8 HD 225
Pounds Second Addition Corrected [tract] 3 HD 59; 4 HD 5
Pounds Second Addition [tract] 3 HD 195; 4 HD 5
Pounds Third Addition [tract] 4 HD 5
Powell, Charles 4 HD 324
Presbury, George Gouldsmith 6 HD 374
Presbyterian Meeting House 4 HD 513; 8 HD 332
Preston Creek 3 HD 275
Preston [tract] 8 HD 218
Price, Ephraim 4 HD 297, 300
Price, James 8 HD 92, 480
Price, John 4 HD 297, 300, 561
Price, Laban 4 HD 297, 300
Price, William 4 HD 297, 300; 8 HD 567
Prince William County, Virginia 3 HD 594
Pringle, Mark M. 8 HD 394, 406
Prison Lands 8 HD 399
Pritchard, Arthur 3 HD 165; 4 HD 544, 552; 6 HD 377, 560, 564; 8 HD 576
Pritchard, Sally 6 HD 560
Pritchards Lott [tract] 6 HD 560
Pritchet, Elijah 6 HD 254
Pritchet, Thomas 3 HD 89
Pritchett, Edward 8 HD 82, 112
Pritchett, Elizabeth 3 HD 226; 4 HD 215; 8 HD 596
Pritchett, John 4 HD 598
Pritchett, John Macnemara 3 HD 226
Pritchett, John McNamara 8 HD 596
Pritchett, John McNemara 4 HD 215
Pritchett, Thomas 6 HD 129
Pritchetts Forrest [tract] 6 HD 195
Pritchetts Regulation Regulated 8 HD 82
Priviledge [tract] 3 HD 463; 4 HD 154, 371; 6 HD 541
Project [tract] 4 HD 220, 263
Promise [tract] 4 HD 383
Pursom, John 3 HD 560
Queen Anns County 4 HD 402; 8 HD 77, 137
Raccoon Ridge [tract] 8 HD 203
Ragged Point [tract] 8 HD 52
Ramsey, David 6 HD 603
Randall, John 8 HD 480
Range [tract] 6 HD 338
Ratcliff, John 4 HD 127
Ratcliff, Thomas 3 HD 306, 619
Ratcliff, John 3 HD 444
Ratcliff, Sarah 3 HD 294, 347
Ratcliff, Thomas 4 HD
Ratcliff, William 3 HD 35, 267, 294, 306
Ratcliffe, Fanney 6 HD 266
Ratcliffe, John 6 HD 266
Ratcliffs Addition [tract] 3 HD 267, 306, 619; 4 HD 1
Rawley, Walter 3 HD 259; 8 HD 205
Rawlings, Moses 8 HD 380
Rea, Peter 3 HD 221, 236, 279, 345, 529, 549, 601; 4 HD 454, 497, 513, 531, 587, 594; 6 HD 70, 184, 219, 271, 344, 346, 486, 502; 8 HD 87, 387, 390, 586
Rea, Sarah 4 HD 513; 8 HD 387
Records, Anne 3 HD 480
Red Oak Level [tract] 4 HD 391
Reed, Ann 6 HD 292
Reed, Eby 3 HD 187, 189, 192

Reed, Ezekiel 3 HD 178; 4 HD 395; 6 HD 292, 407
Reed, Isaac 3 HD 187, 189, 192; 4 HD 393; 6 HD 407
Reed, John 4 HD 239, 249, 393; 6 HD 289, 405; 8 HD 8, 92, 254, 301, 534
Reed, John, Justice 6 HD 396, 433, 445, 446, 447, 489, etc.; 8 HD 80, 195, 212, 229, 254, 259, 260, etc.
Reed, Nancy 6 HD 292
Reed, Susanna 4 HD 239
Reed, William 4 HD 334; 8 HD 65, 472
Reeds Chance [tract] 6 HD 292
Reeds Hazard [tract] 4 HD 147
Reeds Regulation [tract] 3 HD 187, 189, 192
Regulation [tract] 3 HD 431
Reliance [tract] 4 HD 140, 473; 8 HD 474
Reserve [tract] 4 HD 359
Resurvey Callis [tract] 6 HD 307
Ricarton [tract] 6 HD 135, 184
Rich, Peter 8 HD 221
Rich Ridge [tract] 8 HD 335
Richards Delight [tract] 6 HD 507
Richards Discovery [tract] 6 HD 1, 374
Richardson, E., Justice 3 HD 246, 284, 295, 297, 299, 312, etc.; 4 HD 22, 189, 428; 6 HD 281
Richardson, John 8 HD 22
Richardson, Joseph 3 HD 133, 425
Richardson, Rebecca 8 HD 430
Richardson, Thomas 3 HD 133, 290; 8 HD 191, 196, 221, 455, 544, 590
Richardsons Orchard [tract] 8 HD 22
Riddell (Riddle), John 6 HD 10, 432, 633
Ridder, Julius Conrad 4 HD 508
Riddle, Ann 4 HD 625
Riddle, John 4 HD 538, 625; 8 HD 245, 515
Riders Forrest [tract] 4 HD 85; 6 HD 391
Ridout, Horatio 3 HD 394, 455; 6 HD 495
Ridout, Rachel 3 HD 394; 6 HD 495
Ridout, Samuel 4 HD 90
Riggen, Rhodes 4 HD 163
Riggin, Edward 4 HD 571; 8 HD 449
Riggin, Rhoads 8 HD 602
Riley, William 8 HD 542
Ritchie, James 3 HD 594; 4 HD 494
Robbins, Joseph 3 HD 20
Robbs, Alexander 6 HD 617, 620, 624; 8 HD 124, 126
Robearts Begining [tract] 4 HD 506
Roberts, Francis, 8 HD 224
Roberts, George 4 HD 506
Roberts, Jems 3 HD 46
Roberts, Joseph 8 HD 84
Roberts Lott [tract] 6 HD 590
Roberts, Sophia 6 HD 584, 587, 595, 598; 8 HD 594
Roberts, Thomas 4 HD 82
Roberts, William 4 HD 89
Robertson, George 8 HD 622
Robertson, John Senr. 3 HD 485
Robertson, W. M. 8 HD 373, 547
Robertson, William M. 4 HD 454; 6 HD 132
Robertson, William Murray 3 HD 517, 523, 535
Robins Defiance [tract] 6 HD 495
Robins, Joseph 4 HD 314
Robinson, Amasa 6 HD 540

Robinson, Andrew 3 HD 572
Robinson, John 3 HD 302
Robinson, Levi 8 HD 176
Robinson, William M. 8 HD 383
Robinson, William Murray 3 HD 532, 535; 4 HD 240, 594
Robinsons Craft [tract] 3 HD 302; 4 HD 140, 473
Robinsons Discovery [tract] 3 HD 302
Robinsons Lott [tract] 3 HD 181, 380; 8 HD 490
Robson, Joseph 8 HD 506
Robson Pasture [tract] 4 HD 35
Robsons Beginning [tract] 6 HD 233
Robsons Chance [tract] 6 HD 464, 503
Robsons Lott [tract] 3 HD 249; 8 HD 495, 506
Robsons Range [tract] 6 HD 493
Rockingham County, N. C. 3 HD 428
Rodely [tract] 3 HD 414
Rogers Chance [tract] 3 HD 107
Rogers, David 3 HD 121; 4 HD 359
Rogers Endeavour [tract] 4 HD 609
Rogers, John 3 HD 10, 127; 6 HD 440; 8 HD 436
Rogers, Susannah 3 HD 121
Rohobath [tract] 3 HD 224
Roly, Walter 4 HD 227
Roney, James 8 HD 195
Roses Purchase [tract] 6 HD 227
Ross, Mary 3 HD 477
Ross, Anthony 3 HD 477
Ross, Elizabeth 6 HD 407
Ross, James 3 HD 565; 6 HD 227, 368
Ross, John 3 HD 487, 494; 4 HD 239; 6 HD 227, 407; 8 HD 363
Ross, Levin 8 HD 112
Ross, Rebeccah 3 HD 199
Ross, Thomas 3 HD 172, 199, 565; 4 HD 219; 6 HD 227
Ross, William 3 HD 565; 6 HD 227; 8 HD 52
Ross's Chance [tract] 4 HD 232
Ross's Lott [tract] 3 HD 487
Ross's Purchase [tract] 3 HD 565
Rosse's Lott [tract] 8 HD 363
Rosses Chance [tract] 6 HD 475
Rosses Purchase [tract] 6 HD 37, 368
Rosses Range [tract] 3 HD 502
Rowins, Francis (Fras.) 6 HD 352; 8 HD 264
Ruark, Edward 4 HD 359; 6 HD 420
Ruark, James 8 HD 518
Ruark, John 6 HD 326
Ruark, Thomas 4 HD 506
Rumble, William 3 HD 246
Rumbley, David 6 HD 151
Rumbley, John 6 HD 151
Rumbley, William 6 HD 151
Russell, Charles 3 HD 31, 494
Russell, William 6 HD 348
Russum, Mitchell 4 HD 574; 8 HD 627
Ryan, William 4 HD 193
Ryder, Joseph 3 HD 166
Safford [tract] 3 HD 199; 6 HD 93
Salmon, George 3 HD 1; 6 HD 374
Salsbury Plaine [tract] 6 HD 274
Sams Neglect [tract] 6 HD 489, 549
Sandwitch [tract], 3 HD 510
Sandy Hill [tract] 3 HD 447; 4 HD 618; 6 HD 57
Sandy Island Creek 3 HD 76
Sappington, Samuel 4 HD 244
Sarah Land Addition [tract] 3 HD 254; 4 HD 118

Sarah Land [tract] 3 HD 254; 8 HD 169
Sarahs Delight Enlarged [tract] 4 HD 309; 8 HD 425, 583
Sarde, Peter 6 HD 402
Sare, David 3 HD 83; 4 HD 272; 8 HD 265
Sares, David 8 HD 132, 268
Satchel, Andrew 4 HD 106
Savory, Rosanah 6 HD 374
Savory, William 6 HD 374
Scholarship Improved [tract] 3 HD 457; 4 HD 179
Scholarship [tract] 3 HD 402; 4 HD 179
School House Cove 4 HD 324
Schools 4 HD 548; 8 HD 221
Scoggins, Nancy 4 HD 25
Scot, John 3 HD 583
Scott, Gustavus 3 HD 517, 520, 529, 532, 535; 4 HD 113, 240, 350, 388, 489, 531, 590, 594, 597; 6 HD 96, 515; 8 HD 406
Scott, John 3 HD 173, 175, 216, 434, 437, 442; 4 HD 480, 483; 6 HD 224, 525; 8 HD 207
Scott, Margaret 3 HD 532; 4 HD 113, 240, 388, 531, 590, 594, 597; 6 HD 96, 515
Scott, Robert 6 HD 261
Scott, William 8 HD 114
Scotts Purchase [tract] 6 HD 96
Scrivener, William 3 HD 487
Sears, Thomas 4 HD 611
Seberry, Elenor 4 HD 601
Second Chance [tract] 3 HD 355
Secretary Creek 4 HD 379, 566, 568
Sector [tract] 3 HD 259; 4 HD 309
Security to Pains Point [tract] 8 HD 315, 322

Security to Paint Point [tract] 6 HD 281
Security [tract] 4 HD 309
Seers, John 3 HD 562
Seven Oaks Point 4 HD 211; 6 HD 68
Sewars, James 6 HD 555
Sewers, Deborah 8 HD 12
Sewers, Esther 8 HD 12
Sewers, James 8 HD 12
Sewers Land [tract] 3 HD 408
Sewers, Mary 8 HD 12
Sewers, Rosannah 8 HD 12
Shambles [tract] 4 HD 359
Shanks, Abner 8 HD 557
Shapleys Rest [tract] 6 HD 151
Sharpes Point [tract] 4 HD 435; 6 HD 37
Sharps Creek 6 HD 277, 368
Shaw, Ann 6 HD 112
Shaw, James 3 HD 254, 419, 480; 4 HD 65, 77; 6 HD 112, 289; 8 HD 212, 480
Shaw, James, Justice 3 HD 53, 56, 59, 62, 158, 167, etc.; 6 HD 332
Shaw, Neale H. 6 HD 481, 482
Sheep Pasture [tract] 8 HD 216
Shenton, Anne 8 HD 4
Shenton, Charles 6 HD 499; 8 HD 242, 254
Shenton, Elizabeth (Booze) 8 HD 254
Shenton, John 4 HD 553, 580; 8 HD 4
Shenton, Joseph 4 HD 580
Shentons Advantage [tract] 8 HD 77
Sherman, Seth 6 HD 228
Sherwood, Ann 3 HD 312
Sherwood, Philip King 3 HD 312
Shinton, Charles 6 HD 443, 507; 8 HD 143

Shinton, Ichabud 8 HD 512
Shintons Addition [tract] 6 HD 466
Shintons Point 6 HD 466
Shore Ditch (Shear Ditch) [tract]) 4 HD 330
Shores, Edward 6 HD 151
Short, Isaac 4 HD 125
Shorter, William 3 HD 20, 76
Simmons, Philemon 4 HD 193
Skillington [tract] 6 HD 373
Skinner, Elizabeth 3 HD 389, 391
Skinner, James 3 HD 391
Skinner, William 3 HD 389, 391
Skinner, Zachariah 3 HD 391
Slacum, Gabriel 8 HD 104, 108, 171, 172, 529
Slacum, George 6 HD 448, 450, 451, 453; 8 HD 69, 104, 106, 173, 436
Slacum, Job 4 HD 463; Job 6 HD 195
Slacum, Job Junr. 8 HD 145
Slacum, Marcellus 8 HD 258
Slaughter Creek 3 HD 83, 198; 4 HD 83, 129, 140, 272, 399; 6 HD 394; 8 HD 265, 268
Sloop Cove 3 HD 613; 8 HD 100
Sloss, Samuel Shelton 4 HD 118, 157
Small, Richard 4 HD 540
Small, Sarah 4 HD 540
Small Tract [tract] 3 HD 485
Smarts Inclosure [tract] 4 HD 5
Smith, Alexander (Alexr.) 6 HD 289; 8 HD 229, 292, 293, 359
Smith, Amelia 3 HD 434
Smith, Ann 3 HD 50; 8 HD 399
Smith, Arthur 4 HD 609
Smith, David 3 HD 537; 4 HD 65; 8 HD 487, 515
Smith, David, Justice 3 HD 386, 397, 416, 419, 439, 447, etc.; 4 HD 5,

19, 21, 179, 249, 293, 307, etc.; 6 HD 27, 86, 112, 121, 170, 230, etc.; 8 HD 71, 80, 195, 212, 245, 246, 254, etc.
Smith, Edward 6 HD 24; 8 HD 194
Smith, Elisabeth 4 HD 395
Smith Field Composition [tract] 6 HD 274
Smith Field [tract] 4 HD 524, 526; 6 HD 274
Smith, Isaac 8 HD 486, 505
Smith, James 3 HD 302; 4 HD 25
Smith, John 3 HD 1; 6 HD 289, 363, 366, 432; 8 HD 195
Smith, Levin 3 HD 48
Smith, Mathew 6 HD 407
Smith, Matthew 3 HD 109; 4 HD 395
Smith, Matthew Junr. 8 HD 363
Smith, Rebecca 3 HD 48
Smith, Relf 6 HD 475
Smith, Robert 4 HD 185
Smith, Samuel 3 HD 361
Smith, Sophia 6 HD 274
Smith, Thomas 4 HD 225, 626; 6 HD 274; 8 HD 176, 195, 301
Smith, Thomas Junr. 4 HD 524, 526
Smith, Thoroughgood (Thorowgd.) 6 HD 37, 89, 348; 8 HD 394, 406
Smith, William 8 HD 421
Smiths Creek 3 HD 383; 4 HD 339; 6 HD 569
Smiths Discovery [tract] 6 HD 274
Smiths Forest [tract] 8 HD 461
Smiths Industry [tract] 8 HD 301
Smiths Meadow [tract] 6 HD 274
Smiths Mills 6 HD 96
Smoot, Alexander 3 HD 594
Smoot, Alexander L. 3 HD 350
Smoot, Edward 6 HD 481, 482; 8 HD 554

Smoot, Henry 4 HD 572; 6 HD 481, 482
Smoot, John 3 HD 1, 101, 103; 4 HD 405, 538, 611; 6 HD 57, 59, 446, 481, 482
Smoot, John, Justice 3 HD 8, 25, 31, 33, 67, 69, 72, etc.; 4 HD 367
Smoot, Samuel 6 HD 300; 8 HD 554
Smyly, Saml. 4 HD 494
Snake Point [tract] 3 HD 412
Somerset County 3 HD 23; 4 HD 383, 494, 624; 6 HD 332; 8 HD 315, 423, 567, 622
Sothen (Sotherin), Wm. 6 HD 448, 450, 451, 453
Sotherin, William 8 HD 69, 104, 106, 108, 173, 305, 436
Sothern, Nancy 6 HD 141
Sothern, William 4 HD 353; 6 HD 141
South Carolina 3 HD 544
South Preston [tract] 3 HD 383; 4 HD 557
Southeys Creek 8 HD 368
Soward, John 3 HD 502
Soward, Sally 8 HD 52
Sparks, Elizabeth 8 HD 87
Spedden, Hugh 4 HD 145
Spedding, Hugh 3 HD 555
Spencer, Perry 8 HD 459
Spencer, Richard 8 HD 459
Spicer, Jeremiah 6 HD 509
Spicer, Lucrecy 6 HD 509
Spite [tract] 4 HD 229; 6 HD 630
Spocott [tract] 4 HD 324
Sprigg, Richard 3 HD 43; 4 HD 580
Spring Valley [tract] 4 HD 309
St. Anthonys [tract] 8 HD 238, 610, 612, 618

St. Bartholomew(s) [tract] 4 HD 115; 6 HD 405; 8 HD 602
St. Johns Island [tract] 4 HD 297
St. Stephens Creek 8 HD 497, 523
St. Stevens Creek 4 HD 49, 54, 135, 138; 6 HD 100, 617, 620, 624
Stack, Elisabeth 4 HD 556
Stack, Levin 3 HD 463; 4 HD 556; 6 HD 541
Stack, Nancy 6 HD 541
Stack, Nuton 4 HD 556
Stafford [tract] 4 HD 631
Stainton, Charles 4 HD 544; 6 HD 129, 341; 8 HD 607
Stainton, John Hicks 6 HD 341
Stainton, Magary 8 HD 576
Stainton, Nancy 3 HD 78
Stainton, Thomas 3 HD 78
Staintons Industry [tract] 3 HD 78
Staintons Purchase [tract] 8 HD 576
Staitons Purchase [tract] 3 HD 431
Stanaways Forrest [tract] 3 HD 199
Standly, George 6 HD 428
Stanford, Celia 3 HD 42, 158
Stanford, Elizabeth 3 HD 42, 158
Stanford, Richard 3 HD 42, 158
Stanford, Samuel 3 HD 439
Stanford, Thomas 8 HD 150
Stanfords Chance [tract] 8 HD 360
Stantons Purchase [tract] 3 HD 86
Staplefort, Celia 8 HD 385
Staplefort, Edward 3 HD 39; 8 HD 108
Stapleforts Creek 6 HD 373
Stapleforts Desert [tract] 3 HD 489
Stapleforts Recreation [tract] 4 HD 359
Stayton, Handa 4 HD 596
Steele, Henry 6 HD 245, 249; 8 HD 167, 424

Steele, Isaac 4 HD 9; 6 HD 245, 249, 405; 8 HD 167, 424
Steele, James 3 HD 575; 4 HD 9, 65, 343; 6 HD 170, 332; 8 HD 169, 176, 201, 421
Steele, Mary 4 HD 9; 8 HD 169, 201
Steele, William 8 HD 52
Stephens, Edward 3 HD 158; 6 HD 224; 8 HD 158, 161, 163, 194
Stephens, Levin 3 HD 158; 8 HD 158, 161, 163
Stephens, Thomas 8 HD 158, 161, 163
Stephens, William 3 HD 251; 6 HD 457; 8 HD 158
Steple Bumstead [tract] 3 HD 202
Stepleforts Creek 3 HD 185
Sterling, Henry 3 HD 157
Stevens, Benjamin 4 HD 580
Stevens, Benthal 4 HD 574
Stevens, Benthall 3 HD 578
Stevens, Cala 3 HD 46
Stevens, Edward 6 HD 155
Stevens, Frances 3 HD 74, 109, 299; 4 HD 22
Stevens, James Rule 3 HD 145, 150, 180, 440; 8 HD 147
Stevens, John 3 HD 74, 109, 115, 195, 257, 299, 309, 565; 4 HD 22, 174, 377, 548; 6 HD 371; 8 HD 56, 452, 478
Stevens, John, Justice 3 HD 257, 259, 284, 287, 297, 312, etc.; 4 HD 41, 57, 71, 78, 98, 109, 113, etc.; 6 HD 13, 24, 31, 46, 48, 52, 57, 59, etc.; 8 HD 1, 71, 74, 84, 91, 119, 139, 149, etc.
Stevens, John M. 3 HD 150, 559; 6 HD 296; 8 HD 147, 347, 531, 533

Stevens, Levin 8 HD 128
Stevens, Nathan 4 HD 132, 616; 6 HD 35, 155; 8 HD 177, 521
Stevens, Pamela 6 HD 296; 8 HD 531, 533
Stevens, Peter 3 HD 133
Stevens, R. 4 HD 367
Stevens, Robertson 8 HD 531, 533
Stevens, Robinson 8 HD 74
Stevens, Sarah 6 HD 155
Stevens, Thomas 3 HD 46, 133, 195; 4 HD 57; 6 HD 245
Stevens, William 3 HD 495, 565; 4 HD 563; 6 HD 227, 348, 368; 8 HD 56
Stevens's Regulation [tract] 8 HD 56, 452
Stevens's Venture [tract] 8 HD 177
Stewart, Betty 6 HD 415, 418
Stewart, Charles 8 HD 248, 485
Stewart, James 3 HD 65
Stewart, John 3 HD 38; 6 HD 415, 418
Stewart, John Cook 3 HD 353; 8 HD 150
Stewart, Joseph Fookes 3 HD 391
Stewart, Levin 3 HD 391
Stewart, Mary 8 HD 589
Stewart, Robert 8 HD 224
Stewart, Sarah 3 HD 65; 6 HD 486
Stewart, Thomas 3 HD 65, 440, 552; 6 HD 41; 8 HD 150, 394
Stewart, William 6 HD 486
Stewart, William Hayward 3 HD 65
Stewart, Woolford 4 HD 147, 562; 8 HD 276, 385, 589
Stewarts Creek 6 HD 266
Stewarts Discovery [tract] 4 HD 147
Stewarts Lot [tract] 3 HD 279
Stewarts Marsh [tract] 6 HD 415, 418

Stewarts Outrange [tract] 4 HD 147
Stewarts Place [tract] 8 HD 524
Stewarts Second Beginning [tract] 3 HD 23
Stewarts Third Beginning [tract] 6 HD 48
Stoaks, James 8 HD 145
Stoaks, Peter 8 HD 470
Stokes Adventure [tract] 6 HD 213
Stokes Priviledge [tract] 6 HD 213
Stokes's Adventure [tract] 3 HD 329
Stokests Priviledge [tract] 3 HD 329
Stondwick [tract] 8 HD 469
Stone, Will 4 HD 494
Straits 6 HD 141
Streets, Edward 3 HD 122
Streights Meeting House 8 HD 64
Strife [tract] 3 HD 540; 4 HD 609
Sulivane, D., Justice 4 HD 343, 371
Sulivane, Daniel 3 HD 312; 4 HD 548, 597; 6 HD 135; 8 HD 71, 349, 428, 503, 579, 583
Sulivane, Daniel, Justice 3 HD 8, 23, 25, 29, 31, 33, 72, etc.
Sulivane, James 3 HD 8, 25, 195; 4 HD 574; 6 HD 31; 8 HD 22, 71, 149, 349, 425, 493, 542, 577, 579, 583
Sulivane, Mary 8 HD 425, 542
Sulivane, Robert 8 HD 176
Sullender, James 6 HD 529, 532, 534
Sullender, James Smith 6 HD 104
Summers, Elijah 4 HD 607
Support [tract] 8 HD 262
Surveyors Point [tract] 4 HD 266, 269
Sussex County, Delaware 3 HD 81, 113, 164, 187, 189, 192, 302, 494; 4 HD 126, 157, 179, 391, 560; 6 HD 407, 468; 8 HD 168, 377
Sweeting, Richard 3 HD 404
Swiggett, Femy 3 HD 598
Swiggett, James 3 HD 598
Sykes, Elizabeth 3 HD 354, 455; 4 HD 43; 6 HD 495
Sykes, James 3 HD 354, 455; 4 HD 43; 6 HD 495
Sylvys Cove 3 HD 127
Talbot County 3 HD 133, 168, 213, 309, 354, 593; 4 HD 26, 29, 83, 174, 303, 399, 557, 561, 603; 6 HD 437, 439, 475, 495, 627; 8 HD 92, 212, 292, 368, 459, 480, 503, 513
Tall, Anthony 8 HD 520
Tall, Bruffett 6 HD 359
Tall, Elizabeth 8 HD 8
Tall, James 3 HD 467, 500
Tall, John 6 HD 410
Tall, John 8 HD 442, 444, 508, 527
Tall, William 8 HD 8
Talls Contrivance [tract] 4 HD 251
Talls First Venture [tract] 3 HD 467
Talls Forrest [tract] 8 HD 444
Talls Regulation [tract] 3 HD 500
Tan Yard [tract] 6 HD 283
Tar Bay 4 HD 196
Tarcells Neck [tract] 8 HD 246, 276
Tarkill Ridge [tract] 3 HD 226
Taylor, Ann 4 HD 125
Taylor, Prudence 4 HD 232; 6 HD 475
Taylor, Sarah 6 HD 332, 436
Taylor, Thomas 3 HD 30, 502; 4 HD 232; 6 HD 332, 475
Taylor, William 4 HD 109; 8 HD 516
Taylors Addition to Rich Ridge [tract] 8 HD 337
Taylors Creek 4 HD 9; 6 HD 249

Taylors Delight [tract] 4 HD 201; 6 HD 126, 224
Taylors Folly [tract] 3 HD 164
Taylors Good Will [tract] 6 HD 385
Taylors Inheritance [tract] 6 HD 412
Taylors Island 3 HD 164, 181, 249, 380; 4 HD 129, 423; 6 HD 1, 233, 374, 459, 462, 468, 470, 471, 509, 582; 8 HD 1, 495, 506
Taylors Island Chapel 8 HD 65
Taylors Island Ferry 8 HD 450
Taylors Island [tract] 4 HD 300
Taylors Kindness [tract] 6 HD 377, 564
Taylors Neglect [tract] 3 HD 463; 6 HD 332, 541
Taylors Point [tract] 8 HD 622
Taylors Range [tract] 3 HD 117
Tegious Creek 6 HD 151
Teverton [tract] 3 HD 6, 1391 8 HD 134
Thames Street [tract] 6 HD 363, 366
Thicket [tract] 8 HD 461
Third Callis [tract] 3 HD 76
Third Purchase [tract] 3 HD 598
Thomas & Betsey [tract] (Schooner) 4 HD 545
Thomas, Alce (Alice) 3 HD 275
Thomas, Charles 4 HD 251
Thomas, Eleanor 6 HD 579
Thomas, Ellis 4 HD 169
Thomas, John 8 HD 22
Thomas, Joseph 3 HD 472
Thomas, Reuben 3 HD 474, 507
Thomas, Tristram 6 HD 402, 579; 8 HD 64
Thomas, Trustram 3 HD 254
Thomas, William 3 HD 275, 483, 505; 6 HD 563

Thomas's Chance [tract] 3 HD 472, 483, 505, 507
Thompson, Anthony 6 HD 592
Thompson, Betsy 4 HD 600
Thompson Branch 6 HD 385
Thompson, Edwards 4 HD 456; 8 HD 71
Thompson, Joseph 3 HD 67, 69, 159
Thompson, Priscilla (Prissillah) 3 HD 67, 69, 272; 4 HD 160, 275; 6 HD 381, 385; 8 HD 356
Thompson, Thomas 3 HD 29, 272, 309; 4 HD 160, 275; 6 HD 381, 385, 443; 8 HD 356, 486, 505
Thompson, Thomas of Wm. 6 HD 409
Thompson, William 3 HD 69; 6 HD 341
Thompsons Chance [tract] 6 HD 443
Thompsons Meadows [tract] 3 HD 69
Thompsons Range [tract] 6 HD 385
Thomsons Island [tract] 6 HD 495
Tickle, David 4 HD 65
Tickle, William 4 HD 65
Tilghman, Elijah 4 HD 77, 97
Tilghman, Richard 5th 8 HD 485
Timber Neck [tract] 8 HD 121
Timber Swamp [tract] 3 HD 202, 434
Timber Yard [tract] 6 HD 592; 8 HD 433
Tobacco House Cove 6 HD 314
Tobacco Stick Ba1 6 HD 172, 546
Todd, Benjamin 3 HD 166, 206, 326, 327; 6 HD 151, 261, 606
Todd, David 4 HD 185
Todd, Jabin 8 HD 599
Todd, Jacob 3 HD 326; 6 HD 189, 420, 534, 536; 8 HD 63, 305, 485, 486, 505
Todd, John 6 HD 12

Todd, Levin 6 HD 534
Todd, Michael 6 HD 261
Todds Chapel 8 HD 65
Todds Point [tract] 6 HD 450; 8 HD 106, 529
Tolley, Thomas 4 HD 196; 8 HD 495
Tolley, Travers 8 HD 214
Tolly, Anne 6 HD 320, 338
Tolly, Traverse 6 HD 320, 322, 338
Tongue, Thomas 4 HD 330; 8 HD 109
Tootell, John 3 HD 366; 4 HD 94; 8 HD 205, 373, 625
Tootell, John, Justice 3 HD 16, 18, 23, 56, 59, 62, 177, etc.
Tootels (Tootells, Tootles) Venture [tract] 3 HD 366; 4 HD 41, 501; 6 HD 118, 139, 178; 8 HD 365, 368
Tootle, John 6 HD 74, 502
Toppan, Abner 3 HD 42
Town Hill [tract] 6 HD 537
Town Neck Composition [tract] 8 HD 421
Town Point 3 HD 275; 6 HD 495, 569
Town Point Neck 3 HD 4; 4 HD 339
Transquakin River 3 HD 23, 216, 218, 251, 414; 4 HD 201, 255, 573; 6 HD 126, 245; 8 HD 163, 433, 513
Travers, Anne 8 HD 537
Travers, Benjamin 8 HD 214
Travers, Elizabeth 3 HD 164, 466; 6 HD 233, 470, 471
Travers, Henry 3 HD 164, 249
Travers, Henry Hicks 4 HD 126
Travers, Jacob 4 HD 612; 6 HD 394, 399, 425
Travers, John Hicks 8 HD 537

Travers, Levin 3 HD 164, 493; 4 HD 47, 600; 8 HD 242
Travers, Mary 8 HD 242
Travers, Matthew 3 HD 249; 8 HD 214, 249, 537
Travers, Matthias 3 HD 464; 6 HD 441
Travers, Teresa 3 HD 249
Travers, Thomas 3 HD 249, 264, 380; 8 HD 214, 495
Travers, Thomas Brome 3 HD 249
Travers, William 3 HD 249, 380
Travers's Lott [tract] 3 HD 216
Travers's Purchase [tract] 3 HD 431
Traverse, John Ascum 6 HD 314, 322
Traverse, Letitia 4 HD 35, 266
Traverse, Matthias 4 HD 32, 35, 266, 269, 612
Traverse, Priscilla 6 HD 314, 322
Traverse, Thomas 6 HD 320
Traverses Honeysucker [tract] 8 HD 537
Trego, Ezekiel 8 HD 470
Trego, James 3 HD 181, 380
Trego, Newton 3 HD 324
Trego, William 6 HD 359
Trego's Spite [tract] 6 HD 359
Tregoe, Henry 3 HD 502
Tregoe, James 4 HD 229; 6 HD 630; 8 HD 490, 495, 506
Tregoe, Levin 4 HD 229; 6 HD 630
Tregoe Samuel 4 HD 255
Tregoe, Thomas 3 HD 467, 500
Tregoe, William 4 HD 229
Tregoes Division [tract] 4 HD 229; 6 HD 630
Tregoes Venture [tract] 3 HD 500
Treves, Joseph, 6 HD 425
Trice, George 3 HD 239
Trice, John 3 HD 309; 4 HD 574

Trices Chance [tract] 3 HD 239
Trippe, Ann 3 HD 167
Trippe, Edward 3 HD 309
Trippe, Henry 3 HD 167; 4 HD 566, 603; 6 HD 67, 454
Trippe, James 6 HD 439
Trippe, James Junr. 6 HD 288
Trippe, John 3 HD 16, 167; 4 HD 603; 6 HD 439
Trippe, Joseph 3 HD 16, 62, 167, 195; 6 HD 473
Trippe, Margaret 3 HD 535
Trippe, Mary 3 HD 167; 4 HD 201; 8 HD 151
Trippe, William 3 HD 16, 167; 4 HD 563; 6 HD 473
Trippes Bush [tract] 4 HD 293
Trippes Desire [tract] 4 HD 582
Trippes Discovery [tract] 3 HD 16; 4 HD 293
Trippes Inclosure [tract] 3 HD 16, 53, 62; 4 HD 293; 6 HD 473
Trippes Marsh [tract] 3 HD 16
Trot's Creek 3 HD 8
Trouble Enough [tract] 6 HD 164
Trumpabout [tract] 4 HD 94, 98
Trustees of the Poor 6 HD 3, 72, 74, 228, 291
Tryall [tract] 3 HD 246, 295, 475, 477; 4 HD 22
Tryangle [tract] 3 HD 40
Tubman, Ann 8 ND 254
Tubman, Mary 8 HD 254
Tubman, Richard 3 HD 124, 304; 4 HD 32, 35, 506, 520, 585; 6 HD 420, 466, 590; 8 HD 4, 77, 143, 254
Tubs's Desire [tract] 6 HD 110
Tucker, Jacob 6 HD 410
Tucker, James 6 HD 445, 446, 447
Tucker, William 3 HD 50, 148, 254; 8 HD 399
Tuckers Folly [tract] 4 HD 196
Tuckers Lott [tract] 6 HD 320
Tull, Abel 4 HD 393
Tull, Handy 8 HD 307
Tull, Mary 3 HD 494
Tull, Stoughton 4 HD 420
Tull, William 3 HD 494
Tunis, Arabella 8 HD 52
Turcells Neck [tract] 4 HD 147
Turkey Land [tract] 8 HD 279
Turkey Neck [tract] 3 HD 53;
Turkey Nest [tract] 8 HD 425
Turnbull, Matthew 8 HD 182, 185, 188
Turner, Joseph 8 HD 461
Turner, Thomas 4 HD 466
Turpin, Francis 4 HD 391, 393; 6 HD 292; 8 HD 307
Turpin, John 4 HD 179, 391, 393; 8 HD 547
Turpin, Margaret 4 HD 179
Twyford, John 4 HD 391; 8 HD 168
Twyford, Mary 4 HD 391; 8 HD 168
Tybout, Andrew 4 HD 185
Tyler, David 6 HD 450; 8 HD 106, 436
Tyler, Rachel 6 HD 93
Tyler, Solomon 6 HD 93
Tylor, David 4 HD 220
Tylor, Job 6 HD 93
Tylor, Solomon 4 HD 215, 220, 263
Tylors Stave Landing [tract] 4 HD 220
Upper Black Walnut Landing [tract] 3 HD 33; 6 HD 86
Usher, John 3 HD 1
Utophia [tract] 8 HD 119

Vass, Elizabeth (Betsey) 6 HD 464, 493; 8 HD 506
Vass, William 3 HD 351; 8 HD 506
Vass, William K. 6 HD 464, 493
Vaughan, John 6 HD 445, 447
Vaughan, William 3 HD 570
Vaughn, William 8 HD 258
Venture [tract] 3 HD 69, 229, 595; 4 HD 13; 8 HD 411, 415
Vickars, Clement 4 HD 557; 8 HD 218
Vickars Creek 4 HD 557
Vickars, Ezekiel 3 HD 231, 389, 391, 565; 8 HD 16, 56, 177, 329
Vickars, John 3 HD 469
Vickars, Thomas 3 HD 565; 6 HD 184, 379, 483, 486; 8 HD 56, 113
Vickars, William 3 HD 210, 345, 549; 4 HD 224, 513; 6 HD 70, 78, 287; 8 HD 194
Vickars, William 2nd 3 HD 38, 275, 400
Vickars, William of Sarah 3 HD 168
Vickars's Creek 3 HD 275; 8 HD 218
Vickarses Priviledge [tract] 6 HD 379
Vickers, Ann 6 HD 483, 486
Vienna 3 HD 416, 480, 537, 594; 4 HD 77, 163, 494, 538; 6 HD 96, 489, 537, 549, 579; 8 HD 212, 254, 301, 534, 537
Vinson, James 6 HD 312; 8 HD 94, 96, 99
Vinson, Polley Skinner 8 HD 94, 99
Vinton, Richard 8 HD 22
Virginia 3 HD 249, 594; 4 HD 297, 300
Vival- see Wyvill.
Wadles Desire [tract] 3 HD 202, 206

Waggaman, Henry (Hy.) 3 HD 428; 4 HD 555, 571, 587; 6 HD 84, 435; 8 HD 346
Waggaman, Mr. 6 HD 564
Walker, Francis 4 HD 169
Walker, John 6 HD 27, 617
Walker, John Junr. 4 HD 393
Walker, John Senr. 4 HD 393
Walker, Nathaniel 4 HD 562
Walker, Sarah 6 HD 27
Walkers Chance [tract] 3 HD 8
Walkers Lott [tract] 3 HD 8; 6 HD 132
Wall, Ezekiel 4 HD 405; 8 HD 441
Wall, Levin 3 HD 136; 4 HD 529, 584; 6 HD 521
Wall, Thomas 8 HD 534
Wallace, Aaron 3 HD 15, 351, 352; 4 HD 321
Wallace, Beththuly 3 HD 352
Wallace, Charles 3 HD 487
Wallace, John 3 HD 15; 6 HD 536
Wallace, Joseph 3 HD 352
Wallace, Matthew 3 HD 352
Wallace, Richard 6 HD 532, 534; 8 HD 182
Wallace, Staplefort 3 HD 352
Wallace, Thomas 3 HD 351, 352
Wallaces Addition [tract] 6 HD 529, 532, 536, 584; 8 HD 182, 185
Wallaces Chance [tract] 3 HD 351
Wallaces Meadow [tract] 3 HD 14
Walnut Neck [tract] 4 HD 32
Walnut Point [tract] 8 HD 622
Walter, Denwood 3 HD 617
Walters, Anne 8 HD 537
Walters, Clement 4 HD 246
Walters, Thomas 6 HD 10, 289, 432, 567, 633; 8 HD 515, 537

Ward, George 3 HD 35, 43, 282, 493, 560, 561, 577, 583, 604, 611; 4 HD 25, 47, 106, 107, 126, 170, 172, 554; 6 HD 67, 72, 74, 228, 293, 428; 8 HD 91, 165, 176, 205, 206, 289
Ward, Jonathan 3 HD 213; 8 HD 283
Ward, Mary 3 HD 35, 43
Warner, Stephen 4 HD 324
Warner, William 4 HD 324
Warners Chance [tract] 4 HD 324
Warren, William 4 HD 607
Wateres Last Choice [tract] 8 HD 74
Waters, Anne H. 6 HD 630
Waters, George 8 HD 311, 315
Waters Last Choice [tract] 3 HD 91
Waters Lott [tract] 4 HD 405
Waters, Peter H. 6 HD 630
Waters, Richard 3 HD 224; 4 HD 65; 6 HD 405
Waters, Spencer 8 HD 363
Waters, Spencer Martrum 4 HD 393
Waters, William 8 HD 315
Waters's Last Choice [tract] 4 HD 395; 8 HD 531, 533, 574
Web, James 6 HD 228
Webb, Dorothy 8 HD 520
Webb, Joseph 3 HP 309
Webb, Peter 3 HD 309; 8 HD 137
Webster, Catharine 8 HD 425
Webster, Thomas 4 HD 219, 596
Weems, David 3 HD 487
Weems, Rachel 8 HD 109
Weems, William 8 HD 109
Welch, Nancy 6 HD 74
Wells, Mary 8 HD 437
Weston [tract] 4 HD 115; 6 HD 405; 8 HD 602
Wet Work [tract] 4 HD 77, 94, 97
Wheatley, Arthur 6 HD 78
Wheatley, Augustus 3 HD 231
Wheatley, Charles 3 HD 31, 469, 494; 8 HD 74
Wheatley, Edward 3 HD 94, 422, 607; 6 HD 292
Wheatley, Elizabeth 3 HD 231
Wheatley, Ezekiel 3 HD 96
Wheatley, Isaac 3 HD, 469, 487
Wheatley, Job 4 HD 359
Wheatley, Joseph 3 HD 142, 494; 6 HD 292; 8 HD 547
Wheatley, Mary 3 HD 469
Wheatley, William 3 HD 91, 96
Wheelan, Charles, Cath. Pst. 8 HD 254
Wheelear, Samuel 3 HD 30
Wheeler, Fanny 6 HD 603
Wheeler, John 4, HD 77
Wheeler, Joseph 8 HD 256
Wheeler, Thomas 3 HD 408; 4 HD 553
Wheelton, William 3 HD 402
Whetcroft, Henry 4 HD 489
White, Edward 4 HD 115, 163
White, Edward Junr. 8 HD 137, 502, 516, 547
White, Elizabeth 3 HD 53, 56; 4 HD 98; 6 HD 396
White Fryars [tract] 3 HD 444; 6 HD 266
White Haven [tract] 8 HD 329, 356, 552
White, Jacobus 3 HD 53, 56; 6 HD 396
White Marsh 4 HD 103
White Marsh Branch 4 HD 251; 8 HD 132
White Oak Range [tract] 3 HD 510; 4 HD 466; 8 HD 225
White, Robert 6 HD 567; 8 HD 423

White, Sarah Small 4 HD 540
White, Thomas 4 HD 163; 6 HD 228, 291
White, Thomas Junr. 4 HD 540
Whitehaven [tract] 3 HD 272; 4 HD 160; 6 HD 89, 329, 381, 552, 612
Whiteley, Arthur 3 HD 38; 6 HD 254, 379; 8 HD 16, 238
Whiteley, Nancy 4 HD 612
Whiteley, Nehemiah 3 HD 400; 4 HD 147, 562; 8 HD 246, 248, 276, 589
Whiteley, Rosannah 8 HD 276
Whiteley, William 8 HD 221, 452
Whiteley, Zebulon 4 HD 612
Whiteleys Adventure [tract] 6 HD 104
Whiteleys Swamp 4 HD 535
Whites Friendship [tract] 6 HD 274
Whites Warehouse 3 HD 38, 400; 6 HD 287; 8 HD 194
Whitley, Nathal. 4 HD 89
Whitley, Thomas 4 HD 220
Whittington, Ann (Anne) 4 HD 201; 6 HD 48
Whittington, Isaac 3 HD 23
Whittington, William 6 HD 48; 8 HD 248
Whittington, William Junr. 3 HD 23
Whittington, William Senr. 3 HD 23
Whittingtons Adventure [tract] 6 HD 48
Whores Harbour [tract] 3 HD 231, 408, 410
Widows Purchase [tract] 6 HD 574; 8 HD 517
Wiesenthal, And. 8 HD 461
Wilcocks, Daniel 4 HD 65
Wilcox, Thomas 4 HD 386

Willen, Hopkins 4 HD 459
Willen, John 3 HD 202, 206
Willen, Levi 6 HD 151; 8 HD 109
Willen, Sealey 4 HD 459
Willey, Absolem 4 HD 13
Willey, Absolum 3 HD 229, 595
Willey, Frederick 3 HD 434; 6 HD 448, 450, 451, 453; 8 HD 69, 104, 106, 173
Willey, George 3 HD 434
Willey, Hannah 8 HD 411
Willey, Littleton 3 HD 229, 595; 8 HD 411
Willey, Pritchet 4 HD 489
Willey, Rachel 3 HD 434
Willey, Sarah 3 HD 434
Willey, William 3 HD 424
Williams Chance [tract] 6 HD 227
Williams, Dolley 4 HD 82
Williams, Dyer 6 HD 332
Williams Goodwill [tract] 4 HD 229; 6 HD 359, 630
Williams, Jesse 3 HD 475, 477
Williams, Job 6 HD 356
Williams, John 3 HD 40; 4 HD 154
Williams, John, Justice 8 HD 216, 287, 329, 332, 356, 365, 368, etc.
Williams, Joseph 4 HD 558
Williams, Levin 4 HD 65
Williams Lott [tract] 6 HD 314, 322, 326
Williams, Nathan 6 HD 402, 429
Williams, Thomas 3 HD 67; 6 HD 52, 332
Willin, John 6 HD 604
Willin, Levi 6 HD 606
Willin, Thomas 6 HD 604, 606
Willings Priviledge [tract] 6 HD 151
Willis, Charles 3 HD 578

Willis, Henry 3 HD 397
Willis, Joshua 3 HD 377, 578, 579
Willis, Thomas 8 HD 52
Williss, Joshua 8 HD 22
Willmots Adventure [tract] 6 HD 277
Willoughby, William 3 HD 242
Willoughby's Purchase [tract] 8 HD 16
Willoughbys Purchase Resurveyed [tract] 8 HD 16
Willson, Andrew 4 HD 330
Willson, James 8 HD 74, 533
Willson, Robert 3 HD 452; 8 HD 52, 225
Willsons Chance [tract] 3 HD 469
Wilson, Cutty (Cutty Wilson's Creek) 3 HD 43
Wilson, Robert 6 HD 175
Winder, Levin 3 HD 224
Winder, William 8 HD 229, 254
Windows, Charles 8 HD 80
Windows, John 8 HD 80
Windsor [tract] 3 HD 447; 4 HD 618
Winfells Trouble [tract] 8 HD 540
Winfield, J. 3 HD 544
Winfields Trouble [tract] 8 HD 287, 562
Wing, Robert 4 HD 435
Wingate, Ann 6 HD 332; 8 HD 238
Wingate, Dorothy 4 HD 199
Wingate, Henry 4 HD 199
Wingate, James 4 HD 199
Wingate, John 6 HD 523; 8 HD 269
Wingate, Lovy 4 HD 199
Wingate, Nancy 4 HD 199
Wingate, Robert 6 HD 411
Wingate, Shadrach 6 HD 411
Wingate, Shadrick 3 HD 202, 206
Wingate, Thomas 3 HD 111
Wingate, Triphena 4 HD 199

Wingate, William 6 HD 411
Wingate, Zebulon 6 HD 332
Wingates Inclosure [tract] 3 HD 202
Winrow, Charles 3 HD 601; 4 HD 558
Withgot, Henry 3 HD 377
Withgott, Henry 8 HD 22
Withgott, Joseph 3 HD 377; 8 HD 22
Withgott, William 3 HD 377; 8 HD 22
Wndows, John 4 HD 307
Wood, Jonathan 3 HD 137
Woodard, Benjamin 3 HD 206, 565; 4 HD 563; 6 HD 254; 8 HD 16
Woodard, Mary 3 HD 38
Woodards, James (Lankfit) 3 HD 564
Woodland, Isaac 4 HD 211, 279; 6 HD 68
Woodland, John 8 HD 377
Woodland, John Starling 8 HD 269
Woodland, Mary 8 HD 269, 405, 596
Woodland, Richard 4 HD 251, 272; 6 HD 296, 298; 8 HD 269
Woodland, Sarah 6 HD 68
Woodland, Solomon 8 HD 377
Woodside, Abram 4 HD 183
Woodyard [tract] 3 HD 213, 338, 455
Woolford, Anne 3 HD 514
Woolford, Bartholomew 6 HD 172
Woolford, James 8 HD 540
Woolford, Levin 3 HD 172, 213, 249, 338, 380, 400, 495, 514, 564, 577, 583; 4 HD 47, 73, 106, 107, 170, 172, 224, 229, 598, 600; 6 HD 3, 254, 620, 630; 8 HD 16, 150, 495, 497, 506, 610, 612, 618
Woolford, Levin of John 8 HD 56
Woolford, Levin, Justice 3 HD 440, 442, 444, 489, 493, 510, etc.; 4 HD 109, 113, 115, 129, 147, 151, etc.; 6 HD 13, 22, 41, 46, 48, 63,

70, 78, etc.; 8 HD 1, 65, 82, 84, 91, 96, 113, etc.
Woolford, Levin of Thos. 8 HD 490
Woolford, Mary 6 HD 172; 8 HD 495, 497
Woolford, Molley 3 HD 380
Woolford, Priscilla 8 HD 540
Woolford, R. 6 HD 84
Woolford, Roger 3 HD 206; 8 HD 287, 508, 540, 562
Woolford, Stevens 3 HD 206; 4 HD 477; 6 HD 582
Woolford, Thomas 3 HD 224; 8 HD 1, 134, 450, 540
Woolfords Content [tract] 4 HD 477; 6 HD 582
Woolfords Foresight [tract] 8 HD 1, 450
Woolfords Interest [tract] 3 HD 213, 338
Woolfords Meeting House 8 HD 64
Woolfords Pasture [tract] 8 HD 508
Woolfords Purchase [tract] 6 HD 172, 546
Woollen, Benjamin 6 HD 507; 8 HD 143
Woollen, Edward 4 HD 49, 54, 132, 616; 8 HD 418, 523
Woollen, Elizabeth 4 HD 423
Woollen, John 3 HD 571; 6 HD 410
Woollen, Keziah 6 HD 507
Woollen, Levin 8 HD 527, 599
Woollen, Levina 8 HD 523
Woollen, Priscilla 8 HD 599
Woollen, Thomas 6 HD 425
Woollens Possession [tract] 4 HD 423
Worcester County 8 HD 108
Working Ridge [tract] 6 HD 5
Worlds End Bridge 3 HD 489
Worlds End Creek 3 HD 595; 4 HD 279, 287; 6 HD 601; 8 HD 409, 411, 413, 548
Worlds End [tract] 3 HD 229; 4 HD 13, 220; 8 HD 409, 415, 548
Wottles Desire [tract] 6 HD 411
Wright, Cain 4 HD 391
Wright, Edward 4 HD 22, 275; 6 HD 371, 552; 8 HD 157, 508, 571
Wright, Henry 8 HD 520
Wright, Isaac 8 HD 571
Wright, Jacob 3 HD 253, 282, 309; 4 HD 111, 412, 459, 574; 6 HD 283; 8 HD 22, 264, 298, 569, 571, 574
Wright, Jesse 8 HD 571
Wright, Joshua 3 HD 113
Wright, Nancy 3 HD 502
Wright, Nathan 3 HD 74, 109, 168, 206, 309; 4 HD 22, 582; 6 HD 283, 371; 8 HD 478
Wright, Samuel 3 HD 253, 309; 4 HD 582; 6 HD 283, 403; 8 HD 342
Wright, Sarah 3 HD 113
Wright, Thomas 3 HD 502
Wrights Creek 3 HD 406
Wrights Discovery [tract] 3 HD 402
Wrights Lott [tract] 3 HD 410
Wrights Regulation [tract] 8 HD 571
Wrights Third Purchase [tract] 8 HD 307
Wroten, Levin 8 HD 469
Wroten, Mathew 8 HD 469
Wroten, Thomas 8 HD 469
Wrotens Island 8 HD 469
Wyvill, Dorsey 3 HD 272; 8 HD 356
Wyvill, Sarah 8 HD 356
Yerbury, Richard 3 HD 354
York [tract] 3 HD 189

www.ingramcontent.com/pod-product-compliance
Lightning Source LLC
Chambersburg PA
CBHW051050160426
43193CB00010B/1132